INVENTORY 1985

INVENTORY 98

THE
Canoe
Book

THE
Canoe
Book

I. Herbert Gordon

With Illustrations by
Phil Salow

McGRAW-HILL BOOK COMPANY
New York   St. Louis   San Francisco   Auckland   Bogotá   Düsseldorf
Johannesburg   London   Madrid   Mexico   Montreal   New Delhi   Panama
Paris   São Paulo   Singapore   Sydney   Tokyo   Toronto

First McGraw-Hill edition, 1978

1 2 3 4 5 6 7 8 9 0   MUMU   7 8 3 2 1 0 9 8

Cover photo shows (from right) author Herb Gordon and illustrator Phil Salow.

Library of Congress Cataloging in Publication Data

Gordon, I. Herbert.
  The canoe book.

  1. Canoes and canoeing. I. Title.
Gv783.G67   797.1'22   77-18693
ISBN 0-07-023783-2

Dedicated

to everyone who ever thrilled to the challenge
of roaring whitewater,
or camped on the silent shore
of a lake far in the wilderness,
and, of course,
to a bow partner with glossy hair
whose skill with a paddle
I have envied for years—my wife, Gail.

Contents

CONTENTS

CONTENTS

Preface

A Day on the Capitachoune

The sun sparkled off the blue ripples of the Capitachoune River, flowing lazily southeast through the great forests of central Quebec. The breeze was soft as we paddled along, our canoes loaded with food and gear. It was a day made for canoeing.

Or it would have been had the sun continued to shine in an unblemished sky. But the weather changed midmorning with the abruptness of those subarctic climate patterns. The breeze strengthened. The temperature dropped. Low, ominous streaks of cloud whipped across the sky. The dozen paddlers in the six canoes bent to their paddles and stroked harder in the face of the brisk winds.

We ducked into a sheltered cove and stopped early for lunch, stretching and relaxing muscles beginning to ache from the strain. The cooks untied a green nylon stuff bag. Out came lunch: gorp (more about this delicacy later), cheese wedges, hard crackers, lemon drops—all washed down with potable water dipped from the river in which we floated. As we ate, the clouds grew darker along the horizon.

I gulped down the last mouthful of gorp and rummaged through the military-surplus rubber waterproof bag in which I carried my personal gear. I hauled out my blue rain suit. In every other canoe there was an untying of packs and a scrambling for rain gear.

"We'd better get moving," I called out. The cooks hastily tied up the day's food sack and replaced it in the canoe, throwing a poncho across the top of the gear to shed the inevitable rain.

The sky darkened as we set out. The breeze became stronger. At times we fought a stiff head wind. Intermittently, as the river snaked and turned, we enjoyed brief flings when the winds pushed us along.

The first drops of rain began falling. A canoe paddled up alongside.

"Do you have any idea how long it'll be before we reach a campsite?"

My bow paddler, Gail, struggled to keep the canoe pointed downstream. I scanned the map folded inside a clear plastic envelope. Claude Contant, the cooperative outfitter at Grand Remous, Quebec, who had rented us the canoes, had made a number of notations on the topographical maps about where we might find sites. He had traveled this route several years earlier. He had warned us that while some of the suggestions would work, others were merely educated guesses. Open sites for camps, especially for a large party, are rare in the Canadian North Woods. The forests grow rapidly. The forest floor is a tangle of rotting logs, often swampy, snarled with heavy underbrush. Claude had noted a possible open site on a low bluff ahead of us. I pointed this out.

The rain streamed down in torrents. The air was filled with mist. The water looked alive from the violent beating.

I signaled for all canoes to pull up for a showery conference.

"We should reach a possible campsite in about a half hour," I said. "Meanwhile, keep close. Leo, you and Stephanie take sweep. And keep those life jackets on. No sense anyone getting drowned if you swamp in this storm."

Jerry began singing: "I'm humming in the rain, just humming in the rain, what a glorious feeling, I'm all wet again." His cheerfulness sent a wave of warmth along the line of canoes. We began paddling. The rain trickled down our necks, dripped onto our arms, splashed on our faces.

"Hey, look over there."

There was an old cabin on the left bank. A hunk of the roof was missing. "Maybe we could stop there."

I urged everyone to continue paddling. We'd reach the bluff in a few minutes. "We'll have more room in our tents," I shouted through the downpour. We paddled around a bend. Directly ahead was the low bluff. Suddenly, a tremendous bolt of lightning streaked from the black clouds, blurring our eyes and stunning us with the flash of light and cannonlike thunder.

"Get ashore," I bawled. As one, our six canoes swung toward the bank. We drove the bows onto the shore, leaped out, hauled the canoes well out of the water, and splashed through the mud for the shelter of a line of low trees some 50 feet from the muddy river water. A few hundred feet beyond us was a high ridge of trees. They would serve as a lightning rod. The low trees would give us some protection from the pelting rain. Another streak of lightning. And another. The ground shook. The air reverberated with echoing crashes. One thunderous roar after the other rolled across the forest as if some ghostly massed artillery were firing in tremendous concert. At moments the rain was mixed with hail, large as marbles, which slashed into our dripping bodies. We were miserable, waiting either for that one wild bolt of lightning to obliterate us in a cloud of steam, or for the storm to end. Slowly the flashes of lightning drifted to the east. The wind quieted down. The violent rain turned into a light downpour. We began to unwind.

Jerry trotted back to the canoes to make certain rising river water hadn't worked them loose and sent them floating away. Lloyd saw an opening in the trees across a small, swollen stream. He volunteered to wade over and check on whether or not there would be room to pitch our tents. George and Stephanie joined me as I scrambled up the low bluff. We had gone only a few yards when we sensed there wouldn't be enough open space to pitch a tent pole, much less our tents. We headed back down. Lloyd returned.

"Nothing," he said.

"Nothing," we said. I said we'd best try for the old log cabin for the night. It might be habitable.

We sloshed back to our canoes. The rain was barely a sprinkle as we paddled upstream to the cabin. We found that the hole

PREFACE

in the roof, probably caused by a mischievous lightning bolt, could be covered by a tarp. The windows were intact. A rotten beam under the small porch gave way when my wife, Gail, stepped on it, but the floor inside was solid. Most surprising, there were four sturdy bunk beds with the luxury of springs, a small stove which could hold a warming fire, and a rickety table. "We stay," I said.

There was an outbreak of activity. Gear was hauled up from the canoes. The canoes were dragged well ashore, turned over, roped together, and anchored to a birch tree. Leo and Jerry slung a tarp over the gaping hole in the roof. Inside, ropes were strung from beam to beam and were soon festooned with wet clothes. Packs were placed against the walls. Out came dry clothing.

Dotty was in charge of fire. She found a thoughtfully placed bundle of dry kindling under one bunk and within minutes had a fine firing hissing and sputtering away in the shaky heating stove.

Warm and dry, we broke out a bottle of brandy. The cabin was crowded with bodies and talk and laughter.

The wobbly table had been shoved into one corner, strengthened with a couple of nails from the emergency kit, and promptly claimed by the cooks. Since the small stove was too insecure to support even a frying pan, we brought out the two Optimus 111B gasoline stoves, and the cooks set to work.

I still have a record of our gourmet dinner there in the middle of one of the great wilderness regions of North America: Lipton's dehydrated chicken-noodle soup enhanced with dried Chinese mushrooms and slivers of dried ginger, potatoes *au gratin* from the supermarket shelves, an enticing entrée of steak *au poivre* made from freeze-dried

steak, and, as a special treat for being so good in the storm, our one can of freeze-dried ice cream for dessert with coffee, tea, or hot chocolate.

We devoured that meal with all the delicacy of hungry pigs.

As darkness deepened, the single-mantle Coleman gasoline lantern brightened our crowded emergency shelter. Long after the night had closed over the wet wilderness, we still were talking, recounting the storm, reliving the experiences of other days, giggling at dirty jokes, and playing games, knowing that none of us in that remote cabin in northern Quebec would ever lose the memory of the night. It belonged only, and forever, to us.

Eventually the cabin quieted down as we crawled into the sleeping bags doubled up on the bunks or sprawled on the floor. Occasionally a wild gust of wind or a passing shower shook us awake, but we'd fall back to sleep quickly enough.

We were up early. Breakfast was a filling and satisfying combination of freeze-dried eggs served with a hollandaise sauce, Quaker instant hot cereal, raisins, and coffee. Before the last of us had finished eating, others were down straightening the canoes and packing the gear.

As we put in, the wind was a mild breeze. The sun was welcome and bright. The canoes set out. I glanced back. Our flotilla paddled down the river, colorful with wet clothing spread across the gear and hung from every thwart to dry.

Who composed this hardy band of men and women paddling a remote wilderness? A group of travel-tough and experienced canoeists? Not at all. We were ordinary people, city people. Except for the two leaders and two of the others, all were new to the

PREFACE

wilderness. There was a young engineer, a scholarly CPA, a divorce lawyer, a producer of documentary films, a mother taking a vacation from her two children, a homemaker, a teacher, a social worker, two graduate students free for the summer, and a sales representative. Age ranged from mid-twenties to late fifties. We did not share skill or knowledge or exceptional ability. We *did* share a dream of someday doing precisely what we now were doing—canoe-camping in a faraway land where the loudest evening sound was the laugh of a loon echoing across the deepening shadows.

Introduction

Undertaking a canoe journey is not difficult. To the novice, however, even a one-day trip on a quiet lake may seem to pose a host of problems. And a weekend on a flowing river? That seems to present complications of staggering proportions.

However, most of the problems can be quickly resolved as soon as the novice knows that there are answers to his or her questions. For example: Where do you get a canoe? There are hundreds of liveries in the United States and Canada which rent canoes by the day, the weekend, the week, or the month. You will find lists of canoe liveries in every section of both nations in Appendix VI. You also will find some handy hints on what to ask when you arrange in advance to rent a canoe. Do canoe liveries provide transportation for you and your party? Most do. For a fee.

So, you've rented your canoe. Do you leap in and paddle off? It may not be quite that easy. Yet you can become quite proficient at paddling with some guidance—either from an instructor, or from the information contained in this book, or—ideally—both.

You also will find that when you canoe a river, you must know something about how to "read" the water if you expect to avoid trouble, which usually comes in the form of a quick and unexpected dunking. There is considerable information that you can study about what waves and currents tell you about the water you are canoeing.

The more experienced you become in canoeing, the more likely you are to join that adventurous band that canoes through the shrinking wilderness regions left to us. Here is information about where to locate canoe routes, how to obtain maps of the rivers and lakes you hope to canoe, and a word or two about reading and using both maps and compasses. And what to do if you get lost.

Disorganization is the key to outdoor problems. You will learn how to organize a group for a trip of a day or a month. And how to select menus that are mouth-watering, healthful, and simple to prepare in camp. As for quantities, charts will guide you in selecting the amounts you need to fill husky appetites without waste or spoilage.

You also will find guidance in looking for such items as tents, canoe clothing, packs, and specialized canoe gear, along with in-

INTRODUCTION

formation on how to pack and even where and when to look for a campsite.

You may, or may not, want to bring the family hound along on your next canoe trip after you read the chapter on pets.

You won't become an expert in first aid, but you will find invaluable advice on both minor and major medical problems which plague not only the canoeist but everyone who heads into the wilderness.

In a word, here is information of, for, about, and concerned with canoes, canoeing, and canoeists. You don't need to be an expert to navigate the pages of *The Canoe Book*. But you'll be much closer to one when you emerge from a welter of source material found in the appendixes than when you first wrapped your hand around a broomstick to practice the canoe strokes as you started your voyage.

Good reading. And happy canoeing.

THE
Canoe
Book

PART
I

About
Canoeing

1

Canoes and Paddles

A great variety of canoes and paddles are available to the modern canoeist. This chapter will introduce the beginning canoeist to the basic construction and nomenclature of canoes and paddles and describe the similarities and differences among the various kinds available.

CANOE TERMINOLOGY

Canoeing is a specialized activity. In order to get started as a canoeist, it is important to learn the correct terms for the parts of a canoe.

Figure 1 shows the parts of a typical canoe.

1.	Stern deck	6.	Bow thwart	11.	Bang plate
2.	Stern seat	7.	Bow seat	12.	Flotation chamber
3.	Stern thwart	8.	Port (left side)	13.	Keel
4.	Center thwart	9.	Bow deck	14.	Starboard (right side)
5.	Gunwale	10.	Towing link or shackle	15.	Rib
				16.	Gunwale
				17.	Flotation device

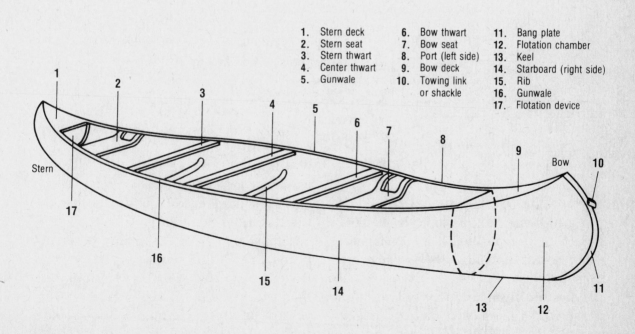

Figure 1

3

ABOUT CANOEING

Cut a wood and canvas canoe in half and it looks like Figure 2. Cut a fiberglass, aluminum, ABS (more about this material later), or Kevlar canoe in half and it looks similar, though it may or may not have a keel, will not have bilgekeels, and will have narrower gunwales (pronounced "gunnels").

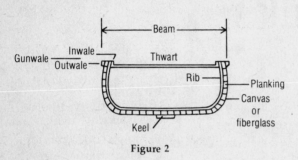

Figure 2

Figure 3 shows a fish-eye view of a canoe. Familiarize yourself with the parts of a canoe. A good canoeist knows the craft well.

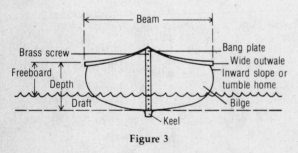

Figure 3

PADDLE TERMINOLOGY

A paddle is a simple tool; the names of its several parts are almost self-explanatory. Centuries of canoeing, however, have sophisticated the shapes of the most popular paddles and given rise to a variety of special designs. The parts of a typical paddle and paddles of various designs are shown in Figures 4 through 6.

Figure 4 shows a single-blade paddle.

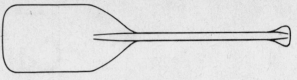

Figure 4

Figure 5 shows a double-blade, or kayak, paddle.

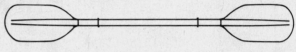

Figure 5

The parts of a paddle are shown in Figure 6.

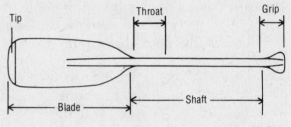

Figure 6

The most popular paddle shapes today are pictured in Figure 7.

CHOOSING A PADDLE

Today's paddles are sophisticated instruments. They may be made out of solid wood, wood laminate, aluminum, synthetics, or a combination of products.

There is one great difficulty with the solid-wood paddle—the grain. The paddle is most apt to snap where the grain twists and bends. Solid-wood paddles still incorporate the rather narrow blade, usually not more than 6 inches at its widest, because it is difficult to find a single piece of wood wider than that with a satisfactory grain for a paddle.

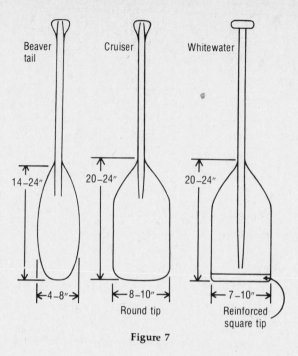

Beaver tail

Cruiser

Whitewater

14–24"

20–24"

20–24"

←4–8"→

←8–10"→
Round tip

←7–10"→
Reinforced square tip

Figure 7

Ash is a favorite among solid-wood paddles, because it is a strong, springy hardwood. Maple runs a close second. Cherry is another wood prized for solid paddles because of its strength. The major drawback to using these woods in paddles is that they are heavy. Cedar can be fashioned into an excellent and reasonably strong lightweight paddle, though the wood is brittle. Spruce is tough and light but somewhat soft. Basswood is springy but soft.

Over the past decades, as the greatest canoe use moved from flatwater and lakes to rivers and whitewater, paddles kept pace with the technological changes that made canoes reliable for the tremendous excitement of running rapids. Laminated wooden paddles have largely taken over the wooden-paddle market. Through lamination, a combination of woods can be selected to make a canoe paddle tough, light, and sturdy, with a springy reaction to water.

In such paddles, the shaft may or may not be laminated.

Sawyer paddles are made of a straight, round-dowel shaft, with blades of laminated blocks of different wood. Hand-laid fiberglass reinforces the blades. Clement shafts are made of laminated white cedar reinforced with hickory. The blades are spruce strips reinforced at the tip with cross strips of hardwood hickory. Summit makes its blades of laminates of red cedar, Sitka spruce, and ash. Another strip of ash reinforces the tip. The shafts are oval laminates of ash and Sitka spruce. The blades are finished with a fiberglass epoxy veneer.

In addition to wood, paddles are made out of almost every synthetic used in making canoes. Paddles made of synthetics may have wooden shafts, though aluminum shafts are more common. Various synthetics are used in the grips and blades. These include fiberglass, ABS, injection-molded plastic, heat-formed sheet plastic, and Kevlar.

Wooden paddles require maintenance; the synthetics, virtually none at all. Some synthetic paddles are so fashioned that any part—blade, shaft, or grip—can be replaced. Others are irreparable once damaged. Broken wooden paddles can be repaired, though after surgery they do not seem to be as dependable.

After each lengthy trip I sand my wooden Clement paddles lightly, using 0 or 00 steel wool, paying special attention to the outer edge of the tip, which is most likely to get chewed up by the rocks; the shaft, where my lower hand holds it; and the grip. After rubbing the paddle down firmly, I spray the entire blade and the upper two-thirds of the shaft lightly with a urethane finish. I soak the grip and the lower one-third of the shaft with lemon oil, then store the paddles in a cool, dry place. Never store paddles in a hot or damp area.

The beginning paddler usually will find that canoe liveries rent better canoes than they do paddles. Generally, the paddles available have narrow blades. The paddles may be beaver-tail shape or smaller editions of regular cruising paddles. If the paddles are wood, you may find that they have become water-soaked and heavy as a result of improper care. The blades of plastic rental paddles may look as though a large and hungry squirrel had nibbled on them.

The narrow blade has an advantage for the beginning canoeist. It moves more easily through the water than the larger blades. The wider the blade, the more cumbersome it is to handle. The novice will have troubles enough without adding to them by grabbing a big, fat blade the first few times out.

The popular wooden beaver tail has a rounded end. Its widest part is about one-third of the way up. It then narrows very gently into the shaft. A good beaver-tail blade, if sliced in half, would have a foil shape, thicker in the center and thinning gently toward the edges. The edges should be about $\frac{1}{4}$ inch thick.

Square-tipped blades are usually found in the hands of whitewater enthusiasts and racers, though more and more are being carried by paddlers on long-distance cruises. The square tip enables a paddler to use the corner of the blade as an emergency pole when he has to dig in for a maneuver. This technique cannot be used with a paddle made from a single piece of wood, as it will damage the paddle.

Blades of 10- to 12-inch widths are common. These move a huge amount of water with each stroke. I find they are awkward

in the fast, divergent currents for any rapids of Grade II or greater, though they are fine for long-distance and flatwater cruising. My own preference is a square-shaped blade $7\frac{1}{2}$ to 9 inches in width and 20 to 26 inches in length. I use the larger size for combination cruising and river maneuvers, the slightly smaller type for playing in whitewater.

In addition to standard-shaped blades, there are offset and angled blades for highly specialized use by downriver and marathon racers.

There are two basic grips: the long-established "pear" and the newer "T." (See Figure 8.) The T was designed to enable the whitewater paddler to hold more firmly to the paddle with his upper hand. I find it a more comfortable grip than the pear and prefer it for both whitewater maneuvering and long wilderness cruises.

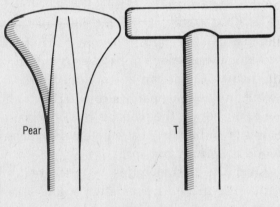

Pear   T

Figure 8

Your selection of a paddle will depend upon several factors: how you intend to use it, how much you want to spend, and your experience.

An excellent paddle for the beginner is the "beaver tail" or a modified flat-tip paddle with a blade not more than 7 inches at its maximum width and not more than 18 inches from tip to throat. If you intend to use your paddle only for a Sunday-afternoon cruise on a nearby lake or an occasional long-distance cruise on flatwater, a solid-wood or a laminated-wood paddle with round-tip blade should prove highly useful. For fast river currents and whitewater work there is no substitute for the square-tip blade. Both laminated wood and synthetics are made with square tips. The tip of a laminated wooden blade must be reinforced with a counter-grain strip of hardwood, fiberglass, or copper. However, the use of metal as a reinforcing strip has its drawbacks. Where the metal is riveted to the wood, the rivets can cause wear, allowing water to soak in. This will weaken the blade and increase its weight.

A shaft may be either round- or oval-shaped. If it is oval, the oval must be at right angles to the blade. An aluminum shaft should be covered with vinyl on the lower third for comfort in holding it.

A fine wooden paddle or a synthetic paddle will have the feel of smoothly finished wood furniture. Your hands will get wet when paddling; a rough finish which may be easy to hold when your hands are dry will soon wear blisters on wet skin.

Because I do not care for the feel of varnished wood in my hands, I sand the varnish finish off a wooden grip and throat, then soak the two areas in oil to keep them waterproof.

Selecting the length of a paddle is troublesome to new canoeists. One rule of thumb is to select a paddle that comes up to your chin if you will be working the bow, but a paddle that comes somewhere between chin and forehead if you are working the stern. Another rule of thumb, used for either canoe position, is to select your paddle by stretching your arms out as far as possible and choosing a paddle over which you can close your fingers on the grip and blade.

You should also keep another factor in mind: cruising paddlers tend to favor slightly longer paddles; those working whitewater often choose slightly smaller ones. I stand 5 feet, 8 inches tall. My favorite paddle is 5 feet, 2 inches long. Gail barely clears 5 feet, 3 inches, but her favorite paddle is 5 feet, 2 inches also. While I have long legs and a short torso, Gail has short legs and a long torso. When seated side by side, we appear to be the same height. Obviously, we are considering the distance from hip to shoulder as the significant factor in choosing paddles, rather than the length of our legs. For whitewater I use a 60-inch paddle. Gail prefers her 62-inch paddle for both cruising and whitewater.

The weight of a paddle is important. The lighter it is, the easier to handle. However, wooden paddles lose necessary rigidity if they give up too much weight in return for lightness. The blade may be shaved so thin that it vibrates in the water.

A well-made paddle will balance nicely when held loosely at the throat.

Sources of Paddles

Sporting goods stores, even those which handle a selection of canoes and paddles, rarely stock more than two or three different brands of paddles. There is a reasonable correlation between price and quality of available paddles. If you cannot find what you want at a canoe supply center, try the manufacturers. Appendix VIII lists manufacturers that offer a variety of paddles.

ABOUT CANOEING

TYPES OF CANOES

A canoe is a craft with a long, slender hull and symmetrical bow and stern. Modern canoes range from 10 to 20 feet in length. The most popular lengths are from 15 to 18 feet. They are designed to be paddled by one or two persons. A true canoe can be any length and carry any number of paddlers. Those used in the old fur trade and as wilderness freighters sometimes carried crews of twenty men. Polynesian outriggers which sailed vast distances across the Pacific were true canoes. So, too, were the mighty Viking longboats which were once the scourge of European coastal cities. Canoes can be paddled, sailed, or propelled by small outboard electric motors or gasoline engines. Our concern is only with the self-propelled canoes found today on almost every waterway of North America.

The variety of designs and the various materials out of which canoes are fashioned are bewildering.

Among canoe designs are the lightweight, cruiser, racer, freighter, whitewater, surfing, slalom, and general recreation canoes. Canoes are made of wood, aluminum, fiberglass, polyethylene, Aramid, vinyl, ABS, wood and canvas, wood and Verilite, wood and fiberglass, Hypalon, nylon-neoprene, polyvinyl chloride, Diolen, and a few other synthetics.

Manufacturers are forever experimenting with new materials and subtle changes in hull configurations to produce better craft for every type of canoeing. Neither they, nor the consumer, would object if in their search they also discovered a way to bring down the soaring cost of a good canoe. A few years ago an excellent canoe could be purchased for less than $200. Today, the same canoe will cost upward of $400, and the cost is still climbing. It may come as a shock to realize that the finest-quality recreational and sport canoes sell for over $1,000, while a fine extra-large freighter canoe will cost more than $2,000.

There are two basic canoes: (1) the popular open canoe and (2) the much more specialized closed ("C") canoe, also known as a "C-1" if designed for the single paddler or "C-2" if designed for two paddlers. The C canoes are quite similar to kayaks. The fundamental difference between closed canoes and kayaks is that a C is designed to be paddled while either kneeling or seated, while a kayak may be paddled only while seated. Kayaks have top decks which slope downward. Closed canoes have top decks which may slope slightly up at the bow and stern. Although closed canoes may be used for all types of canoeing, they were created as whitewater craft.

Open canoes vary in length from about 10 feet to as long as 25 feet. Canoes between 10 and 13 feet are "subcompact" models for the lone hunter or fisherman who needs a reasonably lightweight craft to use by himself, or for use by youngsters. The adult who plans to use a canoe only for his own hunting or fishing would do well to consider one of the lightweight 10- to 11-foot models.

Craft between 12 and 13 feet long, while still in the lightweight range, offer more carrying capacity and are suitable for larger children or the adult who may wish to take a friend or child along occasionally on a fishing trip. These are highly maneuverable craft, relatively easy for a person to paddle alone. They are best suited for flatwater and easy trips.

Canoes between 13 and 15 feet long are bastard craft, lacking the lightness of the subcompacts and the stability and useful-

CANOES AND PADDLES

ness of the longer canoes. They are most popular for use at summer camps by youngsters or as a second family canoe for use around a lakeside home or camp.

The most widely used canoes range from 16 to 18 feet. The shorter canoes are more maneuverable. The longer boats are easier to paddle on a straight course. A longer canoe will ride higher in the water than a shorter canoe with the same weight aboard, offering less hull drag, a distinct advantage on long cruises.

Hull configuration also plays an important role in determining a canoe's specific function. A canoe designed for cruising has a flat bottom and a long, straight hull. A flat-bottom canoe is the most stable for recreational canoeing. A straight-hulled canoe is easier to keep on a straight course.

Figures 9, 10, and 11 show how hull configurations and cross sections at midthwart are utilized in making three distinct types of canoes.

The most important element to consider when choosing a canoe is the material from which it is made. Following is a general discussion of canoes of the various materials available.

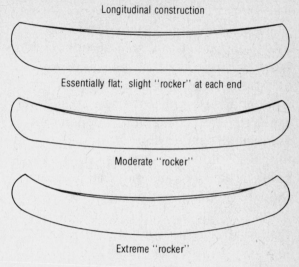

Longitudinal construction

Essentially flat; slight "rocker" at each end

Moderate "rocker"

Extreme "rocker"

Figure 10

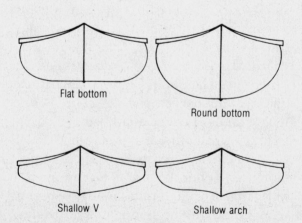

Flat bottom

Round bottom

Shallow V

Shallow arch

Figure 9

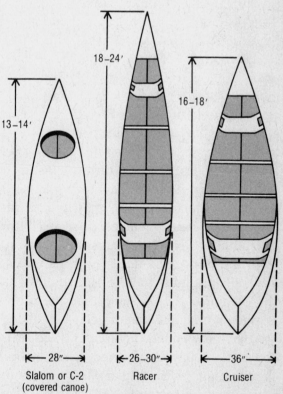

13–14′

18–24′

16–18′

Slalom or C-2 (covered canoe) — 28″

Racer — 26–30″

Cruiser — 36″

Figure 11

Wood

The most beautiful canoe ever built was made of wood. It still is. Just looking at a wooden canoe gives me a feeling of sheer delight. A wooden canoe is a handcrafted work of art. Despite some hesitation in the canoe fraternity to admit it, wooden canoes are superbly serviceable. If properly cared for, they will last for decades. They can absorb a tremendous amount of punishment—though certainly not as much as canoes made from aluminum or the tougher synthetics—and remain intact. They are easy to repair. Unlike other canoes, they do not need flotation blocks or bags, because wood floats.

For whatever reason—the pace of modern life, changing tastes, or the fact that wood requires maintenance—the wood canoe is slowly vanishing from the canoe scene. Its disappearance has been quicker in the United States than in Canada.

Making a wooden canoe involves considerable handwork and may take up to a month. The first step, as in making every canoe, is to form a mold. Pre-cut ribs, usually white cedar, are steamed and bent around the mold and fastened to the keel and the inwales. These, in turn, are fastened to the stems. The ribs are then planked, usually with clear red or white cedar (the colors are sometimes intermixed for artistic effect), and the canoe is removed from the mold. The decks, thwarts, seats, and rails are added along with the last of the planking. At the same time the canoe is given a final alignment.

After the wooden canoe is finished, it is covered. It may be covered with canvas, Verilite, or clear fiberglass, through which you can see and admire the wooden planking. If the canoe is covered on the outside with canvas, the canvas is coated with a silica-base liquid and allowed to cure under heat for a couple of weeks. Then the canvas is lovingly sanded to a satin-smooth finish, the outside gunwales are attached, and the craft is painted with a marine spar or high-density polyurethane.

Aluminum

Since Grumman introduced aluminum canoes after World War II, they have dominated canoeing. The American Canoe Association estimates that in 1977 fully 70 percent of all canoes made in the United States were aluminum. Why? Because aluminum makes a fine, maintenance-free canoe. Unless it is thoroughly maltreated by slamming it around a rock in a fast-flowing set of rapids, an aluminum canoe will be available for your children, your grandchildren, and who knows how many future generations of their descendants to canoe the same waters you canoe today. Assuming, of course, that those waters will remain canoeable for as long as an aluminum canoe will last.

Aluminum has its drawbacks, some aesthetic. An aluminum canoe tends to be noisy, whereas other canoes are silent. The slap, slap of water against an aluminum hull is like a miniature drum. When an aluminum canoe bumps into a rock, the boom can be heard across the river, embarrassing the canoeists, who should have known better and would have escaped detection by their fellow canoeists if they had been in a canoe made of some other material. Some people complain that canoes made of aluminum are either too hot or too cold. This argument is fallacious. An aluminum canoe may heat up more quickly in the sun or cool down more quickly on a chilly day, but it is no hotter or colder than any other kind of canoe.

Aluminum canoes do dent and bend. Since aluminum has no memory, the dents and bends stay until they are removed in a shop or by solid stomping with a pair of heavy shoes when in the field. I have seen aluminum canoes as full of dents as a pock-marked rural highway in the spring, still floating along stalwartly.

It is fortunate that aluminum canoes can withstand such brutal treatment and survive intact, for they are difficult to mend. The usual technique is to rivet a patch over a cut or hole, not an easy operation in the wilderness.

There is nothing extraordinarily difficult about the manufacture of an aluminum canoe. A sheet of corrosion-resistant aluminum alloy is shipped off to the manufacturer. The sheet is placed over a mold and pressed into shape at a pressure of some 3,000 pounds per square inch. Since a canoe is symmetrical, the same mold is used to press both halves of the canoe. The half shells are cleaned, trimmed, and drilled so that later they can be riveted together. Then they are treated by heat to a temper of T-6, or about 35 percent stronger than the original sheet of aluminum.

Finally, the two halves are riveted together. Since aluminum is thin and weight must be minimized, the type of riveting used is important. At one time many owners complained that the rivets rusted or came loose. This problem has been corrected by the use of anodized Alumilite rivets. There is no substantial difference in the effectiveness of flush and round-head rivets, but the more careful builders tend to use flush rivets to satisfy canoeists who fear that round-

head rivets might shear off in an accident. On the other hand, if an accident is powerful enough to shear off a rivet, it probably will shear off a lot more than a rivet.

The most complex part of the assembly is the fastening of the keel. The usual method is to place a gasket atop the keel, put the hull halves on top of the gasket, lay a plate over the halves, and rivet all the parts together. (See Figure 12a.) A less satisfactory method is to place the two canoe halves overlapping and rivet them to the keel. (See Figure 12b.)

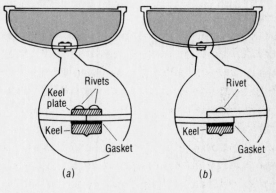

Figure 12

The standard Grumman aluminum canoe is made out of sheet .050 inch thick. The so-called "light" models are made out of aluminum .040 inch thick. The lightest aluminum skin, only .032 inch thick, is used to make Alumacraft's 185 CL. The strongest sheet aluminum, .061 inch thick, is preferred by canoe liveries as well as by those whitewater enthusiasts who don't mind a slightly heavier canoe if it can withstand the rocks and obstacles that lurk in the whitewater runs.

Fiberglass

Fiberglass (polyester plastic reinforced with glass fibers) is becoming one of the most popular materials for making canoes, especially those of highly sophisticated design used for racing, whitewater, and slalom craft. One reason is that fiberglass can be molded into intricate hull designs not possible with other materials. Fiberglass is the major material used in the manufacture of kayaks, C-1's, and C-2's.

Making a fiberglass canoe is not as complicated as making a wooden canoe, but it may take a conscientious builder a week to turn one out. The process begins with a "male plug," really a wooden canoe with all the features of the fiberglass boat. This plug is treated with a special wax. The wax is covered first with a black gel and then with layers of fiberglass soaked in resin to make a "female mold" about $\frac{3}{8}$ inch thick. When thoroughly set, the female mold is removed from the male plug and carefully checked on the *inside* to make certain there are no flaws or blemishes. The female mold looks, in effect, like an extra-large canoe.

The interior of the female mold is liberally coated with a special wax. Then a gel coating is applied. This gel coating is the *outside* of the finished canoe, which is built from the outside in, within the female mold. Next, a piece of glass cloth is placed inside the mold, wetted with a laminating resin, and, in a better-made canoe, smoothed out by hand with a brush and roller. Varying thicknesses of glass cloth may be used. For example, a builder may use three layers of 10-ounce glass cloth and one of 6-ounce cloth.

But the process is always the same: Each layer of cloth is wetted with catalyzed polyester resin and hand-laid inside the canoe. The roller removes the excess resin. If excess resin is not removed, the result will be a heavy and brittle canoe. If patches of glass are not wetted sufficiently. the section will delaminate. The longer the fibers used in the cloth, and the denser the fibers in proportion to the resin, the stronger and more expensive the canoe. After the basic layers of cloth have been laid in, woven roving (a basket weave) or mat (a pressed felt) is added to strengthen the bilges and add stiffness in critical areas.

Some manufacturers use what is called a "chopper gun" to spray the fiberglass on, instead of hand-laying the cloth. Chopper guns use a lot of resin and short glass fibers with about half the strength of the fiberglass cloth. Such canoes are heavier than the hand-laid boats, considerably cheaper, and not nearly as serviceable.

After the basic fiberglass canoe has thoroughly cured, it is removed from the female mold and smoothed. The gunwales, seats, decks, and thwarts are then added.

Kevlar 49

A discussion of this material in *Canoe*, the magazine of the American Canoe Association, said: "If aluminum was called the 'wonder material' of the canoe market in the 30s and 40s, then Kevlar 49 can only be called the 'miracle material' of the 70s and 80s."

Harry Roberts, the editor of *Wilderness Camping*, referred to Kevlar in a glowing commentary as "tough stuff . . . the greatest thing since sliced bread."

And *Explorers Ltd. Source Book* found " . . . it has outstanding advantages over all other materials. On a pound-for-pound basis it's five times stronger than steel, which means that maintaining the same strength factor, a craft can be made dramatically lighter.''

And what is this synthetic which has excited these authorities? It's a golden-yellow fiberglass polyamide called Aramid, originally developed by DuPont in the late 1960s as a tire cord to replace steel cord.

The material is woven into fabrics in much the same way as fiberglass is processed into cloth. Almost the same techniques are used in making canoes out of Kevlar 49 as are used in making boats out of any fiberglass. The result, however, is a canoe which is both substantially stronger and substantially lighter than canoes made out of other materials. On the average, a canoe made of Kevlar 49 will weigh 25 to 50 percent less than one made of fiberglass, aluminum, or wood.

The advantages of such a craft are obvious, especially since the material can be fashioned into the highly complicated curves, angles, and forms of the most sophisticated canoes designed. However, since Kevlar 49 is expensive—it costs about three times as much as fiberglass—and more difficult to work with than fiberglass, canoes made of Kevlar may cost from 50 to 150 percent more than canoes made of fiberglass.

Kevlar is an ideal material for ultralight racing boats. It is equally suitable for a cruiser used on lengthy canoe-camping trips. Imagine the advantages of portaging an 18-foot canoe weighing from 40 to 55 pounds as compared with a standard canoe weighing from 75 to 85 pounds.

Kevlar 49 is also being used increasingly by top-of-the-line fiberglass-boat builders as a reinforcing material along those sections of a canoe that need extra strength.

ABS

One of the best ways to explain materials made with ABS (acrylonitrite-butadiene-styrene) is to compare a sheet of such material to a sandwich. The sandwich is made of cross-linked vinyl, ABS, and a closed-cell foam. A typical sheet might consist of an outer layer of vinyl skin, two layers of ABS, three layers of foam, two layers of ABS, and a final layer of vinyl. Each layer has its own importance. The outside layers of vinyl protect the ABS from deteriorating under ultraviolet light. While ABS resists penetration by sharp objects, it is too rubbery to make a sturdy canoe hull; the foam layers add the necessary stiffness and help to absorb blows. The resulting sandwich not only is rigid but has unusual durability and a reasonably low weight factor.

To manufacture a canoe using ABS, the sheet material is heated to between 305 and 315 degrees Fahrenheit, at which temperature the foam layers expand. The heated material is then pushed into a female canoe mold and shaped by hydraulic rams which force the material into every cavity of the mold. Instead of the hydraulic rams, a vacuum may be used to force the material into the mold.

The canoe shell is allowed to cool briefly. The mold is taken away and the shell is ready for such accessories as seats, thwarts, gunwales, and deck plates.

When the foam expands during heating, it forms millions of closed-cell air bubbles, which provide sufficient flotation so a swamped ABS canoe will float. However, the flotation is minimal. At best, it is substantially less than that of an aluminum or fiberglass canoe with flotation blocks inside the bow and stern. To compensate, better manufacturers will add flotation blocks or line the underside of the seats with flotation material. The drawback to the latter technique is that it makes seats so thick that it is difficult to kneel without catching one's feet under the seat.

ABS canoes have proved to be unusually durable. Their wide acceptance among canoe liveries is testimony to their ability to stand up under every conceivable kind of usage. If a craft made of ABS rams an obstruction, it will spring back to its original shape. Twice I have seen an ABS canoe wrapped around rocks like a horseshoe. In both instances the canoe popped back to its original shape once it was hauled free, though slight wrinkles in the hull indicated where it had been cruelly bent. The wrinkles can be removed by heat. The removal of the wrinkles should be handled by an expert, not by a garage mechanic with a blowtorch.

The ability of an ABS canoe to bounce back after a collision with a standing wave with an immovable center makes it an excellent choice for whitewater. ABS craft slide easily off rocks and are therefore unusually fine for canoeing rivers during those lean summer months when sandbars are more common than water.

Like fiberglass canoes, ABS craft require little maintenance. Unlike fiberglass or wood canoes, however, ABS canoes are difficult to mend. The greatest weakness in designing canoes of ABS is that the material does not take kindly to minute bends necessary to sophisticated hull designs for specialized canoeing.

Within the industry, ABS canoes are known as Royalex by most manufacturers, though Old Town refers to its canoes made of ABS as Oltonar.

Polyethylene

Although polyethylene has been in use for a number of years in kayak manufacture, it has found its way into canoe manufacturing only recently. Basically, this material is a plastic resin blended with ultraviolet inhibitors, heat stabilizers, and the desired color and then formed into sheets 4 feet wide by 18 feet long and about $\frac{1}{4}$ inch thick. Heated to 350 degrees Fahrenheit, the sheet is placed on a vacuum mold and sucked into the desired shape. After cooling, the canoe hull is removed from the mold and the necessary hardware is added, along with flotation blocks under the bow and stern decks (polyethylene, unlike ABS, has no flotation capability).

Polyethylene is a tough material. Though it tends to scratch rather easily, it has an excellent ability to resist impacts and a "memory," which "reminds" the material to return to its original shape. Polyethylene canoes and kayaks are extremely strong and offer the flexibility to handle more easily in shallow water and on rocky stretches than aluminum or fiberglass craft.

Although the synthetic is inexpensive and durable, it can be shaped only with the use of expensive molding equipment. A single mold may cost upward of $40,000, and the cost inevitably will rise.

At the present time polyethylene canoes are marketed by Coleman under the name of Ram-X, and by Keewaydin under its trade name of K-Tek. Because of the high cost of the molds, manufacturers so far have tended to limit their designs to the most popular canoe styles. However, because polyethylene can be molded into more precise shapes than ABS, specialized canoes of this material are likely to be on the market soon.

CANOES AND PADDLES

CANOE SHOPPING

With more than 100 manufacturers producing some 700 models of canoes, kayaks, and kits, finding a canoe to satisfy your particular needs can be complicated. Only after you have some experience with canoeing, and have tried several different models, will you appreciate the differences in canoes.

It is almost impossible for the beginning canoeist to understand the difference between two canoes that look alike, just as it is quite a chore for the novice skier to figure out the difference between an easy-riding, soft ski especially designed for the beginner and a tough, high-performance competition ski. With experience comes an increased knowledge of how design affects what a canoe will do—as a cruiser on a long trip through the Canadian wilderness; as a lively, bouncing craft to dare whitewater; or as a lean and mean downriver racer designed only to win races.

Whenever you find the opportunity, compare canoes. Look closely at how they are made. You can become an expert in quality manufacturing if you check out canoes carefully. Are the seats made out of flimsy bars of aluminum with a piece of plastic to sit on, or are they firmly fastened to the sides of the canoe? Are they well made and comfortable? Are the seats movable? Are the thwarts fastened sturdily, or slapped together? Is there room under the seats for your feet when you paddle kneeling? In an aluminum canoe are all rough edges carefully smoothed? How about flotation blocks in the bow and stern? When you deliberately capsize the canoe, does it tend to float upright, or turn bottom up and fight your efforts to right it? Is that fiberglass canoe made of cloth, or by a chopper gun? Even an ex-

pensive wooden canoe can be made a bit cheaper by skimping on the fittings. Is it made with clear white cedar ribs that are set close together, or common-grade cedar set 4 inches apart?

As to costs, "chopper" fiberglass canoes range from $125 to $250; good fiberglass canoes begin at around $300 and range up to $600. Aluminum canoes cost between $300 and $400. Hand-built wooden canoes range from $750 to $1,000; wood and canvas, from $750 to around $1,100. Kevlar 49 canoes are priced from $700 to $1,200; Royalex, Oltonar, Ram-X, and other forms of ABS and polyethylene canoes, from $400 to $600. The most expensive canoes made are the huge freighters, from 20 to 25 feet in length, which can carry loads up to 7,000 pounds. These range from $2,000 to $5,000.

Almost every canoe manufacturer has a catalog describing its canoes, how they are made, and what they are best suited for. Send away for the catalogs. Appendix VII contains a list of canoe manufacturers.

If you are looking for the most comprehensive information published on canoes, study the annual buyer's guide issues published by *Wilderness Camping*, 1597 Union St., Schenectady, New York 12309, and by *Canoe*, 4260 E. Evans Ave., Denver, Colorado 80222.

Buying Your Own Canoe

It is as much of a mistake for the novice canoeist to rush out and spend several hundred dollars for a sleek canoe after only one weekend on the river as it is for the novice skier to race off and plunk down several hundred dollars for skis, bindings, boots, and poles after one weekend on the slopes. Neither buyer is in much of a position to evaluate equipment. Since canoe liveries are almost as plentiful as ski rental shops, there is considerable opportunity in most areas of the nation for the excited novice to try a lot of canoeing—and a lot of canoes—before buying.

One essential factor which should be kept in mind when purchasing a canoe—in addition to the price—is how it will be used. If your paddling will be confined to playing in a lake outside a summer cottage, you may well settle for an inexpensive chopper fiberglass canoe. If your choice is whitewater, you must have a sturdy craft that can take the punishment of fast channels and hard rocks and bounce back in one piece. If you intend to use your craft only for quiet fishing in remote corners of rivers and lakes, a relatively small canoe will be ideal. A substantially larger canoe will be necessary if you plan to do long-distance cross-country canoeing.

Here are some other points to consider:

- Canoes between 10 and 15 feet in length are popular with young paddlers and, because of their low weight, also with the single fisherman who wants a limited paddling craft that is easy to handle.
- Sixteen-foot canoes are good for general recreational use. They also are a good compromise length for whitewater because they are short enough to be maneuverable, yet long enough for downriver cruising.
- Seventeen- and 18-foot canoes are the most popular for the wilderness cruiser, because their excellent beam-length ratios make them relatively fast. They track well on flatwater. Seventeen-footers are also popular with whitewater buffs.

- Round-bottom canoes are less stable and narrower than flat-bottom canoes, but they are also faster.
- Flat-bottom canoes are more stable than round-bottom canoes.
- The wider the beam and the greater the extension of the full lines into the bow and stern sections, the greater the stability and capacity of the canoe. For example, depending upon design, 17-foot canoes can carry from 600 to 1,200 pounds.
- Asymmetrical canoes with a fuller stern than bow will ride better at high speeds than symmetrical canoes, which tend to ride lower in the stern at higher paddling speeds.
- All things being equal in terms of design, the longer canoe is faster than the shorter canoe.
- A canoe with a rocker bottom is more maneuverable than a straight-bottom canoe but also more subject to being blown about by the winds.
- Canoes with high ends and free boards (that part of the canoe that projects above the water) are more susceptible to winds.
- A canoe without a keel is more maneuverable in whitewater than a canoe with a keel. Incidentally, canoes are built with keels for hull strength, not so that they will track better.
- A shoe (or river, or flat) keel will provide more protection to a canoe than the long, thin lake keel, and will not hang up as much on rocks.
- Wooden canoes and canoes with wooden parts (such as gunwales, thwarts, or seats) require constant care. ABS, aluminum, and Kevlar 49 canoes require the least maintenance.

CANOES AND PADDLES

Care and maintenance of fiberglass canoes are generally limited to minor repairs.

- Canoes of the same model and design made by the same manufacturer may vary in weight by as much as 6 to 10 pounds. If weight is critical, check the weight of the canoe on a scale before you buy. A good bathroom scale will do the trick.

- Canoes made of wood or with wooden parts must be stored under cover to protect them from sun, wind, and rain. However, all canoes should be stored the same way, regardless of the material they are made of.

TRANSPORTING A CANOE

Hauling a canoe around the country generally is no more complicated than hoisting it to the roof of an automobile and seeing that it is firmly anchored. There are two types of commercial gadgets that are useful. One is a canoe rack, a simple set of two aluminum rods that fasten to the rooftop very much like a set of ski racks. Better sets are adjustable in width to accommodate either one or two canoes.

The inverted canoes are lashed to the racks either with rope or sturdy shock cords and reinforced with ropes anchoring the front end to the front bumper and the rear end to the rear bumper. There is only one knot really useful in tying down the front and rear ends to the bumpers—the pulley hitch (illustrated in Figure 106, page 140). In fact, so much power can be applied with this knot that an enthusiastic canoe owner must be careful about damaging either the canoe or the car roof.

For the canoeist who wants to haul his own canoe, canoe racks often are available for rent through canoe liveries.

Another, and increasingly popular, method for transporting one canoe is to use two or four polyurethane "chocks" especially designed to fit on the gunwales so the inverted canoe actually rests on the chocks rather than grinding into the car roof. As is necessary with canoe racks, the canoes still must be anchored with shock cords and tied front and rear to the car bumpers.

It is possible to haul three canoes atop a standard automobile when two can be mounted side by side. The third canoe is placed pyramid style, right side up, between the two inverted bottom canoes. This is a tricky procedure and is not recommended as a standard practice for hauling canoes on highways. It can be utilized, however, as a field expedient when you're deep in the bush and following an abandoned logging road for miles to your put-in point.

Another field expedient for hauling canoes on a rooftop is to fashion two cross braces out of poles and tie them to the roof; then tie the canoes to the poles, lashing front and rear ropes to the bumpers.

Obviously, canoes also can be hauled on trailers. For moving more than two canoes, special canoe trailers are available. Some can transport up to twelve canoes at one time. These are popular with canoe liveries. Some liveries will rent canoe trailers to groups.

2

Paddling

Like many active sports, canoeing demands the mastery of certain skills. Simply keeping the canoe on a straight course in flatwater requires knowledge of strokes and a little practice; canoeing rivers and running whitewater stretches demand a much broader mastery of stroke technique.

PADDLING THEORY

As soon as you begin paddling, you will learn that the stern is the position of greatest control in the canoe. The person with the authority to make final decisions—the captain—is the one who controls the stern. If you are paddling alone in a canoe, you sit in the stern, or at least well back in the craft. From that position you can make your canoe do anything you want it to do. You do not have such control in the bow.

Imagine that a canoe has a central pivot point, like a weather vane. If you push the stern in one direction, the bow goes the other way. If you pull instead of pushing, the opposite happens. (See Figure 13.)

However, this is not the case in the bow. The bow of the canoe goes in the same direction it is pushed or pulled by the bow paddler. (See Figure 14.)

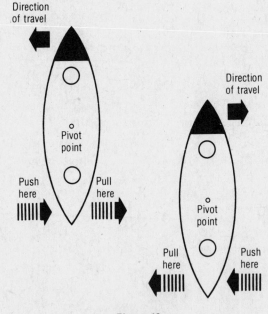

Figure 13

The words "push" and "pull" have equivalents in canoe terminology.

The pry and sweep strokes push water away from the canoe. The draw stroke, in effect, pulls water toward the canoe.

In addition to the pry, sweep, and draw strokes, there is a forward stroke and a back stroke. The forward stroke pushes the canoe ahead, the back stroke pulls it backward, or acts as a brake and brings it to a halt.

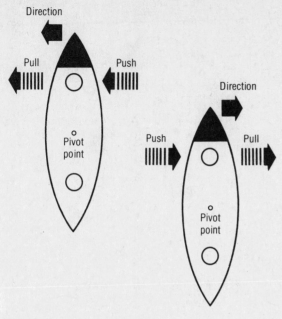

Figure 14

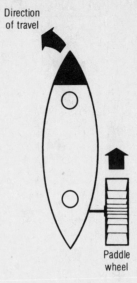

Figure 15

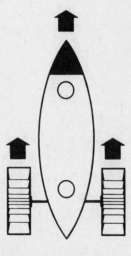

Figure 16

All canoe strokes are based on those strokes or combinations of two or more of them.

If a paddler is in the stern of his canoe and paddles with straight forward strokes on one side of the canoe, the result would be exactly what would happen if an old Mississippi side-wheeler had one big paddle wheel at one side of the stern. (See Figure 15.)

To correct this veering off in one direction, a boat builder might put two wheels on the boat. (See Figure 16.)

If both paddle wheels were the same size and moved at the same speed, the boat would travel in a straight line. You could achieve the same effect by putting two paddlers side by side in the stern of your canoe.

Another way of correcting this problem by the use of paddle wheels would be to place one wheel forward on the port side, the other aft on the starboard side. (See Figure 17, page 20.)

Unfortunately, this solution would not prove totally effective unless both paddles were in the same relative position on the canoe. If the paddles were located in the same position as the paddlers, the forward paddle would be much farther back from the bow, the aft paddle much closer to the stern. The result would be that with both paddle wheels exerting the same force, the

ABOUT CANOEING

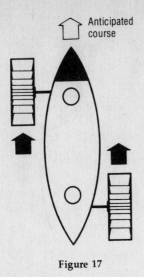

Figure 17

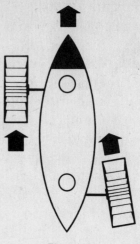

Figure 19

canoe would still wander somewhat off course. (See Figure 18.)

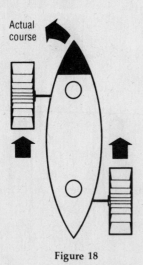

Figure 18

There are several ways this arrangement could be adjusted to push the canoe in a straight line. One would be to turn the rear paddle wheel faster than the forward paddle wheel, or to turn the paddle at a slight angle. (See Figure 19.)

Translated into canoe terms, this is a J-stroke effect, an important stroke which will be discussed later in this chapter.

PADDLING: HOW TO

Before we begin a discussion of the practical application of theory, you will find it helpful, if you are a novice, to get up, go out into the kitchen and grab a house broom, and practice the strokes while sitting in a chair.

Modern paddles are sophisticated tools. To be used with greatest efficiency, they must be used properly. Keep firm control of the paddle. If you paddle on your left, close your right hand over the top of the handle, with the fingers facing forward. Reach down with your left hand on the shaft to where you feel comfortable. Some experts advocate holding the shaft about 6 or 8 inches above the top of the blade. However, find a position which is comfortable for you. Start by holding the shaft about 1 foot above the blade and adjust it as you feel comfortable. (Note: If you paddle on your right, your left hand is wrapped around the top of the handle, and your right hand holds the shaft.)

PADDLING

BOW STROKES

THE POWER STROKE.   The first bow stroke is a straight, reach-well-forward, pull-straight-back power stroke. On this stroke, hold your paddle so that your upper hand is just beyond the edge of the gunwale, and your lower hand is as close to the canoe as you can hold it. This vertical position is the best one for getting the greatest forward motion and the least side thrust out of each stroke. Be careful not to rub the paddle against the canoe. (See Figure 20.)

water, then thrust it back in with a solid stroke, pushing squarely down and back with the upper hand, pulling back with the lower hand. The stroke should be parallel to the keel (see Figure 21*a*). If the paddle is held at a sloppy angle, the stroke follows the arc of the gunwales and causes the boat to turn (see Figure 21*b*). (Remember, for the canoe to move as it does in the drawings, the stern paddler must be doing something at the same time. We'll get to him in a moment.)

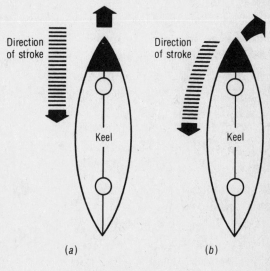

Figure 21

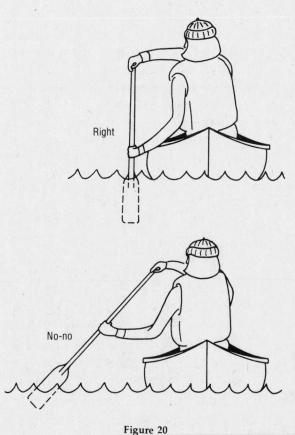

Figure 20

When lifting the canoe paddle from the water and swinging it forward for another stroke, raise it only high enough to clear the

To reduce air resistance, turn the blade to an almost horizontal position when lifting it out of the water. (This technique is called "feathering.") As quickly as the paddle is pulled from the water, let all your muscles relax for a moment, then swing the paddle forward. This one moment of relaxation, brief though it is, gives the muscles a chance to rest, thus enabling you to paddle with more vigor and less energy loss throughout the day.

I prefer a seated position for all flatwater

canoeing. Some canoeists will disagree with this, insisting that kneeling is the only way to paddle. There may be times when I'll kneel simply to change muscle positions to prevent cramping. But sitting is much more comfortable than kneeling, even with knee pads.

I sometimes sit with my ankles crossed and my knees braced against the sides, or with one leg tucked under me and one leg extended. Others prefer sitting with both legs tucked back or both legs extended. Be careful not to jam your feet under the seat; you would be in serious trouble if you swamped with your feet stuck under there.

However, it's important to remember that in bad weather or in whitewater, kneeling is a safer position than sitting. It lowers the center of gravity and gives better control of the canoe through the action of the knees and hips against the sides of the boat.

THE REVERSE, OR SIMPLE BACK STROKE.
The second most important stroke—bow or stern—is the reverse, or simple back stroke. It is not an instinctive stroke. Novices tend to forget they can use it. Often it's the last stroke taught or the last learned. But don't minimize its importance. When everything is going wrong, use it. It will slow you, stop you, or reverse the movement of the canoe. It is the one stroke that gives you time to think while you figure out what to do. It can be used in the flattest of flatwater or in the most turbulent whitewater. (See Figure 22.)

THE DRAW STROKE.
The paddler stretches out and pulls the paddle sharply and directly to the side of the canoe. Recovery is important. The amateur tends to bang the paddle against the canoe. With a little ex-

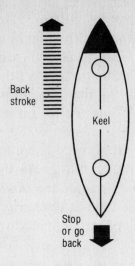

Figure 22

perience you will learn to shove the top of the paddle forward, twist the shaft, and slice the blade out of the water as it comes within a hair of touching the canoe. (See Figure 23.)

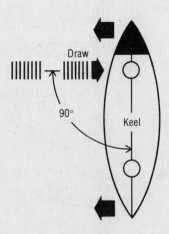

Figure 23

It would appear to the untrained eye that the draw stroke would tilt the canoe toward the paddle. Actually, the opposite happens. In the draw stroke, as the water from the face of the blade pushes against the side of the canoe, the canoe tilts away from the stroke. The advantage is that the paddler can lean much farther out on the draw side and still maintain the balance of the canoe when a long, strong draw is critical, especially in stormy weather or in a fast maneuver in whitewater.

THE PRY STROKE. Now, opposite the draw? The pry, sometimes called the push, push-away, pry-away, or even the "pray" if you need to put it into service fast to avoid a head-on argument with a rock swimming hell-bent toward you in fast water.

Novices are usually instructed in a sort of gentle push-away stroke, accomplished by putting the paddle in the water and pushing it away without touching the canoe. (See Figure 24.) The far more powerful stroke, though, is a pry using the bilge of the canoe as a fulcrum for the paddle. (See Figure 25.)

The pry is especially useful in whitewater or for a very fast maneuver. This stroke bears practice by flatwater canoeists, too, although in flatwater one can be less concerned about the force of the stroke.

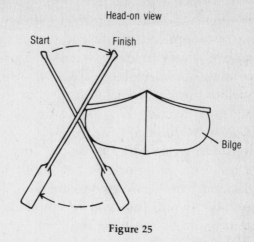

Figure 25

THE SWEEP STROKES. Neither the draw nor the pry provides any forward momentum. They are useful in maneuvering the bow from side to side. The practical sweep stroke accomplishes simultaneous forward and side movement. Begin by dropping the paddle into the water well forward and sweeping it in a quarter circle. If you need greater side movement, the stroke becomes a half sweep. (See Figure 26.)

The quarter sweep is the more useful of the two strokes; this reasonably short, quick

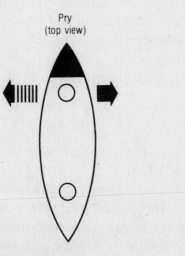

Figure 24

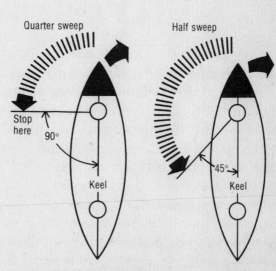

Figure 26

stroke enables you to change course slightly. If you need to make a greater course change, you can use several short sweeps or a pry, depending upon whether you need forward as well as turning momentum.

THE BOW RUDDER STROKES. Using your bow paddle as a rudder is simple. Stick it into the water at an angle of about 45 degrees, and *hold it still*. If you have forward momentum your canoe will veer in the direction the rudder is pointing. (See Figure 27.)

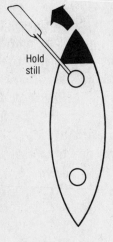

Hold
still

Figure 27

The cross-bow rudder is done *without changing the position of the hands on the paddle*. Lift the paddle up, turn your body to the opposite side of the canoe, and, with one hand holding the top of the paddle pulled back and the other hand holding the shaft forward, put the blade in the water and hold it still. This is a moderately good rudder stroke when you already have forward motion. (See Figure 28a.) You can make it more effective by using a draw stroke, known to the trade as a "cross draw". It is a handy stroke in very shallow water where you can-

not put the paddle deep into the water and you need a light and quick stroke. It is also a good stroke for maneuvering in whitewater. (See Figure 28b.)

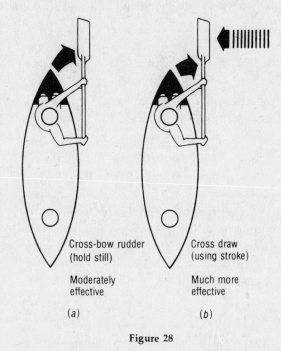

Cross-bow rudder
(hold still)

Moderately
effective

(a)

Cross draw
(using stroke)

Much more
effective

(b)

Figure 28

If you would normally paddle on the right side, then you would do a right rudder, and the left stroke would become the cross draw. All bow paddlers should keep in mind that since the stern has the greatest control of the canoe and is the "captain," the bow paddles on the side opposite the stern.

STERN STROKES

THE J STROKE. The basic stern stroke is the so-called "J." With the J stroke you can canoe well. However, with an understanding of how to use a stroke slightly different from the J stroke, you will canoe with more precision, more control, and less effort.

When both bow and stern are paddling

straight and equal strokes, the canoe will veer to the side opposite the stern paddler's; by his position at the rear of the canoe, the stern paddler's power of thrust is greater on the craft than the power of thrust in the bow. (See Figure 29.)

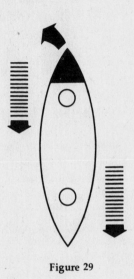

Figure 29

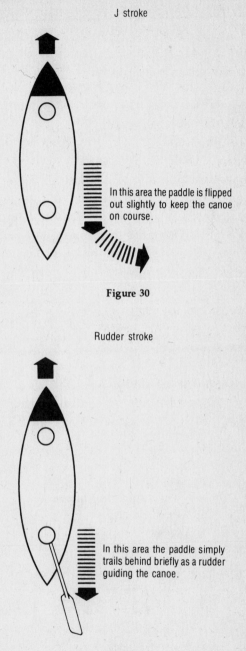

J stroke

In this area the paddle is flipped out slightly to keep the canoe on course.

Figure 30

Rudder stroke

In this area the paddle simply trails behind briefly as a rudder guiding the canoe.

Figure 31

To keep the canoe on course, the stern paddler must make some adjustment in his stroke. One way to do so is by using the traditional J, or flipping the paddle slightly out at the end of the stroke to keep the canoe on course. (See Figure 30.)

The weakness of this stroke is that while the muscular effort of the first part of the stroke propels the canoe forward, part of the momentum is lost by converting the forward motion to a side motion at the end of the stroke.

Modifying this stroke slightly requires less muscle and still serves the necessary purpose of keeping the canoe on course. To do so, end the stroke with the blade vertical to the water, and use the final part of the stroke as a rudder to hold the craft straight. (See Figure 31.)

THE MODIFIED J STROKE. Now we come to the modified J stroke or, as some call it, the parallel turn. In this stroke the paddle moves in a straight line, much as though the paddler were going into a rudder position. However, as the paddle sweeps back, the hand on the paddle grip rotates to the outside so the stroke ends with the *thumb pointed straight down*. If the blade is held in a straight line as it moves backward in this stroke, the force of the blade moving at an angle will keep the bow straight while the blade turns.

This particular stroke takes considerable time and a fisherman's patience to master. The amount of outward rotation of the upper hand varies with the amount of pressure necessary to keep the canoe on course. One stroke may require the thumb to rotate fully downward. In the next, only a slight downward rotation may be necessary. In some cases—as in the J and rudder strokes—only a straight, simple stroke without any fancy flips, twists, or torques at the end is necessary. (See Figure 32.)

THE STERN RUDDER STROKE. The simplest "stroke" of all for the stern paddler is to use the paddle only as a rudder. (See Figure 33.)

It sounds elementary, doesn't it? Yet many of us, as novices, had difficulty using the stern paddle as a rudder and discovered that, without any more work than moving the rudder to the right or left, we could swing the bow of the canoe in one direction or another. Perhaps the rudder presents difficulty to the novice because the novice fails to *put the blade well into the water and hold it there*. If the stern paddler wants the canoe to swing to the right, he would position the paddle as in Figure 33*a*. If he wants it to swing left, he places the paddle as in Figure 33*b*.

Obviously, there must be forward momentum for a stern rudder movement to make an impression on the course of the canoe.

A warning to bow paddlers: When you're paddling your heart out and don't seem to be making the usual headway, sneak a peek back. Your stern paddler could be merely coasting and ruddering.

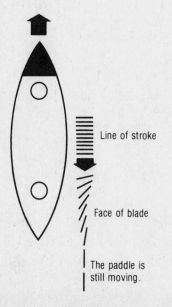

Line of stroke

Face of blade

The paddle is still moving.

Figure 32

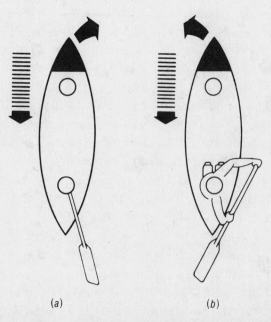

(a)   (b)

Figure 33

PADDLING

The remaining stern strokes are the same strokes learned by the bow paddler. The reaction of the canoe is precisely the opposite to what happens when the bow paddler does them, because of the "pivot point" principle. (See Figures 34, 35, and 36.)

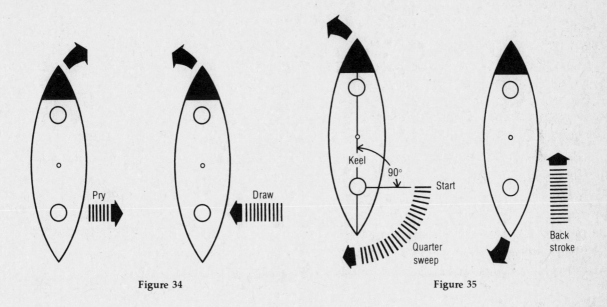

Figure 34

Figure 35

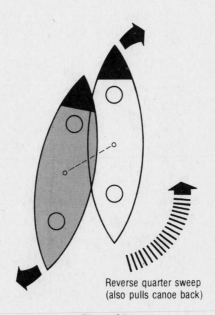

Figure 36

3

Underway

Once you've become a tolerably efficient armchair-and-broom paddler, it's time to put in for the real thing. It's not necessary to carry most canoes all the way into the water before climbing in. Sand, gravel, and the small rocks around shore will inflict virtually nothing but slight scratches on hulls made of aluminum or any of the tough synthetics. (However, if you're handling a wooden canoe with a canvas hide, you must be considerably more conservative in your launching techniques.)

Canoes may be launched in one of two modes. If the water next to the shore is quite deep, the canoe can be placed parallel to the bank. Until you've gained experience, one paddler should hold the canoe steady while the other steps carefully in, keeping the weight absolutely centered over the keel. When the first canoeist is secure, the second steps in, being especially cautious about accidentally pushing the canoe from shore while stepping aboard.

Most of the time, however, you will launch your canoe with the craft pointed toward the center of the stream. When launching in this mode, the bow should be slid into the water with the other end barely resting on the bank. One canoeist steps up to the canoe, tucks the stern between his legs, and leans forward, holding the canoe firmly by both gunwales. The bow partner steps in, works his way forward, and takes his seat—being cautious at all times to keep his weight centered directly over the keel. The stern paddler then puts one foot in the canoe, shoves off with the other, and then carefully takes his seat.

When moving forward or aft in a canoe, keep your weight centered. If you keep one hand on each gunwale when moving in the canoe, your weight should stay safely centered. You'll fall into trouble—or water—when you casually place both hands on the same gunwale and shift weight.

Being able to set out a canoe without mishap is important, too. When canoeing wilderness rivers and lakes, one often reaches take-out points on portages where the shore is a steep bank and the water too deep to stand in. How does one get a canoe ashore in that situation? With muscle, sweat, and difficulty! The only workable technique is to nuzzle the canoe against the bank. Usually the stern does the nuzzling while the bow climbs ashore. Then the bow steadies the canoe so the stern can climb awkwardly across gear and thwarts to the bank.

UNDERWAY

Continue to heave, pull, and drag until the whole heavy canoe is well ashore. The tough canoe hide is undaunted by the experience. However, show the canoe some respect. Don't jam it into rocks or otherwise maltreat it.

Once underway, rock your canoe from side to side. Your body should shift to counter each tilt. Do this three or four times and get some feeling for how far your canoe will tilt with safety.

Next, the paddlers should take turns standing up. Keep your paddle in the water. There will be times when you want to stand to see what's ahead. Get the feel of it.

After you have familiarized yourself with basic strokes on the water, try some maneuvers. Paddle a figure eight. Make the canoe turn in circles tighter and tighter until it is practically spinning. Move the canoe sideways by a combination draw in bow, pry in stern. Finally, paddle backward 100 yards, retaining full control over the direction of travel.

In order to do this last maneuver properly, the bow paddler paddles a sturdy back stroke, looking backward as he does so. The stern paddler pivots on his hips until he is facing the stern and uses a stroke akin to a series of draw strokes and pry strokes. By keeping the paddle extended as far backward as possible, however, the stern paddler controls the direction of the canoe.

Paddling is normally done on one side. It should never be necessary for the stern to shift the paddle from one side to the other side in order to maintain control over the direction of the canoe. If the stern does change sides, he does so either in response to a specific situation which can be handled in no other way or because he wishes to change sides—in order to practice paddling the opposite side or to relieve the pressure on his muscles. He does not change from side to side to side to side to control the direction of the canoe. The surest sign of the ill-trained canoeist or the uninformed novice is that he will do precisely that: shift the paddle from one side to the other as often as every few strokes in order to keep the canoe under control.

There is a singular exception to this rule. If you watch a downriver race with keenly trained and highly skilled paddlers driving a slender needle of a canoe at an unbelievable pace, you will see that the paddlers switch sides every half dozen to a dozen strokes. When you and your partner want to travel like demons across the water, do likewise.

FLATWATER

Even the most experienced team constantly makes minor adjustments to keep the canoe on course. The secret is in the word "minor." After a while one develops an almost sixth sense of the direction in which and approximate speed at which the canoe is moving. Every slight variation from the course is met by a slight corrective maneuver. It is in this area of adjustment that the novice makes most of his early mistakes. (See Figure 37.)

The experienced canoe team, on the other hand, would make a slight adjustment at position 2, then continue downriver. (See Figure 38.) Notice: It would take the same number of strokes to move from position 1 to position 5, but the experienced team will go at least 25 percent farther.

For the inexperienced paddler, the difficulty of maintaining a steady course is compounded by the very fact that he is traveling on an unfamiliar medium—water. The flu-

ABOUT CANOEING

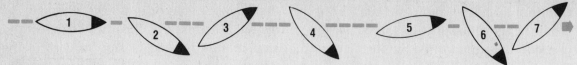

1. On course.

2. Discovering he is paddling off course, canoeist tries corrective maneuver.

3. Overcorrects, then paddles hard to amend mistake.

4. Overcorrects again.

5. Almost makes it, but still must make adjustment.

6. Overcorrects again.

7. Overcorrects again. Wants to go home.

Figure 37

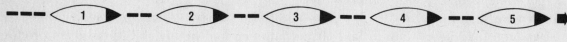

Figure 38

idity of the water, the shifting of currents, the play of the wind upon the canoe, the movement of waves and ripples—all affect one's sense of direction. Take the case of a light, playful tail wind. The wind will kick up ripples of waves and send them racing along the water. If you watch the water while paddling, you will feel that you are going slower when the tail wind is pushing the ripples past you and faster when the wind dies away and the water becomes calm. This is an illusion. With the tail wind you are moving at a brisker clip even though the waves racing past the canoe may give you a momentary feeling that you are actually drifting backward. To avoid losing your sense of speed and direction, paddle with stationary objects as "aiming stakes."

If you are on a lake, your basic aiming stake can be a spot on the far horizon; if you are on a wide river, it can be a particular hill, tree, or rock. Keep the bow "aimed" at the particular target. This will help you determine whether you are traveling in a straight line or weaving back and forth. *Shift the aiming stake frequently*, especially on river

travel. It also is very helpful to check the banks from time to time. Thus, you have two points of reference: the basic aiming stake ahead and the bank. Unless you have two reference points, the current and the curves of the river will conspire to throw you off course. (See Figure 39.)

The mistake in following only the riverbank or lakeshore is obvious once you study yourself in relation to the body of water. (See Figure 40.) Unfortunately, it is not nearly so obvious when you are a small canoe on a large body of water. Obvious or not, the error of using only the bank or shore as a reference point causes a lot of unnecessary work.

Crossing from one riverbank to another is known as "ferrying" or "setting."

This maneuver is easiest in slow water. In a gentle current it is possible to ferry across pointed almost directly toward the opposite bank. (See Figure 41.) In fast-flowing water the angle of the canoe in relation to the current might be as slight as 10 or 15 degrees. (See Figure 42.)

Both of these ferry maneuvers should be

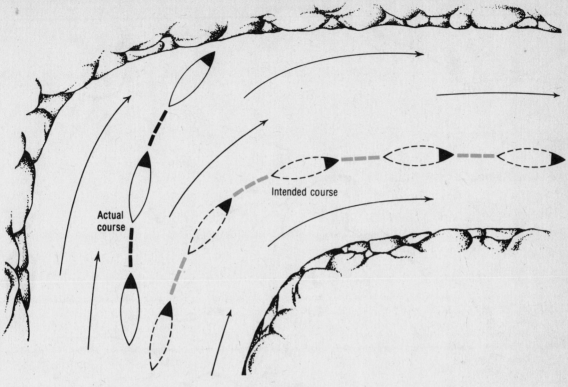

Actual course

Intended course

Figure 39

practiced by every canoeist until he can accomplish them as easily as paddling gently downstream.

In order for canoeists to successfully take out where there is almost any kind of current, from light to modestly heavy, the canoe must be properly positioned. The canoe is swung bow upstream and nosed into the shore at an upstream angle to the current. (See Figure 43.) Nosing in at a downstream angle is an invitation to trouble. Attempting to put the canoe straight in, as in Figure 44(3), could mean the current would sweep the canoe back out (4).

Under normal circumstances, look for any kind of obstruction when coming ashore in a swift current and put in just below it. The obstruction could be a rock or a shallow hollow on the shoreline. Water flowing around the obstruction creates a back eddy of calm water. (See Figure 45.)

WIND

Few moments in canoeing are more blessed than when, after a long and wearying day, the wind suddenly springs up with a light, steady breeze at your back, pushing you along, saving wear and tear on the muscles. But for each one of those blessed moments, there is another not quite so blessed when the wind is head-on, slowing your swift forward progress to an aching fight against the uncooperative elements or blasting your canoe to one side or the other, stubbornly challenging you to use all of your

ABOUT CANOEING

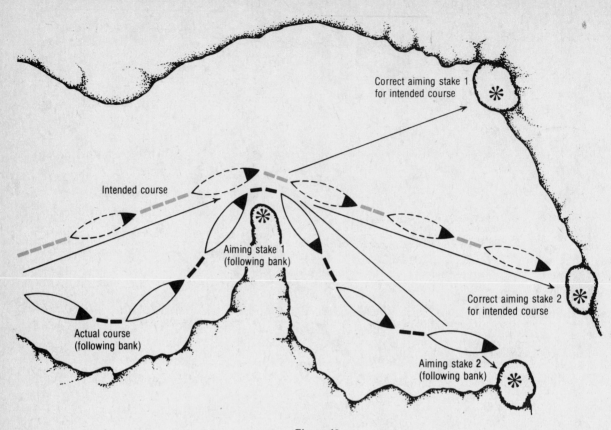

Correct aiming stake 1
for intended course

Intended course

Aiming stake 1
(following bank)

Correct aiming stake 2
for intended course

Actual course
(following bank)

Aiming stake 2
(following bank)

Figure 40

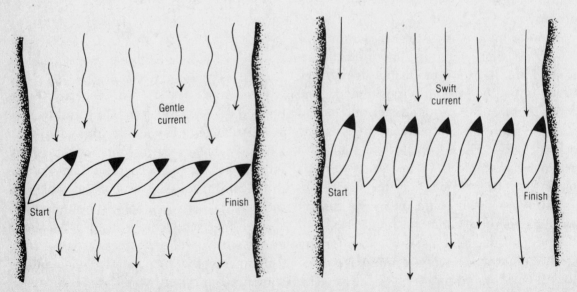

Gentle
current

Start

Finish

Swift
current

Start

Finish

Figure 41

Figure 42

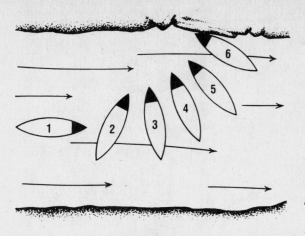

Figure 43

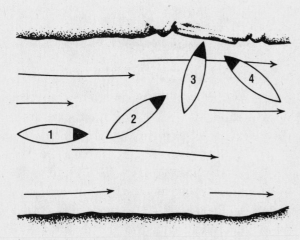

Figure 44

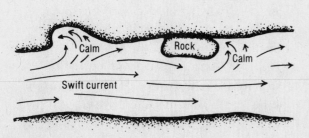

Figure 45

skills to maintain directional control over your craft.

Light breezes are no particular problem in either river or lake canoeing, regardless of the direction from which they come. They will make your forward progress easier if they come at you from the stern, slow you down if they are head winds, and cause you to use more pry or draw strokes if they shove against you from the side; but with muscle and modest skill you can handle any of these. When the winds increase in power, however, trouble sets in and real canoeing skill is essential.

Tail winds can be fun. If they are reasonably light, you face no problem on flatwater. Rig up a temporary sail and let the air speed you effortlessly on your way. You'll find the opportunity arises seldom enough.

To hoist a good jury-rig sail in a matter of seconds, the bowman—never the stern—should stand up, grab a poncho, hold the bottom down with his feet, spread his arms, and let 'er blow. With a little experimentation it also is possible to cut a couple of saplings, attach each side of the poncho to a sapling, and use this as a sail. It is important even when running with a light wind for the stern to control the direction of the canoe. This usually is done through the lazy technique of steer ruddering.

In a light tail wind, trim the canoe so that the bow rides at a higher level than the stern, because a canoe will behave much like a weather vane in the breeze. Work this effect to greatest advantage by keeping the bow as high as possible in relation to the stern.

The situation changes when canoeing a river, where shifting currents, bends, and rapids (even slight ones) add to the complexity of paddling. A light breeze has a tendency to hold the canoe in the direction it is blowing. At times this may prove a considerable help, but when you're trying to navigate a set of rapids, the wind will be handicap. Under such circumstances, grin and paddle. Forget the mast except on long, clear stretches where a jury-rig sail can be tossed up in seconds and taken down equally quickly. Breezes can cause trouble when there is a sudden need for a change in course while someone is holding a sail aloft.

While lake canoeing in light winds it also is possible to lash two canoes together and erect a poncho sail between them. The canoes are lashed catamaran style with a long pole fore, a second aft, and the canoes reasonably parallel to each other. To keep water from piling up between the two canoes, space the bows 3 to 4 feet apart and the sterns 5 to 6 feet apart. Erect the sail at the front of the canoes. The two bow paddlers may do so by holding a poncho between them. And the stern paddlers? Relax and steer.

Paddling into a head wind or crosswind is another matter.

First, the head-wind problem. If you paddle directly into a head wind with no shift in the direction of the canoe, you will offer the smallest possible target to the wind. But with the slightest movement off course, the wind will start to push the canoe broadside.

If you are paddling at an angle to a wind pattern, a change of sides by one or both paddlers may make progress much easier. Suppose you are paddling—stern on the right, bow on the left—with the breeze coming in from starboard. To keep on course in this situation will require a continual J-stroke pattern or some determined prying. (See Figure 46.)

If you shift sides, however, the bow can

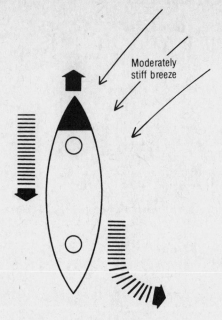

Figure 46 *Even considerable J paddling or prying by the stern results in losing forward motion.*

paddle with a straight stroke and the stern with a modest sweep to hold the course. (See Figure 47.) If the wind velocity increases, both paddlers must shift to the same side to hold course. (See Figure 48.)

At times, especially on large lakes, you must paddle at an angle to the wind in order to avoid broaching in waves, regardless of whether this keeps you on your true course. Windblown waves are highest on long lakes with powerful breezes. Such waves can reach heights of 3 to 4 feet, quite rough enough to capsize or swamp your boat.

If a canoe hits these huge waves head-on, as the bow drops into the trough between waves, the stern still riding high, the approaching wave may sweep over the canoe. (See Figure 49.) A maneuver used to avoid this disaster is a deliberate "quartering," or cutting the wave at an angle. This maneuver presents the largest possible bow area to

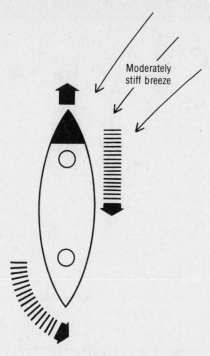

Figure 47 *Changing sides makes it easier to hold course without losing so much paddling energy.*

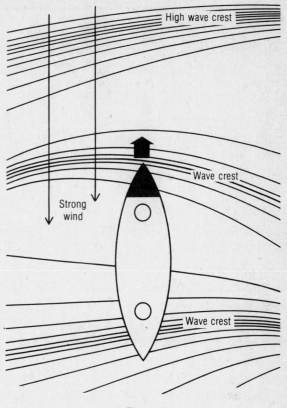

Figure 49

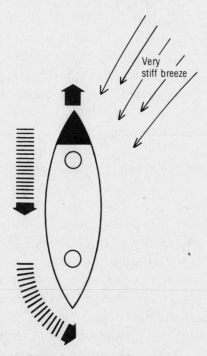

Figure 48 *Both paddles on same side to hold course.*

ride over the wave and the least danger of plowing head-on into it.

However, as soon as you quarter, you're faced with another danger: broaching. This problem develops when the bow rides up an oncoming wave at one angle and the stern drops into the trough at exactly the opposite angle. Both bow and stern must fight constantly to keep the canoe from being swept at a right angle to the waves and rolled over by the next wave. In this situation, the bow must maintain a rapid forward paddling momentum while the stern keeps the canoe from swinging into the trough. (See Figure 50.)

Running before a breeze is a breeze—except when the tail wind is strong enough to start kicking up high, mean waves. A tail

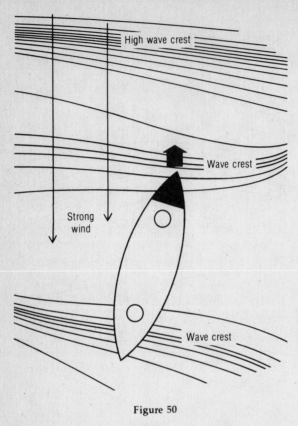

Figure 50

overboard. A word of warning: The painter must be fastened at or near the waterline. If it is too high (fastened, for example, to the stern deck or to the side of the stern seat), the anchor may actually pull the stern into the water instead of stabilizing the craft.

READING WATER

The early-morning sun splashed across the valley. Wisps of mist spiraled lazily upward from the glass-sheen surface of the river. Two ducks, flying fast and low, swept past. The rat-a-tat-a-tat-a-tat of a woodpecker drilling into a dead trunk for his breakfast echoed through the calm air.

While Jerry and I loaded the canoe we could hear the ominous rumble of a stretch of modest whitewater, though at that time, with our lack of experience, the word "modest" probably should have been "ferocious."

We pushed off with Jerry in the bow while I took the stern.

The current carried us toward the first bend faster than we had anticipated. We could see numerous rocks jutting out of the water and occasional white standing waves.

From the corner of my eye I saw two other canoes moving quickly through the same stretch, but following a channel well to the right of us. The two canoes maneuvered with the agility of acrobats, leaping from one clear stretch of water to another. Our progress came to an abrupt halt atop a rock. We both cursed as we struggled to get the canoe off. Finally, I climbed onto the rock, which was covered with foaming water, struggled against the slippery surface for a foothold, and gave a mighty shove. The canoe slipped back into the water. I grabbed for a gunwale and almost turned the canoe over as I tumbled inside. The canoe bounced, scraped, and gyrated through the rapids.

wind on an open lake really sweeps across the water, piling up the waves as it travels. In a stiff breeze both the wind and the waves move faster than the canoe. As the waves get bigger, outracing the canoe, the boat begins to bob up and down perilously as the waves roll forward. This action throws the bow up until the canoe fails to mount the waves and slides back. When this happens, an onrushing high wave can overrun the stern.

Once again, a quartering maneuver will help. But again the other problem promptly presents itself: the threat of broaching in the troughs. In a tail wind a sea anchor can provide enough drag to keep the canoe from being swung broadside to the waves. A sea anchor can be fashioned from a large pot or kettle tied to the stern painter and tossed

UNDERWAY

The noise of the aluminum hull as it banged into rocks sounded like a broken-down truck loaded with empty oil drums rattling across a rutted dirt road.

Suddenly, all was calm and peaceful. We had made it. And there was not more than 6 inches of water sloshing around in the bottom of the canoe.

We bailed the canoe out and started off again. Rounding a bend, we saw the two canoes which had slipped so gracefully through the rapids. They were floating side by side in the center of the river while the four people aboard relaxed and enjoyed the sunshine.

We pulled alongside. I apologized for the intrusion, but, I said, I was puzzled at how easily they had seemed to skim through those violent rapids, while we'd had such trouble. Was there a secret?

One man said he didn't think it was a secret so much as a matter of learning to read the water. His words are as true now as when I first heard them: "You will never really learn how to canoe until you can read the water."

The waves and currents of the river tell you what lies ahead of your canoe and beneath the surface. Waves and currents tell you the gradient of the river and the location of rocks and obstructions of all sorts (including those deceptive rockopotamuses, which rear up under canoes when the river seems virtually calm, and the angry rockagators, those vicious animals which give you a bad time in the rapids).

River waves are different from ocean waves. In the ocean, the wave moves and the water stands still. In a river, the water moves and the crested waves stand still, forming what are known as "standing waves" or "haystacks."

Haystacks are the canoeist's delight—for the bigger and more regular they are, the deeper and clearer is the channel beneath them. Standing waves occur in a series of scallops spaced rather evenly, beginning with a large wave, followed by a series of smaller waves. They are formed when a fast current flows into a deeper and lower channel; they are the result of the dissipation of the energy of the water as it slows down on reaching the deeper channel. Learn to recognize them. The regularity of the standing waves is a certain indicator of an open run. Danger exists only if the first two or three haystacks are huge enough to swamp an open canoe when water sweeps over the gunwales as the craft bounces through. (See Figure 51).

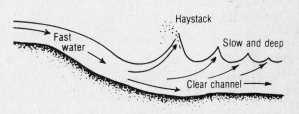

Figure 51

The same wave patterns occur when water is flowing between rocks. The water flowing over and around rocks and ledges will dissipate its force on the obstructions. Water flowing down a clear channel will develop the characteristic scalloped wave pattern that marks the deeper water without obstructions. (See Figure 52.)

Submerged rocks indicate their presence by creating everything from slight "pillows" to foaming standing waves. Greater turbulence on the surface indicates fast water

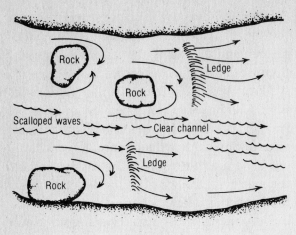

Figure 52

with a foaming crest, the typical haystack. Depending on the size of the rock and the flow of the water, it may be anything from a wave no more than a few inches high to one several feet high. (See Figure 55.)

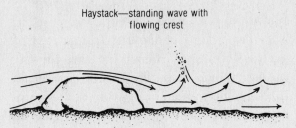

Figure 55

and/or a close-to-surface rock. A partially submerged rock may blend with the river's surface, or the glare of the sun reflecting off the water downstream may blind you to the rock's presence. In such cases you will be amazed at how obvious the rock becomes when you're solidly lodged atop it.

Learn to recognize where the rocks are by studying Figures 53 and 54.

When the current is strong enough, the turbulence is marked by a standing wave

Experience will teach you when you can safely ride the water pouring over a rock and when you must avoid it. The deciding factor is the amount or depth of the water flowing over the rock. The surface of the water over a deeply submerged rock is smoother and more glasslike. (See Figure 56.)

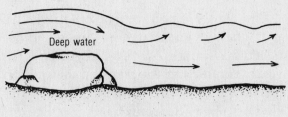

Figure 56

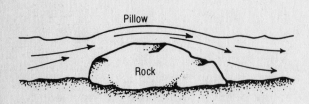

Figure 53 *In a slow current a rock's position will be marked only by a slight "pillow."*

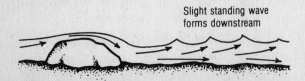

Figure 54 *In a faster current, there will be greater turbulence.*

When the river is wide and shallow, it is possible to find channels which may be passable. You must peer diligently for long, narrow "streets" of deeper, regular waves. Broken, irregular waves and a choppy surface indicate where the water flowing over a rocky bottom may be only a scant few inches deep. The deeper channels ("deeper" in the sense that 6 or 8 or 10 inches is deeper than 2 to 3 inches) are marked by the scalloped wave pattern. When in doubt, keep clearly in mind that the larger and more regular the wave pattern, the deeper the channel beneath the surface. (See Figure 57.)

Reading water also requires an understanding of current flow. When a stream or river flows around a bend, the current on the outside is the fastest and deepest. When the gradient is steep and the water swift, the centrifugal force which pushes the current to the outside of the bend is the same force which undercuts the outside bend and cuts the deepest channel on the outside of the curve.

On a sharp bend the surface current flows diagonally toward the bank, then rolls over, down, and inward across the bottom, thus making room for more surface water. This spiraling action in high water will create heavy, sometimes dangerous wave patterns which can force the unwary canoeist against the outside bank, swamping an open canoe and pinning a closed canoe against the outer edge. (See Figure 58.)

All obstructions in the water create wave patterns and deflect the river flow. (See Figure 59.)

The depth and speed of the current affect your canoe's course. In fast water the canoe approaches an obstruction faster, and the canoeist must exercise more skill and effort to avoid trouble. When you move from a fast to a slow area, you usually are moving from a shallow to a deep section of the river.

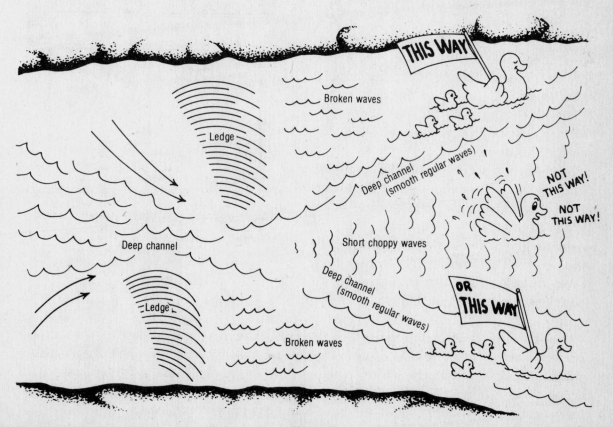

Figure 57

ABOUT CANOEING

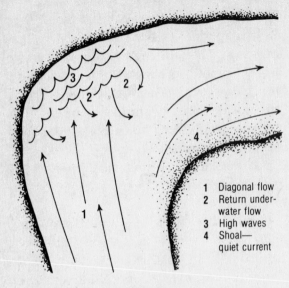

1 Diagonal flow
2 Return under-
water flow
3 High waves
4 Shoal—
quiet current

Figure 58

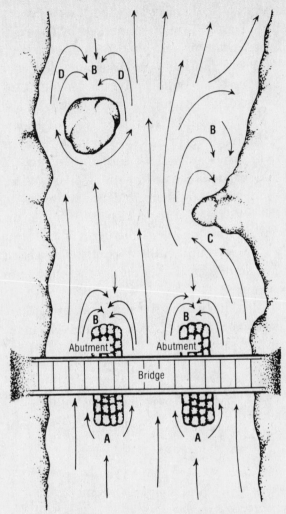

A river loses almost all of its current when it widens into a lake.

Rock gardens look formidable and perhaps impassable to the novice. The experienced canoeist knows there are visible signs which will guide him through.

The most important of these are the "V's." These are your directional signs. Follow them for a safe ride.

When the V's begin to look like upstream "U's," beware. U's are formed by the water flowing around a single obstacle. They have very hard centers.

The tongue of smooth water forming a V is the channel between the rocks. Standing waves indicate a clear channel below the V. Turbulence indicates smaller rocks. (See Figure 60.)

River currents flow at different rates in different places. The current is faster in the middle and slower near the shore, where friction slows it down. The direction of the current generally parallels the shore; however, there are numerous exceptions to this

A Water piles up on the upstream side of an obstruction.
B Upstream current as water flowing around an obstacle reverses its flow.
C Current deflected at an angle to the main current, creating turbulence.
D Turbulence on either side of a rock projecting above the water.

Figure 59

rule. The diagonal sweep of the surface water at a sharp bend is one example; other examples include the many places where the water is deflected by obstructions and the changing shoreline.

Take time to study the river. Climb a bank

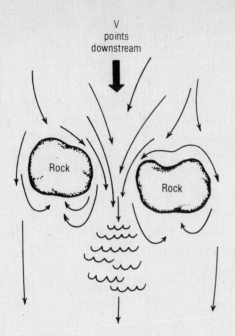

V
points
downstream

Rock

Rock

Figure 60 *"U" formed by water flowing around an almost submerged rock means trouble.*

and look down at even a Class-I set of rapids. Look for the currents. See what the water reveals by its wave patterns. When paddling, glance back at the turbulence behind you and see what it looks like as you slide downstream. It is far simpler to get a good view of the rocks and ledges once you are below them than it is as you approach them.

SAFETY ON THE WATER

They are no longer officially called life jackets. The U.S. Coast Guard refers to them as Personal Flotation Devices, or PFDs. When you are in a canoe or a kayak, wear one.

Visit any river that is popular with weekend canoeists. Occasionally you will see skilled veterans paddling among the novices. There are two ways to distinguish the veterans. They have their own canoes. You can distinguish the private from the rented,

because rented canoes usually have a plaque affixed or stenciled telling the world where the canoe can be obtained.

And the veterans are wearing PFDs. Not the novices. Day hot? Life jacket uncomfortable? Water reasonably calm? Then why wear it? After all, the seats are hard and the life jacket makes a soft cushion for a bony fanny. Unfortunately, if something goes wrong, it doesn't do much for the drowning canoeist.

There are a number of different styles of PFDs. However, when you buy or rent or borrow one, there are only a couple of factors you must consider in making your selection. First of all, is the PFD recommended by the U.S. Coast Guard? If it does not have the seal of approval of the USCG, *don't put it on*. Second, you must wear a PFD designed for a person of your weight. A canoe livery in Pennsylvania recently lost a massive lawsuit when a client drowned even though wearing a USCG-approved PFD which the livery had included with the canoe. Unfortunately, the particular PFD was a child's model. Since the man was a novice canoeist, he had no way of knowing this, although according to witnesses he did mention that it seemed rather small.

The least expensive, and therefore the most widely used, of the approved PFDs is the so-called "horse-collar" type. (See Figure 61.) This fits around the neck and over the chest. It is not an especially comfortable PFD to wear, but in an upset it will help hold the head of a person out of the water, vitally important if the person is injured or unconscious.

We had a particularly graphic illustration of how well these awkward life jackets work when a canoeist with our party broached in a heavy set of rapids and fractured his arm

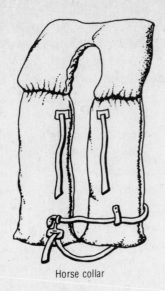

Horse collar

Figure 61

when the canoe flipped over. The foaming water sent the canoe and the two canoeists churning downriver. For a moment there was a lot of laughter among the other canoeists, for no one seemed in any danger. The two heads of the unseated canoeists were well above water, held up by horse-collar, ensolite PFDs. Not until another canoe paddled to the side of the injured man did anyone realize that he was half unconscious from pain and that only his life jacket had saved him from probable drowning by forcing his head above water.

A word of caution, however, about horse-collar jackets. The cheaper ones consist of kapok sealed in plastic compartments. If the seal is punctured, the kapok jackets become waterlogged and useless. Slightly more expensive are horse-collar PFDs filled with closed-cell foam. These cannot become waterlogged. However, if used as seat cushions or badly mistreated, even these in time will lose some of their flotation capacity. Some closed-cell jackets are encased in nylon; others are covered with a rubberized coating.

The fabric-covered PFDs are much more comfortable when you're paddling under a hot sun.

The second style in life jackets is the vest type. Two basic methods are employed in the construction of these PFDs. One is made of closed-cell foam. The other, an aristocrat among PFDs, is made of segmented plastic air tubes. (See Figure 62.) The better vest styles are covered with fabric, sometimes interspersed with netting to provide as much ventilation as possible. The comfort of the fabric or net cover is worth the additional price.

While experienced canoeists tend to prefer the vests, they do have a slight disadvantage. They are not as likely to float an unconscious person head up as the horse-collar style. On the other hand, the vests restrict the paddler's movement less than the horse-collar jackets, and in case of an upset in whitewater, they provide more protection from rocks.

Vest type
(plastic air tubes)

Vest type
(closed-cell foam)

Figure 62

The canoeist should *never* wear a water-skier's waist belt. It may be adequate to provide some buoyancy to the water-skier who loses his balance and is paddling about waiting for the powerboat to swing around and pick him up. It is worthless to the canoeist in trouble.

Not always looked upon as a safety device is the painter, or rope, which should be tied to the canoe. For casual weekend canoeing, I would recommend a painter of 10 to 15 feet. For the wilderness canoeist, the painter ought to be at least 25 feet long. A good rope for this purpose is $\frac{3}{8}$-inch braided nylon with a breaking strength of 1,500 pounds. I find that hauling with a rope of $\frac{5}{32}$- or $\frac{1}{4}$-inch diameter is rough on the hands.

The rope can be used when docking, or in case of an upset. It is handy to have a rope to get a swamped canoe under control.

Since a painter can be a safety device, it should be treated like one. It should be kept coiled and placed inside the canoe so it will not entangle your feet should your canoe nose-dive in rough water. A sturdy rubber band is excellent for keeping the rope from snaking its way all over the bottom of your craft. (See Figure 63.)

A bailer is both a safety device and a convenience. The best bailer I've ever run across

is also the cheapest—a large plastic Clorox bottle with the bottom cut off and the cap left on. (See Figure 64.) Every canoe should have one. Tie a long cord to the handle, with the other end tied to a thwart or the stern seat.

Figure 64

In rock gardens and other forms of rough water, water inevitably will slosh into the canoe over the gunwales. Some canoeists tend to ignore the water slowly gathering in the bottom of the canoe. In whitewater, however, you cannot ignore the increased chances of swamping. An inch of water sloshing back and forth is tantamount to having a huge dog shifting from side to side, sometimes causing just enough of an unexpected tilt to send you careening over the side.

When the water is more than a mere slosh, bail it out while you're floating in peaceful water. If this is not possible, consider making a swift eddy turn behind a rock, or going ashore, and getting rid of the water.

In addition to bailers in each canoe, carry a large sponge. It is ideal for wiping sand, mud, and small amounts of water from the inside of the canoe. (See Figure 64.)

Although helmets are rarely used by pad-

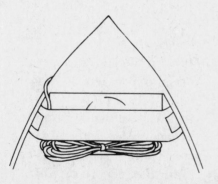

Figure 63

dlers in open canoes, they are a necessity for the kayaker and those who travel in closed canoes (C-1's and C-2's). Closed canoes should not be confused with open canoes with a fabric cover attached. While it is possible to eject oneself from a closed craft when it capsizes, it also is possible for the occupant to hold himself in the craft and use the Eskimo roll to come right side up. The Eskimo roll is accomplished by making a complete underwater roll, emerging with sufficient force to put the craft erect. It cannot be used in an open canoe or an open canoe equipped with a fabric cover. The maneuver is performed basically in a C-1, or kayak. Since kayaks tend to upset where all craft do—in heavy waves or whitewater—the upside-down paddler may be swept along for some distance before reemerging in the sunlight. A knock on the head from a rock while upset is a dangerous way to end a trip; hence the need for a light but strong helmet.

Occasionally, open-canoe paddlers wear helmets, though I would not number them among the items of necessary safety equipment. (See Figure 65.)

Despite all kinds of safety equipment, there will be canoeing accidents. The most common are not normally dangerous. A canoe capsizes and the occupants suddenly find themselves in rough water. Now what? The canoeists should move *instantly* to the upstream side of the canoe, hold on, and float with it until they reach calm water. Failure to do so can turn a minor problem into a major tragedy. Holding on to the downstream side of a swamped canoe is a disaster if you become trapped between a rock and a canoe filled with 1,000 pounds or more of water. Once we helped another party haul a young woman out of a rock

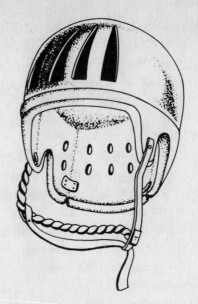

Figure 65

garden after just such an accident. Fortunately, our group included a physician, who administered first aid while we waited for an ambulance. Later I learned she had suffered thirteen fractures of the ribs, a broken collarbone, and serious internal injuries. She was fortunate that the accident occurred within minutes of a telephone, not on some distant and lonely wilderness waterway.

A canoe may get away from the paddlers after a capsize, leaving them stranded on the rocks that dumped their canoe. If this happens, another canoe should come to their rescue if possible, or the stranded canoeist must take to the water and float through the rapids to quieter water. Do not swim in the turbulence of whitewater. Float on your back, feet downstream to fend off rocks.

Because a canoe filled with water will float, it is usually best to remain with a capsized canoe, using it for support or as protection against rocks in rapids. Unfortunately, all canoes do not float equally well.

Aluminum canoes have flotation blocks under the bow and stern decks. While some ABS canoes float without flotation blocks, they usually need some type of flotation block to add to their natural buoyancy. Sometimes such blocks are placed in the stern and bow; in other cases the seats are lined underneath with flotation material. Line seats may be so thick that it is difficult to paddle in a kneeling position with the feet under the seat. Avoid such a canoe. There will be times when it is essential to kneel, and it is no fun if you capsize and your feet are caught under a low seat. If you do find yourself in such a canoe, kneel so your feet are not wedged under the seat, or remove your shoes so your feet will not be caught if the canoe goes over.

There are times when it is better to leave a capsized canoe and strike out for shore than to remain with the craft. If the water is cold, it is essential to get out and to safety as quickly as possible. If the canoe is being swept into a dangerous situation, there is no wisdom in deciding to remain with the canoe and face more trouble.

Every canoeist has an immediate responsibility when a craft capsizes. That responsibility is the safety of the canoeists in the capsized craft. They are your first concern. After someone in your party has reached them, and you are satisfied that they are in good hands, you may concern yourself with the recovery of canoes and equipment. It may sound elementary to stress this primary concern, but I have seen many incidents where everyone in a group was so excited about grabbing a paddle floating away or worried about the canoe, that they overlooked the two paddlers trying to find their way to safety. Once the safety of the water-soaked canoeists is assured, then it is time

to recover equipment, right canoes, empty the water, get the soaked canoeists into dry clothes, share a drink of brandy, laugh at the misfortune, and start off again downriver.

Rescuing a free-floating canoe is usually a relatively easy task. The swamped canoe's painter can be tied around the stern seat of the assisting canoe and paddled into shallow water. If the swamped canoe does not have any gear lashed into it, the rescue can be done in midstream using a "canoe-over-canoe" rescue technique, which is accomplished as follows:

The bow paddler in the rescue canoe turns and faces the stern. Both paddlers then reach down for the swamped canoe. While drawing it across at a right angle to the rescue canoe, they roll it carefully on its side, so that the water pours out as the canoe is hauled aboard. They pull the swamped canoe aboard, so that it is completely upside-down and still at right angles to the rescue canoe. After they have drained the last of the water from the upside-down canoe, they right it and slide it back into the water. By the time one canoe has accomplished this maneuver, another canoe has hauled the capsized canoeists aboard. The operation is complete when the two canoeists have been transferred back into their own craft.

If a canoe capsizes in reasonably shallow water, the two wet canoeists may be able to roll the canoe so that it is floating bottom up, lift it into the air until the last of the water drains out, and plop it back into the water right side up. You must remember, of course, that air pressure will hold all the water in an upside-down canoe as you try to hoist it in the air unless some air can bubble in under the gunwales. When lifting a capsized canoe, tilt it slightly to release the trapped water. Sometimes it is necessary to hoist one end in the air first, then the other.

It is not easy to recover a canoe that has broached against a rock with the upstream gunwale in the water and the full power of the river pinning the craft underwater. If there is gear in the canoe, take it out before attempting a rescue of the craft. To do so, you may find it necessary to stack the wet packs and other gear on a nearby rock in the middle of the rapids or place the gear aboard the second canoe.

If the first effort to get the canoe out is futile, relax. Unless the canoe has been damaged by the broach, it is not likely to suffer from staying against the rock while you figure out what to do next. One end of the canoe is often farther downstream than the other. If all hands concentrate on edging it farther and farther into the current, the canoe may be dislodged and sent on its way. If hand power fails, consider mechanical help. One useful implement is a sturdy pole, at least 2 to 3 inches in diameter. Use it as a wedge to force the canoe free. A pole can be cut from a tree and chopped and trimmed with the emergency hatchet every canoe party carries as standard equipment.

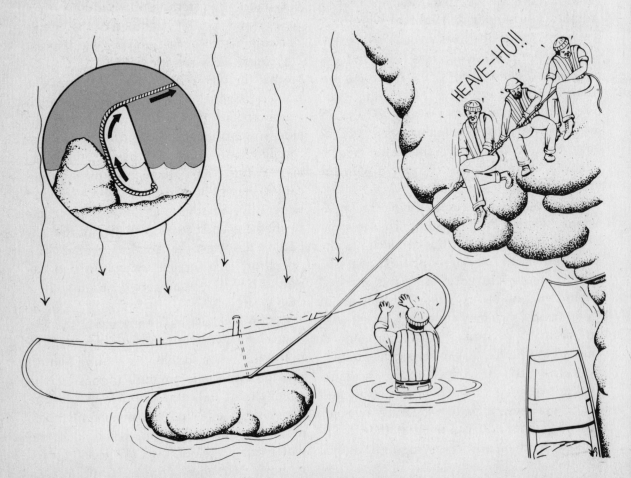

Figure 66

UNDERWAY

When all else fails, sling a rope to the canoe and pull it from shore. In this case, attach the rope so that it passes over the top of the canoe, down the bottom, and around the keel, and fasten it to the canoe at the point where the center thwart is attached to the gunwale. As power is applied, the canoe will roll upstream. (See Figure 66, page 46.)

If the muscle power is inadequate, try the power hitch, a system of converting a rope to a pulley with its 2-to-1 mechanical advantage. (See Chapter 16 for some practical knots for the canoeist.)

4

Whitewater Techniques

In those distant days when only the Indians knew the grace and utility of the canoe, whitewater was treated with infinite respect. Though the Indians startled early Europeans with their skill at navigating rapids, they displayed a strong sense of caution about where they took their craft.

However, when the need arose to canoe through rough water, Indian paddlers rose to the occasion. One early traveler described how she felt as a passenger in an Indian canoe:

> We went with a whirl and a splash—the white surge leaping around me—over me. The Indian, with astonishing dexterity, kept the head of the canoe to the breakers and somehow we danced through them. I could see, as I looked over the edge of the canoe, that the passage between the rocks was sometimes not more than two feet in width, and we had to turn sharp angles—a touch of which would have led us to destruction—all this I could see through the transparent eddying waters but I can truly say I had not even a momentary sensation of fear, but rather of giddy, breathless, delicious excitement.*

Eventually European settlers also learned how to navigate a canoe through rapids. Like the Indians, they did so with caution and out of necessity—to portage every stretch of whitewater would have added an intolerable burden to cross-country travel.

Whitewater canoeing as a sport did not emerge until the development of the Grumman aluminum canoe after World War II. For the first time canoeists had a craft that could absorb an amazing amount of punishment and survive with only a few dents and scratches. The sport has been gaining popularity ever since, spurred by designers who have produced increasingly sophisticated hulls for whitewater canoes, manufacturers who have developed new materials which make canoes sturdier than ever, and paddlers who have developed a greater understanding of the hydrodynamics of canoeing than even the most skillful Indian or early French fur trader.

How far canoeing whitewater has developed as a sport can be seen from the book *Canoeable Waterways of New York*, by Lawrence Grinell, first published in 1948. In it he described a trip down the upper Hudson

*Anna Brownell James, *Winter Studies and Summer Rambles*, reprinted, McClelland and Stewart, Toronto, 1965.

River as it flows out of the Adirondacks through a wild and beautiful valley. The trip took three days. One disaster followed another, with upsets and loss of gear. Today experts run the same trip in less than a day.

Whitewater canoeing is not for the novice. It requires skill and practice. Not until the paddler can use every important stroke with an instant flick of the wrist should he attempt even Class-I whitewater. It is not prudent to learn how to canoe while paddling through rapids.

ADVANCED PADDLING

In addition to the basic strokes, the white-water canoeist must add several more: the brace strokes, the stern circular, and sculling. Of these, none is more important than the brace.

THE BRACE STROKES. I can think of no better way to describe the importance of the brace stroke than Robert E. McNair did in his excellent pamphlet, *Basic River Canoeing*:

> The paddle brace is . . . the most significant addition to canoeing skills in many years. At last we put full reliance in our paddle and use it not only to propel the

canoe in any direction, but also to steady it, to lean it into turns, to correct impending capsize, and event to right the (closed) canoe from an upside down position.*

In the low brace stroke the paddle is extended far out and the face of the blade is pressed against the water. If you are about to capsize in that direction, pushing down hard on the blade is like pushing against solid ground. When used with full power, the stroke will right a tipping canoe or hold a canoe upright against the opposite force of wind or waves. In the "ready" position the paddle is extended, but no pressure is applied until necessary. (See Figure 67.)

The high brace may be used like the low brace, to avoid an impending disaster; it may also be used to pull the canoe rapidly toward a specific point or to grab a changing current. In the high brace the upper arm is straight. Both the upper and lower arms are fully extended. As in the low brace, the canoeist leans as far as possible while thrusting the paddle into the water. Bury the blade deep. If the canoe tilts away from the paddle, a sharp draw will right the canoe. If the canoe should threaten to capsize toward the high brace side, shift instantly to a low brace

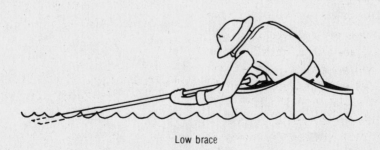

Low brace

Figure 67

*Robert E. McNair, *Basic River Canoeing*, American Camping Association, Inc., Bradford Woods, Martinsville, Indiana, n.d.

to stave off trouble. The high brace also is used as a key maneuvering stroke when entering or leaving an eddy. (See Figure 68.)

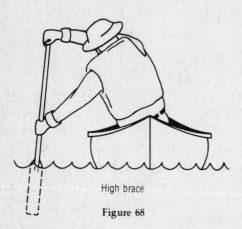

High brace

Figure 68

The novice often fails to place reliance in his paddle when using brace strokes. It may seem as though the outward lean means disaster. It does not. Where the currents are swift and numerous, a firm, vigorous brace may be the only stroke with which you can cross them safely.

THE STERN CIRCULAR STROKE. A stern stroke that can be converted instantly to a brace or back stroke is one which Davidson and Rugge have termed the "stern circular stroke."* It is a good description of a stroke I had long used without thinking of giving it a name. Here, again, the paddle never really leaves the water. (See Figure 69.)

THE SCULLING STROKE. There will be times when it is necessary for the bow to keep the paddle in the water constantly for balance and control. This is especially true in heavy water. The bow must be able to use a draw, a back stroke, or a brace instantly to hold the canoe on course in swift channels. The stroke used in such situations is a sculling stroke, an endless series of figure 8's. (See Figure 70.)

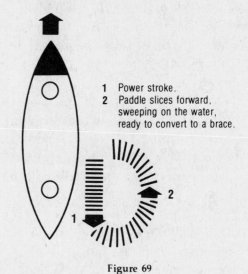

1 Power stroke.
2 Paddle slices forward, sweeping on the water, ready to convert to a brace.

Figure 69

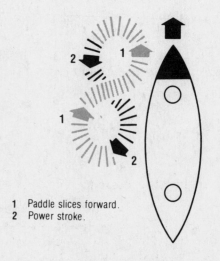

1 Paddle slices forward.
2 Power stroke.

Figure 70

*James West Davidson and John Rugge, *The Complete Wilderness Paddler*, Knopf, New York, 1975, p. 185.

EDDY TURNS AND FERRIES

The eddy turn is the advanced canoeist's best friend. With it the canoeist can whip a canoe behind almost any rock jutting out of the water and take a rest, pause before plunging ahead, or use the maneuver to play games when the mood strikes.

Downstream of every obstruction jutting above the water is an eddy. The water flows upstream below the obstruction, and downstream on either side. (See Figure 71.)

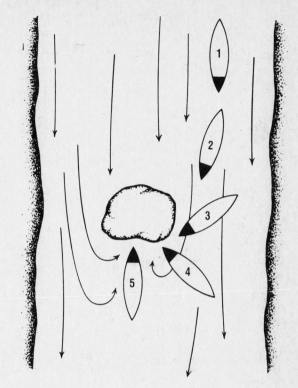

Figure 72

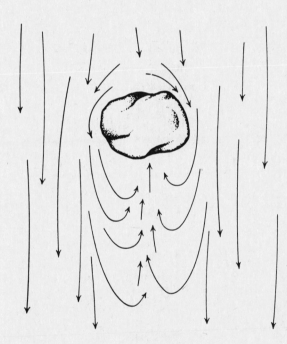

Figure 71

The swifter the current, the clearer the boundary between the upstream eddy and the downstream flow. The eddy turn swings the canoe into the upstream eddy.

Figure 72 shows how the eddy turn works. The canoe is aimed so that it will pass close to the rock (1, 2, and 3). As the bow swings into the upstream eddy (4), the

stern swings downstream and in line with the bow in the quiet water behind the rock (5).

When attempting an eddy turn, you must lean the canoe toward the *inside* of the turn, whether you enter the eddy from the right or the left. As the canoe drives into the upstream flow it also has a downstream movement. The canoe tends to skid across the reverse flow of the eddy. If not counterbalanced, it will flip downstream, just as a car will tip over if you attempt to drive it around a tight turn at high speed.

Although the eddy turn is actually a single, rather complicated maneuver, it can be described step by step.

When approaching the rock from the left, the stern paddles on the right and the bow paddles on the left. The technique is illustrated in Figure 73.

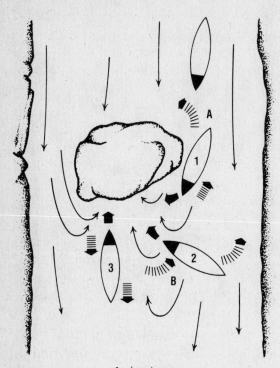

A Low brace
B High brace

Figure 73

(1) The stern aims the bow so that it slices sharply past the rock. The moment the bow enters the quiet upflow of the eddy, the stern leans to the inside of the turn, using his paddle in a low brace.

(2) As soon as the bow enters the eddy, the bow paddler throws his paddle forward in a high brace at about a 45-degree angle, keeping the blade parallel to the keel, while the canoe pivots around the paddle. Then the bow paddler may use one or two strokes to help push the bow into the rock.

(3) As the stern snaps into the upstream current, the stern paddler holds the canoe in line with the rock and uses whatever forward paddling is necessary to keep it nosed up there.

When the canoe approaches the rock on the right with the stern paddling on the right and the bow on the left, as in Figure 74:

(1) As quickly as the bow crosses into the upstream eddy, the bow paddler reaches out with a vigorous high brace draw, reaching toward the middle of the eddy flow. The stronger the draw and the longer the lean, the more stable the canoe.

(2) The stern paddler, using a low brace and quarter sweep, drives the stern into the eddy behind the bow, then uses whatever power is necessary to edge the canoe up to the rock, as in (3).

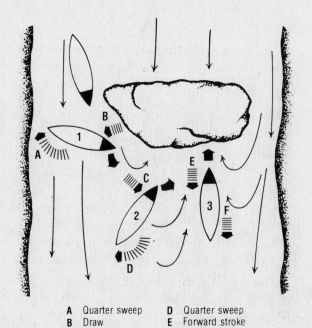

A Quarter sweep   **D** Quarter sweep
B Draw   **E** Forward stroke
C High brace   **F** Forward stroke

Figure 74

Mistakes most frequently made by novices are the following:

- Not leaning the canoe *into* the turn and putting confidence in the paddles.
- Not slicing the bow close enough to the rock.
- The bow beginning the draw while the canoe is still in the downstream current. Instead of pulling the canoe into the eddy, this serves only to push it farther downstream.
- Not turning quickly enough. Here, the canoe will enter the eddy well down from the rock and the paddlers may or may not be able to drive upstream in the weak eddy current below the rock.
- Not approaching the rock with enough momentum to drive it well across the eddy line.
- A combination of any two or more such faults. Result: You either miss the eddy turn altogether or discover how swiftly the canoe can flip you into the water.

Entering the security of the eddy is one maneuver. Leaving it is quite another, though the same judgment and control are required to depart safely—and remain dry— as to arrive safely.

Take a good look at the current differential at the line where the downstream current and the eddy meet; you'll realize the absolute necessity of being in full control of your canoe. You're not heading into the security of a "landing field" but back into the turbulence of the water.

Back the canoe down the eddy far enough so that you can drive vigorously forward and swing quickly at a broad angle into the current. Again, lean *into* the turn. If the bow paddler is on the inside of the turn, he reaches out and grabs the downstream current with a high brace. The working face of the blade must be parallel to the current so that the current will help pull the bow downstream.

The stern paddler sets the point at which the canoe reenters the current. If he is on the outside of the turn, he uses a low brace to help keep the canoe in a downstream lean.

If the bowman is paddling on the outside of the turn, he reaches far forward to slice the blade into the current parallel to the keel and at right angles to the current, at the same time using a pry stroke as necessary.

The stern paddler, on the inside, may use a high brace to stabilize the turn as the current sweeps the craft downstream. If swift maneuvering is necessary, he may use a reverse sweep to help pull the bow quickly around.

Many canoeists new to the eddy turn fail to achieve sufficient forward momentum to drive the canoe out of the eddy and into the current. A good exit requires strong forward momentum. If the canoeists merely stick the nose of the canoe into the current, the craft usually rotates back into the eddy. (See Figure 75.)

When the current is not too swift, it is possible to drop into the welcome quiet of the eddy by setting into it stern-first. In this maneuver, the canoe travels close to the rock, with both bow and stern usually back-paddling to slow the downstream momentum. The stern paddler swings his end into the eddy, first using either the pry or draw. The force of the downstream current then swings the bow into the eddy current. The

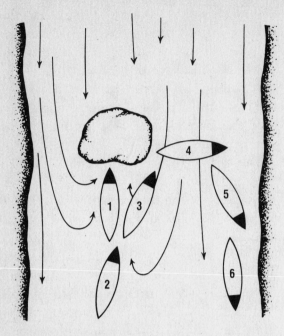

1 Canoe rests behind the rock.
2 Canoeist backpaddles in the eddy for room to drive forward.
3 Picks up momentum to return to the main current.
4 Drives across the current line, canoe leaning *down*river.
5-6 Straightens out the canoe to resume trip.

Figure 75

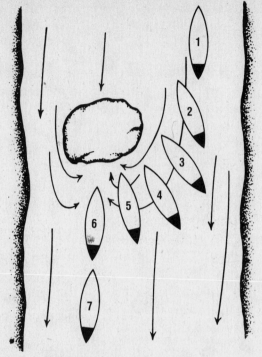

1 Canoe edges close to rock.
2 Stern paddler starts to pull stern toward the eddy.
3 Paddlers backpaddle, stern first, into the eddy.
4 Relax.
5 Canoe starts downstream.
6 Canoe edges out of eddy at weak lower end.
7 You're on your way!

Figure 76

canoe is backpaddled as necessary to the security of the downstream face of the rock.

When it is time to leave, the canoe is driven downstream through the weak currents at the lower end of the eddy. In a strong current it is difficult or impossible to paddle downstream across the eddy line, because the current keeps pushing the bow back into the eddy. (See Figure 76.)

There will be times when you will want to scoot out of one eddy and maneuver *upstream* or across the river without starting downstream. To ferry the canoe upstream or across the stream, the angle of movement must be exceedingly fine. If the angle is too broad, you'll be on your way downstream willy-nilly. (See Figures 77 and 78.)

RUNNING WHITEWATER

Paddling through the rapids requires a combination of skill, judgment, and that all-important ability to read the water. They all come together the first time you start into a foaming rock garden. Suddenly the water looks like a violent, distorted mass of rocks, currents, V's, chutes, standing waves, and pillows, with angry rockopotamuses and hungry rockagators everywhere. The contortions of the rapids become far less menacing as you learn how to handle them.

The first and most important lesson in running whitewater is to keep the canoe aligned with the current. Since the current

WHITEWATER TECHNIQUES

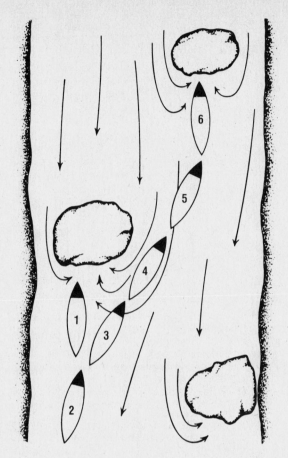

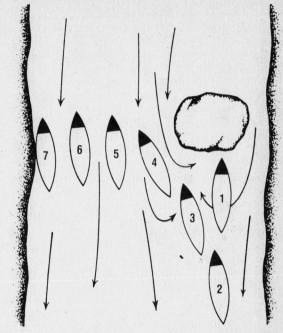

Figure 78 *Canoe drops back, drives forward at a sharp upstream angle. Then, being paddled only at a sufficient angle to compensate for the flow of the current, it crosses the stream in an upstream ferry.*

Figure 77 *Canoe drops back, drives forward, crosses eddy line at a sharp upstream angle, and drives into next eddy current.*

does not always run parallel to the bank, neither do you. If the current sweeps 30 degrees around an obstruction, by a combination of pry and draw strokes, you, too, swing into a 30-degree angle as you whip through a chute. The penalty for failing to keep your canoe aligned with the current can be brutal.

With a little more skill you can ease your craft past the obstruction by keeping it parallel with the currents while setting your course far enough in advance so that you don't have to swing broadside of the current. (See Figure 79.)

How far ahead should the canoe team begin to set a course to avoid that rock? Obviously, the farther the better. There will come a time, of course, when, because of the speed of the current and the number of obstructions, there is no possibility of edging out of harm's way gently. Do not make a fast stern swing to go around a rock. You may move the bow aside, but the stern will only complicate matters by pushing the canoe broadside to the rock. The reason for this unfortunate result is that the bow and stern do not turn on the same axis. The bow may make a fast adjustment, carrying the prow safely past. But the stern, 15 to 18 feet behind the bow, is swinging on an entirely different arc, something like the back end of a car skidding around a turn. The result is disastrous. (See Figure 80.)

Figure 79

in the bow and a pry in the stern, or a pry in the bow and a draw in the stern, depending upon which side each is paddling and by what course they hope to avoid the obstruction. In this case, the course of the canoe is actually on a diagonal without a turn. (See Figure 81.)

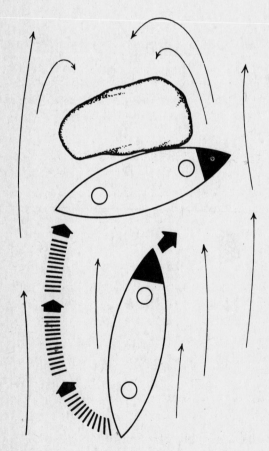

Figure 80

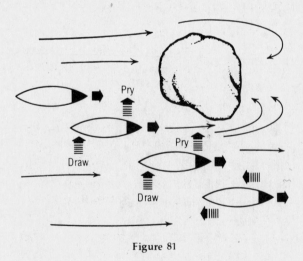

Figure 81

The draw-pry combination must be used vigorously, because it takes a good deal of power to shift the entire canoe sideways. This maneuver also reveals clearly why whitewater canoes have flat-shoe keels, or

To avoid a fast-approaching obstruction, push the canoe diagonally past it. This is done by a combination of a high brace draw no keels at all. Any keel impedes the sideways movement of the craft.

When in doubt about a shifting maneuver to avoid trouble, remember the great ally you have in the back stroke. Applied quickly and vigorously, the backpaddle may slow you sufficiently so that either the current itself will carry you past the obstruction or you will have time to realign the canoe and pass safely on through the thunder and roar of the whitewater.

Every canoe eventually faces the unalterable prospect of ramming into a rock. When this happens, do your best to strike aft of the center thwart. This will help the current swing the bow downstream. Striking forward of the center thwart usually means you'll end up firmly broached against the rock.

If you broach, you face the instant danger of capsizing. This is not an appealing prospect unless the day is hot, the water is reasonably safe, and you are in the mood for a quick dip. The capsize is most likely to occur *upstream*, because water sweeping under a canoe stalled sideways in the current acts like a rug being jerked out from under the craft. In even a modest current an upstream capsize is lots of trouble, because water pouring over the gunwale will overwhelm the canoe almost instantly, locking it firmly against the obstruction.

If you broach, pay swift attention to the upstream gunwale. Now is the time to throw a fast low brace for a recovery stroke. Only if you stabilize your craft can you draw a relaxing breath and make an intelligent decision about what to do next.

The downstream capsize is most likely to occur when the canoe is pushed sideways over a low ledge or barely protruding rock. When running difficult water, canoeists can

usually prevent this by kneeling, so that their weight is appropriately low.

If and when your canoe does ride up onto a rock, and there is no danger of broaching, the current will sometimes swing the canoe loose. If this does not happen, you must either (1) step out of the canoe *on the upstream side* and push it off, thoughtfully holding on to the canoe so you can slip back in when it is free; or (2) remain aboard, but shift your weight, use your paddles as levers, or rock the canoe until it wiggles free. Once freed, you may well find that the canoe has swung stern downstream. Should this happen, don't hit the panic button and attempt to realign the canoe. Instead, pivot your hips, face downstream, and check what lies ahead. You could be plowing into more rocks. If so, paddle backward until you reach a spot where it is safe to swing bow downstream.

Broaching against rocks is by far the most common danger you face in your initial attempts to handle rapids. But a fast current and a sharp bend also can be a trap, depending upon the sharpness of the bend and the depth of the water. On those lazy summer days when the stream flow is low and the bend casual, the wise canoeist will seek the *outside* of the curve, because this is where the water channel is deepest. However, when the water is high, the current fast, and the bend sharp, the extreme outer edge can involve the canoeist in genuine difficulty. The inner curve then becomes the safest course to follow. (See Figure 82.)

There are two techniques for challenging a fast current and a sharp bend. One is to angle the bow toward the *inside* of the bend. Paddle forward in the main current until you can swing the canoe into the slower back eddy at the end of the curve. This is

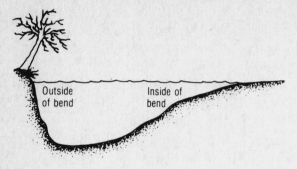

Figure 82

swing the bow downstream in the slower back eddy below the curve. (See Figure 83.)

Here are some general hints which you may find helpful while you're improving your canoeing skills.

difficult. When the water is deep and swift, the forward technique is better left to covered canoes and kayaks. A technique more interesting than hugging the shallow inner curve, but less difficult than the forward drive, is to backpaddle while holding the stern of the canoe toward the inside of the bend, maintaining this course until you can

- With a little bit of luck, a novice canoeist can usually navigate a short, easy set of rapids. Don't mistake this good fortune for skill. Remember, when luck runs out you survive the rapids because you have the ability necessary to enjoy the challenge and excitement of running them.

- Scout unknown rapids. Scramble up the bank, look them over, and determine the best route. Choose alternatives to use if the route you charted from the bank turns out to be impassable.

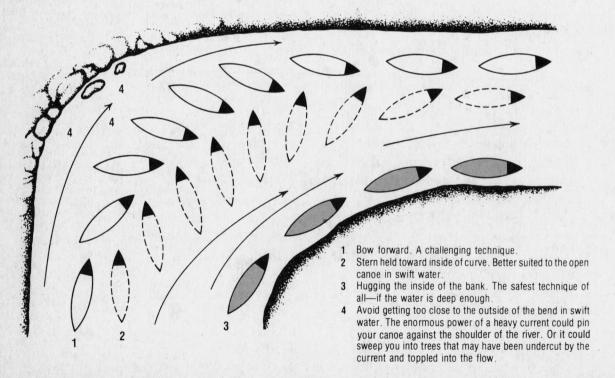

1 Bow forward. A challenging technique.

2 Stern held toward inside of curve. Better suited to the open canoe in swift water.

3 Hugging the inside of the bank. The safest technique of all—if the water is deep enough.

4 Avoid getting too close to the outside of the bend in swift water. The enormous power of a heavy current could pin your canoe against the shoulder of the river. Or it could sweep you into trees that may have been undercut by the current and toppled into the flow.

Figure 83

WHITEWATER TECHNIQUES

- Remember, V's point downstream between rocks.
- The faster river flow is in the middle of the stream because of the friction on the water at the banks and the bottom. On a casual downriver cruise you'll make better time with less effort by remembering this.
- When all your other observations fall apart in the rock gardens, follow the main currents for the most fun and the safest course through.
- In rough water when you suddenly spot a lovely, smooth stretch in the middle of turbulence, beware. The smooth stretch is the backflow of an unseen rockagator.
- When you are hunting your way over a ledge and cannot find a V, seek the largest, heaviest, smoothest current pouring over a section, especially if the flow ends in a series of standing waves.
- If you swing stern downstream in the rapids, check downstream before attempting to straighten your canoe in order to avoid swinging it into swiftly approaching rocks.

Now for some danger signals, the avoid-them-at-all-cost obstacles that confront the river paddler.

A sharp drop may be runnable if the drop ends in that familiar standing-wave pattern, one or two large ones followed by a scalloped series of smaller waves. (See Figure 84.) However, when the drop ends in a hydraulic jump, there will be trouble. A hydraulic jump occurs when the water spilling over a ledge digs a hole below the drop. (See Figure 85.)

Water flowing over a dam or ledge plunges

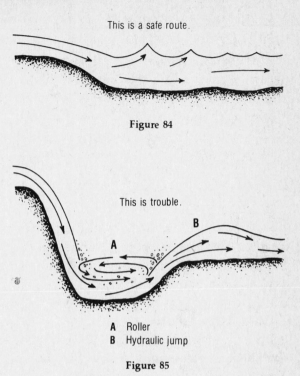

This is a safe route.

Figure 84

This is trouble.

A Roller
B Hydraulic jump

Figure 85

to the bottom, then curves up. The water on the surface rolls back toward the drop, creating a foaming roller. A boat that attempts this run may well be caught up in the foaming roller and remain trapped, rolling over and over. If the canoe does not get caught in the back wave, it may still be impossible to drive it out because of the hydraulic jump; considerable force is required to paddle over a hydraulic jump. These problems are compounded by the fact that the back wave is all foam, so the paddle has no purchase.

If, through a major navigational error, you find yourself heading into a drop that may have a roller at the bottom, your best technique is to ram your canoe forward with all the vigor and muscle at your command. If you're lucky, your momentum will drive you past the roller and up and over the hydraulic jump beyond. Dig your paddle deep to get purchase beneath the foam.

If your canoe is caught in the roller, the most often recommended exit is to dive *below* the water, swimming hard underwater until you emerge downstream from the hydraulic jump. I can't argue in favor of this escape method, because the smart canoeist will be wearing a life jacket, which won't be helpful in swimming underwater. Moral: Don't get caught.

The same heavy drop, aerated back roller, and hydraulic jump may be seen when water is high and pouring heavily over a rock, creating a "souse hole" or "white eddy." The difference between these and the hydraulic jump is one of degree. Leave them alone, too.

Haystacks, those high standing waves on a steep gradient or below a V, indicate a fine, rock-free course to follow, but the 3-foot haystacks on a big river can slosh enough water over your gunwales to swamp an open canoe. When in doubt, leave these to the closed craft.

Occasionally you may find a haystack created by two currents pouring into a chute from two directions, resulting in a pyramid wave. Canoeing the dead center may prove difficult; your paddle may not reach the water as you ride to the top, causing the canoe to slide, stern first, back into the trough between the waves. Quartering is an invitation to broach, too, though a quick brace stroke may save the moment.

Competence in reading water, handling currents, negotiating swift bends, darting through rock gardens, and challenging standing waves comes one step at a time in canoeing. It isn't necessary to practice on foaming rivers that challenge the most skillful canoeists. Practice wherever there is current. On a placid river there still will be an occasional rock or a bridge abutment that will offer an eddy current. Practice making eddy turns wherever there is current. Slow motion is a fine way to absorb an understanding of what both the bow and the stern paddler must do.

As you learn on the quiet currents, move on. The next set of rapids may be a great place to have some fun. Why try to put only miles behind you on a river trip? You may make half a dozen miles instead of 10 or 20, but they may be the most exciting 6 miles you've canoed.

Eventually you'll gain the experience necessary to challenge the wildest of rock gardens and maneuver through the most exciting whitewater on the river.

5

Classifications, Systems, and Evaluations

A river is not dead water. It has relatively calm stretches. At times it is as sluggish as a swamp. It flows into lakes, and races out. It is a liquid animal that bends and twists, rolls across rocks and sand, and drops over ledges. It ranges from swift and narrow to wide, flat, and inviting. Every foot of it is subject to the interplay of currents, the gradient of the bed, obstructions from rocks and bridges, and the vagaries of a long dry season or a wet and rainy spell that turns creeks to rivers, and rivers to rampaging waterways.

Because canoeists are highly mobile, they often find themselves on unfamiliar waterways. This brings us to the first rule of river safety: "The canoeist must always know whether or not he is capable of handling *that* river before he discovers, too late and with a sense of shock, that he is not."

A sensible paddler does not risk life or canoe on water too wild for his skill or wrong for his craft. A canoeist can take certain precautions which will give him a good indication of what he will be up against when planning a trip on a new route.

- Talk to someone who has canoed there before—but make certain each of you is speaking the same language in describing rifts, riffles, rapids, and river flow.

- Look it up in one of the many superb guidebooks increasingly available for both major and minor rivers in the United States and Canada. Be sure, however, that the publication is no more than five years old. Huge dams, major lumbering operations, and resorts can spring up in a few years, completely outdating publication.

- Study it on a topographical map, which will tell you much about the river. (Later we'll get into more detail about what a map will reveal.)

- Understand what the rate of water flow does to a river.

- Know your own ability as a canoeist, and that of your partner.

CANOEIST COMPETENCE RATINGS

First—look at yourself. The Appalachian Mountain Club rates canoeists who participate in its expeditions on a scale of I through V. Check their system against your own degree of canoeing competence.

Class I: Beginner. Is familiar with basic strokes and can handle a canoe competently from the bow or stern in flatwater.

Class II: Novice. Has the ability to handle the more advanced whitewater strokes in either bow or stern, or as a solo kayak paddler; knows how to read water; can negotiate easy and regular rapids with assurance.

Class III: Intermediate. Has learned how to negotiate rapids requiring a linked sequence of maneuvers; understands and can use eddy turns and basic bow-upstream techniques; is skillful in either bow or stern of a double canoe, or in a single kayak, in intermediate or Grade-II + rapids.

Class IV: Expert. Has established ability to run difficult, or Grade-III + rapids, in both bow and stern of a canoe, C-1, C-2, or kayak; understands and can maneuver in heavy water.

Class V: Leader. Is an expert canoeist and has the experience, judgment, and training to lead a group of any degree of skill on any navigable waterway.

To the foregoing, I would add a further classification—"Debutant," in the French sense of the word, to describe one who has almost no familiarity with a canoe whatsoever.

RIVER RATINGS

It is not enough to know your own degree of skill. You also must know how a river, or various sections of a river, are rated. There are several rating systems. Some river authorities classify rapids on a scale of I (flatwater) to X (impassable falls). However, the most respected system is the International Rating System. The following grade levels have been established by the IRS:

Grade I: Easy. Flatwater or smooth-flowing water, light riffles, clear passages, occasional sand banks and curves. The most difficult problems would be caused by artificial obstructions such as bridge piers.

Grade II: Medium. Rapids of medium difficulty, regular waves, clear and open passages with moderate current between rocks, very low ledges.

Grade III: Moderately difficult. Numerous high and irregular waves. Rocks and eddies with passages that are clear but narrow and require a considerable degree of expertise to run. Inspection required if they are unknown rapids. Open canoe will have difficulty.

Grade IV: Difficult. Long and powerful rapids and standing waves, souse holes, and boiling eddies. Powerful and precise maneuvering required; inspection mandatory. Cannot be run in open canoe.

Grade V: Extremely difficult. Long and violent rapids that follow each other almost without interruption. River filled with obstructions, big drops, and violent currents; gradient extremely steep. Reconnoitering may be difficult. Can be run only by top experts.

Grade VI: Extraordinarily difficult. Paddlers face constant threat of death because of extreme danger. Navigable only when water levels and weather conditions are favorable; full safety precautions essential. Violent whitewater better left to paddlers of Olympic ability.

WATER LEVELS

The characteristics of a river change when the water level changes. The volume of water the river carries determines how the water behaves. As you might expect, a set of Grade-II rapids can turn into a raging Grade IV when the water is abnormally high, while the springtime Grade IV becomes a pussycat when water levels drop in the late summer. Even calm stretches become turbulent and dangerous at flood stage because of the tremendous force of underwater currents slammed this way and that by rocks and other obstructions, shooting upward with the force of a jet stream, and creating unbelievably powerful surface currents.

Naturally, a system has been devised for judging water levels; it is also called the International System. You should be aware of it so that you can evaluate the water level for any season. Here, in brief, is the International System:

L (*Low*). Below a level for good paddling, and below normal stream flow. Shallow areas turn into dry banks, and low areas become muddy sandbars.

M (*Medium*). Normal river flow. Medium water generally provides good water for rivers with a slight gradient, but does not provide enough depth for good passage on the steeper sections.

MH (*Medium High*). Higher than normal. Faster than normal flow on the slight gradients; and the best level for the more difficult river sections, with enough water for good passage over ledges and through rock gardens.

H (*High*). Water is becoming difficult to handle. The river is above normal level. Canoeists refer to the increasingly powerful currents as "heavy." There may be some small debris on the water. At High stage, only covered craft should be used. Large, placid rivers become especially dangerous.

HH (*High-high*). Very heavy water. Hydraulics are complex and powerful. Small rivers and rivers with slight gradients become treacherous. More debris. Should be canoed in covered craft, by experts only.

F (*Flood*). Abnormally high water. At this level the TV crews show up to take pictures. Low-lying areas may be underwater. The current is extremely violent. Large chunks of debris are common. Not for boating of any kind.

In sum, three elements must be evaluated before you can come to a competent judgment about your skill on a new—or even a known—river: (1) your ability as a canoeist, (2) the class of rapids you will encounter, and (3) the river flow. Putting all three together, you should have no trouble in deciding whether you can canoe a 12-mile stretch of the Keepahfloughing River between Puttin Pasture and Taakoute Village when a friend tells you:

"I know you don't know much about this stretch, but there are five or six sets of good Class-II rapids on the upper section, and a couple of hot Class III's in the lower stretch when the river is running Medium. Of course, with the rains of the past week the river might have built up to Medium High. In that case, the river will swallow up a couple of the Class II's. There's a rock garden that usually isn't much trouble; now it ought to be maybe a II or a III. Of course, if the river is Medium High we won't have any trouble with those ledges above the Class III's. And there's that one set of standing waves where the Mussumup Creek joins the Keepahfloughing that ought to be wild with more water flow. It'll be a helluva trip."

You'd better believe it. A helluva trip for

fun and excitement if you've got the experience and a canoe that can take the water of this stretch. Or a helluva good reason to stay home if you haven't.

PART II

Wilderness Canoeing

6

The Wilderness Trip

In every canoeist's life there comes one inevitable moment when dreams turn to distant waters and cool forests. The dream is insidious. It cat-paws stealthily into the primordial labyrinths of the soul until suddenly it becomes an urge that can only be satisfied by such a trip. Fragments keep bringing the dream instantly to mind. The smell of a wood fire. The northbound flight of geese in the spring. An evening sun exploding its dying passions in an orgy of reds and oranges found only where the air is sweet and the water clean.

Canoe voyages become complicated when a group is involved and paddling the desired distance takes several days or longer. Wilderness outings are the most complex trips.

If you do not need to own your canoe to take a wilderness voyage, what do you need? First—you must have leadership. Second—you must have organization.

How can I stress the need for leadership? Among many younger people, the thought of a structured group is almost anathema. Tragically, these are the very people who tend to have the most trouble when they take this attitude into the out-of-doors. No one ever is really in charge. Decisions are made as a group—but such decisions are

ignored by those who wish to ignore them. Since no one really is in charge, no one really is responsible. Chores are shared by everyone, which means that those willing to do so, work hard, and those who want to be carried along for the ride relax and do nothing.

Whether a group plans a trip as the result of a friendly get-together or the efforts of one person, it must be clear beyond doubt—and in everyone's mind—that there is one ultimate leader. The final responsibility for the success of the journey belongs to him or her.

The leader must be competent in both canoeing and camping. The group must have faith in his leadership abilities and abide by those hard decisions which he must make for the group.

He will decide, for example, whether the canoes will run a set of rapids loaded or empty. He must decide who may run the rapids and who must portage around. If disputes arise in a large group, the leader must resolve them as best he can. He is the one who takes charge in an emergency, who organizes a rescue team if necessary, and who may well be invested by the group with the authority to banish someone who insists on behavior destructive to the harmony of the group.

If you are the leader of a group, accept your leadership role with the responsibility it deserves. The health, safety, and welfare of those who travel with you are in your hands. If you join a group on a wilderness trip, support the leader. He cannot succeed without your assistance.

No wilderness group can survive in peace and cooperation without some type of formalized structure in which each group member gives an equal effort to the jobs that must be done.

I use a duty roster in job assignments. The roster describes the jobs and rotates every job among everyone participating. (See Figure 86.)

I give a copy of the duty roster to each group member at the start of a trip. Jobs are distributed to teams of two. I mix the names so that those who canoe together do not work together. This system is a great aid in creating friendships on a wilderness trip. If a trip lasts only three or four days, I do not change the work assignments. If a trip extends over a couple of weeks, I shuffle the work teams every week.

Each group member participates in all of the jobs that make canoeing and camping a pleasure. Following are brief descriptions of various camp assignments:

Cook. This is *the* job of the day. Cooks prepare all food. Meals are served only when everything is ready to be served. They may be served family style or cafeteria style.

Bull cook. Well, it has to be done. This team washes all pots, pans, and dishes and cleans up the kitchen area.

Fire. A pleasant task, especially on a chilly morning. Builds the fire, keeps it going during the meal, maintains a plentiful supply of wood and kindling, and takes

DATE:	Mon.	Tues.	Wed.	Thurs.	Fri.	Sat.	Sun.
COOK COOK	Stephanie Howard	Phil Shelley	André Felicia	Marian Herb	Stephanie Howard	Phil Shelley	André Felicia
FIRE WATER	Phil Shelley	André Felicia	Marian Herb	Stephanie Howard	Phil Shelley	André Felicia	Marian Herb
BULL COOK BULL COOK	André Felicia	Marian Herb	Stephanie Howard	Phil Shelley	André Felicia	Marian Herb	Stephanie Howard
AREA CLEANUP SAFETY	Marian Herb	Stephanie Howard	Phil Shelley	André Felicia	Marian Herb	Stephanie Howard	Phil Shelley

Figure 86

charge of the wood-gathering detail, which is composed of everyone not otherwise at work on community tasks when we make camp.

Water. Brings in all the necessary water for cooking, drinking, and dish washing at the campsite. Sees that one full pot of water is always on hand in camp.

Area cleanup. Keeps every campsite clean. Disposes of garbage properly. Biodegradable material normally is scattered in the underbrush, except in well-traveled areas. What can be burned is burned. We carry cans and foil out with us.

Safety. Is responsible for seeing that all safety standards are observed: that canoeists wear life jackets; that canoes are properly loaded and gear is lashed in; that no unsafe practices occur in camp, especially involving knives, hatchets, and fire. Also handles sweep canoe.

It is a good idea to announce daily job assignments at dinner each evening. Each assignment lasts one day. Changeover takes place at sunrise. If a job is a problem, ask for help.

Jobs rotate "up the ladder." Since cooks and bull cooks have the most difficult jobs, they alternate with jobs involving less work. If there are more than eight persons in the group, then group members have some time off their official duties. If there are twelve on a trip, we do not expand the work teams to three instead of two. Two work better together than three.

Adults usually take their job assignments seriously. Not so with teenagers. In more than eighteen years as a scoutmaster and subsequent work with PATH, an outdoor program for boys and girls of high school age, I have found that some of them do whatever wiggling and jiggling they can to get out of their assignments—especially those they don't care for. The only solution is to keep a constant check to make certain each person knows his assignment and allow no one to "trade off" with another group member.

I am opposed to a group larger than ten on a wilderness trip. Ten people means five canoes and, if the group is sleeping in two-man tents, five tents. Five canoes are a reasonable number to maintain constant contact with each other. Pitching five tents, however, may prove a large problem in wild country where you have to scrounge for every possible campsite.

The exception to this "rule of ten" would be a group that already belongs to an organization. Even in this instance I frown upon large groups invading the wilderness. The impact of twenty or twenty-five people on wilderness camping areas is devastating. The amount of wood they consume is horrendous; so is the damage they cause to an area simply by pitching tents and working in it.

There is a sensible minimum as well as a maximum number for wilderness canoe trips. Wilderness travel is usually not advisable for two people alone, no matter how experienced, capable, or wood-wise they may be. I suggest a minimum of three canoes for every kind of backwoods travel on this continent. The more remote the area, the more important it is to have a three-canoe minimum.

CHOOSING A TRIP

What determines where you will travel on a wilderness trip? Although the dream is where it all begins, choosing a trip demands more than a deep yearning to canoe in Canada, Alaska, the St. John's in Maine, or any other remote and isolated river or region. Consider your idea of where you would like to travel against some limiting factors: cost, your group's level of expertise and experience, and the ability of the weakest novices to undertake such a journey. *Never* make any assumptions about the level of skill, the competence, the physical stamina, or the emotional attitude of any member of your prospective party without solid evidence on which to base your assessment.

A canoe party is no better than its weakest and least capable team. Because you always travel as a group, one slow canoe brings everyone down to its rate of travel. Consider whether every member is physically capable of making the trip. Gear your plans accordingly.

There are a million miles, more or less, of magnificent waterways in North America. You can work out almost any trip that stirs your imagination. But keep it realistically within the capacity of each participant.

In choosing a trip, consider your objectives. Distance? Fishing? Quiet loafing? A wilderness experience that combines all three? You might consider how I evaluate trips of a week or longer.

Moderate. Flatwater (lake and/or river). Total distance not over 60 miles. Not more than one or two short portages a day. Averaging only 10 miles of paddling a day, this allows for at least one full day's stopover somewhere along the way at a quiet, remote place that appeals to you.

Moderately strenuous. Mixed water (flatwater and some active rapids which can be run). Not more than one or two portages a day. Distance not over 75 miles. This

means averaging better than 12 miles a day in order to allow for a full day's stopover.

Strenuous. Mixed or river water with rapids which may range to Grade III or more difficult, not all of which can be run. Portages may be frequent; lining may be necessary; campsites may be difficult to locate. From 100 to 150 miles; one to two weeks.

Consider also whether you can terminate your trip in the event of an emergency. If not, can you shorten it?

Finally, after you have selected your route, advise a totally reliable friend or relative of when you will leave, your full route, and when you plan to reach your take-out. When we travel the Canadian wilderness, we make this arrangement: If we do not reach our destination within twenty four hours of the designated time, a search and rescue operation is put into effect.

SELECTING A ROUTE

I've taken wilderness canoe trips every summer for years. These have ranged from trips which could be easily completed in one week, with one or two days spent doing nothing but loafing, to three weeks of arduous travel. The Megiscane River trip fell somewhere in between, but closer to the latter. We selected it because it came close to the requirements we had in mind.

A wise selection begins with several questions. Who will be on the trip? Is it for a family with youngsters? For adults only? For experienced canoeists with considerable camping experience?

The group dictates the choice. So, too, do the money and time available. Sure, it's possible to go on a wilderness trip on a river that meets every one of your requirements—

but happens to be on the Arctic flow which terminates in Hudson's Bay. The only way to your put-in point is via plane. You may either fly out or return to civilization via the excellent trains which operate in Canada. Here the problem is resolved with one more question: Can you afford it? If you can, go. If not, look closer to home.

In every state there are rivers and lakes available for long-distance canoeing. You may locate them through river guides (see Appendix II), contacting your state department of parks or conservation (see Appendix II), contacting state and national forest or park officials (see Appendix II), or talking to friends who have similar interests and have been there first.

It was midwinter when I contacted Claude Contant, the highly respected wilderness outfitter who operates Les Canots Voyageurs, Grand Remous, Quebec, Canada. I outlined what I had in mind for next summer.

Our group was looking for a remote waterway where we would find ourselves crowded if we saw more than one or two fishermen or other canoeists a week. We were interested in a single river, or river and lake combination, that we could reach without excessive costs.

Our group would be composed of persons in good health, adults ranging in age from mid-twenties to late forties, both men and women, some with limited camping and canoeing experience.

I wanted the trip to be completed in fourteen days, allowing at least two full day's stopover whenever we chose, keeping in mind the strong possibility that we could get "stormbound" for a day.

We did not want a route which would

demand that we arise at 5:00 A.M., be underway by 6:30, and continue until 6:00 in the afternoon. Rather, we were interested in a moderately strenuous voyage in which we wouldn't have to be in our canoes before 8:30 A.M. and could start hunting for a campsite by 3:00 or 4:00 in the afternoon.

We were more interested in creating, or re-creating, a canoe trail than in following one of the hundreds maintained by federal and provincial authorities throughout Canada. On this trip we hoped to find the solitude that the French fur traders knew two centuries ago.

We would be fully self-contained. We would have competent leadership for canoeing-camping, trained in first aid and carrying a fully equipped first aid kit.

The trip must allow for alternatives in case of unforeseen emergencies or unforeseen delays. It must be deep in the "bush," as the Canadians refer to the genuine wilderness of the north country.

With these specifications in hand, Claude began scouting the upper Quebec country. In his initial reply, he wrote:

Everything considered, I would suggest the Megiscane on the James Bay watershed. It starts on the Canadian National Railway at Monet, criss-crosses the railway a couple of times, and ends at Senneterre, 180 miles downstream.

The river has no falls. Most rapids are easily (?) run. The worst are Class IV. [Which, indeed, they really were.] Campsites are available. The description I have is enthusiastic. It dates from 1972. Lumbering in the area has started to some extent.

There are several variations on this trip, some of which you may wish to consider.

Among the variations: The trip could be terminated at the 120-mile mark when the Megiscane flows past the railroad; at 150 miles when the river and rail line again meet in the Canadian wilderness; or at the 180-mile mark, Senneterre.

The Megiscane sounded like what we were searching for. Claude sent me two sets of maps of the region, a small-scale and a large-scale series, and I pored over them in our Manhattan apartment. Then I made the decision. This year, the Megiscane.

MAPPING IT OUT

The vast central region of Canada is a complex geological formation called the Precambrian shield. In part it is one of the oldest formations in the world, more than 2 billion years. A few hundred million years ago the region was covered by oceans, which left deposits of sedimentary rock. The oceans receded. The land's drainage system was reshaped as the younger rock formation was worn away to the ancient bedrock. Then came the glaciers of the Pleistocene era, which fully retreated only 12,000 years ago.

Today, it is a mixture of bedrock where old mountains have been worn to low and rolling hills, rivers following drainage systems millions of years old, and areas where the landscape is young and unweathered. It is a region of irregular valleys and cliffs. It is a country in which there are fine canoeable rivers and tens of thousands of lakes. It is a land without spectacular mountains, but with varying topography which breaks the monotony of utterly flat country. Unlike the Midwest in the United States, there is a combination of young and old land formations in the Precambrian region, creating a great number of rivers with excellent stretches of whitewater.

The general geology of an unvisited region is a factor in your decision to canoe there. If your group is made up of skilled canoeists, you might well consider a spring trip to a young mountainous region where the rivers are wild, high, and exciting in spring runoff. If your group is made up of families, it probably would be prudent to consider a single large lake where you could spend a week slowly paddling and camping around its perimeter.

A good canoe guide to the area, if one is available, is a necessity for the wilderness canoeist, novice or veteran. If no such guide is available, it is important to talk with others who have canoed the area. It is mandatory that you explore the region in advance through the superb topographical maps which cover almost every inch of North America—and indeed much of the world. For those who would explore the wilderness on their own, far beyond the areas covered by guidebooks, maps may well be the chief source of preplanning information.

In our case, having canoed the region in the past, and having extracted as much knowledge as I could from Claude, who in turn had spoken with people familiar with various sections of the Megiscane, I turned to the maps as the last preparatory step to the summer canoe adventure.

For those who must acquire a fundamental knowledge of maps and compasses, I recommend two publications: *U.S. Army Field Manual, Map Reading, FM 21–26* (U.S. Government Printing Office, Washington, D.C. 20402) and *Be Expert With Map and Compass* (written by Bjor Kjellstrom, published by Scribner's, and available in most bookstores). See Appendix IV for a detailed report on how to obtain topographical maps in both the United States and Canada.

THE WILDERNESS TRIP

The first maps I studied were the small-scale 1:250,000 series, in which 1¼ inches on the map is equal to 5 miles on the ground. While these maps lack the fine details so helpful to cross-country canoe travel, they do provide a magnificent overview of a large area. This is important in considering what the entire region is like and whether or not there are possible alternate routes should major problems necessitate any changes in travel plans. Two of these maps covered the total route.

The next maps I prowled through were the far more detailed 1:50,000 series, in which 1¼ inches on the map is equal to 1 mile on the ground.* It took a dozen of these large-scale maps to cover the same distance as the two small-scale maps. Note the difference in what the two maps reveal of the same location. (See Figures 87 and 88.)

The first thing I checked on the maps was the average gradient from our put-in point to our take-out point. We would begin at an elevation of approximately 1,450 feet and expected to end at an elevation of approximately 1,050 feet, a drop of only 450 feet, or an average of less than 3 feet per mile. If the drop were constant this would have meant we would canoe a slow and sluggish river with no interesting currents.

However, as the maps revealed, we would be canoeing a good distance on lakes. Since these have virtually no gradient, that meant that all the elevation changes would be found on the river stretches. On the Precambrian shelf, rivers tend to wander only short distances before emptying into lakes, then turn again into small rivers, and

1:250,000

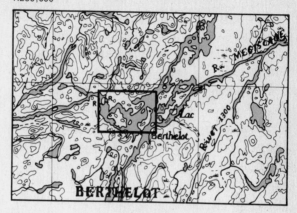

Figure 87

1:50,000

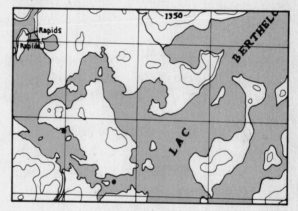

Figure 88

back to lakes. The river stretches are short and their gradient changes often abrupt. A lake and river combination might change only 40 feet in 10 miles, but if all of that 40 feet takes place on a 2-mile stretch of river, you can anticipate that for at least those 2 miles you'll be traveling consistently in water ranging from Grade II to Grade III. If the drop is one single waterfall, the portage around it will be well used.

*The U.S. Coast and Geodetic Survey also publishes maps of 1:62,500, only slightly less revealing than the 1:50,000 series, and highly detailed 1:24,000 maps, in which 2⅝ inches on the map is approximately 1 mile on the ground. While the latter are tremendously detailed, it takes twice as many 1:24,000 maps to cover the same area as either the 1:62,500 or the 1:50,000. The bulk involved is not worth the effort to carry them.

Only careful scrutiny of a map will indicate where the steep gradients occur and what type of water you may encounter. The maps prepared by the Surveys and Mapping Branch of the Canadian Department of Energy, Mines, and Resources will indicate where rapids may be found. If the aerial photographs from which the maps were prepared were made at a time of heavy floods, the rapids might appear ominous, when in a normal summer season they are pussycat stretches with a lot of rocks. If the photographs were taken during a season of unusually low water, a canoeist in a normal season might find himself cursing the existence of rapids not even indicated on the map.

Only one section of the river bothered me as I crawled across the maps tracing our route. Within a space of less than 4 miles the map showed two distinct sets of rapids. In that same distance it appeared that the river could drop as much as 75 feet, indicating at least Grade-II water. Since the rapids were clustered in two sections, we would probably run into no less than Grade-III or Grade-IV rapids. (See Figure 89.)

I called Claude to ask about this area. He was frank:

I've not talked with anyone who's been through there in at least 10 years. I've been told that one or two sections are pretty rough. Once there were portages at all of the rapids. I'm afraid that since the river is so little used by canoeists today, the portages may have grown over. When you get through, keep a record of what it was like. Good luck.

The fact that this river was so seldom used didn't bother me. It added a sense of excitement. I mentally calculated how our group would react if the going got a little tougher than we had bargained for. I decided it would be a great experience.

COMPASSES AND DIRECTIONS

When you head into a land of unknown waters, an excellent compass should be as much a part of your equipment as a fine knife or a sturdy rope. A cheap compass is worthless.

Compasses come in five key styles: fixed-

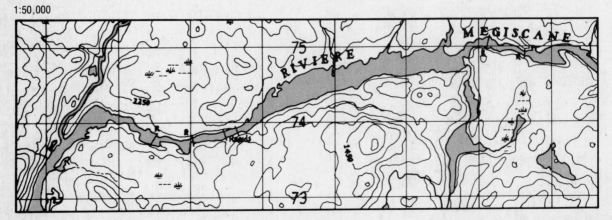

1:50,000

Figure 89

dial, orienteering, floating-dial, lensatic, and cruiser. (See Figures 90 and 91.)

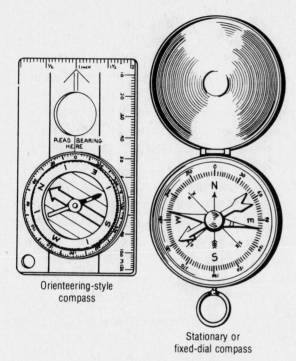

Orienteering-style compass

Stationary or fixed-dial compass

Figure 90

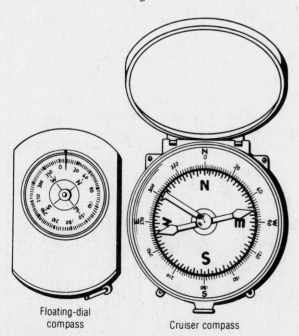

Floating-dial compass

Cruiser compass

Figure 91

Fixed-dial compass. This is the type of compass that most of us are familiar with. It consists of a magnetic arrow inside a round casing with either degrees or named directions marked in a circle around the housing. For hundreds of years these were the chief compasses used by travelers. Now, however, they are better left to children for playing games at home.

Orienteering compass. This is a remarkably good compass with a built-in protractor. With it you can work out a direction and distance on a map without having to orient the map. The less expensive models are less accurate than the lensatic type (see below) when you are attempting to obtain an azimuth by sighting along the compass. Both the orienteering and lensatic compasses can be preset either from a map or from the ground to give you a direction to follow once you arrive at a given position.

Floating-dial compass. This compass uses a magnetized dial instead of a needle. When the compass is aimed in the direction you wish to travel, simply look at the dial and read the direction by degrees.

Lensatic compass. Any person who ever served in the armed forces is acquainted with this compass. While basically this is a floating-dial compass, the lensatic compass has an aiming device attached to it which makes it one of the more precise hand compasses made. Unfortunately, the aiming device usually is reliable only on the expensive models. Cheap imitations of the Army lensatic compass have poor sighting devices.

Cruiser compass. This compass is similar to the compasses used by surveyors. Like the fixed-dial compass, it has a free-swinging needle. You read the direction by noting where the dial is intersected by the north end of the magnetic arrow. While highly accurate, these compasses are large, heavy, and cumbersome to use. They also are expensive.

In canoe travel through the wilderness I use two compasses. One is a fine lensatic compass. The other is a fixed-dial compass, the Finnish-made Suunto KB14. This particular model is the most accurate hand-held compass yet devised. It can give you a reading within ⅙ of 1 degree of accuracy. You'll need that razor-thin accuracy to locate a landmark across any substantial distance.

Each of my compasses is an expensive model. The Suunto sells for about $40. The lensatic I use costs around $25. There are cheaper versions. Since there may be a time when my life or safety depends upon the accuracy of my navigational instruments, I have no intention of cutting corners on reliability to save a few dollars.

We always carry two full sets of maps. I keep one set; the sweep canoe holds the second set. I also recommend that everyone on a trip has a complete set of maps, so that each person can practice navigating by map and compass.

Preparing a map at home for use in the wilderness is much simpler than preparing a map in the wilderness. Working by camp light, using rocks for desks, and kneeling on the ground are not conducive to the careful evaluation necessary to work out advance details when there are few other sources of information about your trip. Even if you do have access to river guides and information from other canoeists, it is helpful to prepare a map for wilderness work.

My canoe route often meanders across small sections of several maps. If it does, I cut out the essential parts of the maps and glue them into a single map to save space.

Next, I trace the entire proposed route in permanent ink or with a felt tracing pen to simplify reading my course in the canoe. It is helpful in a canoe to be able to tell at a swift glance the precise route you should take through that maze of islands and unreadable shoreline that surrounds you.

Finally, depending on the length of the trip, I will add a final step: the 3-mile system. The easiest way to do this is to take a length of string, measure it against the mile scale at the bottom of the map, and mark the string in 3-mile segments. Next, place the string so as to follow the proposed course, and mark every 3 miles on the map. Alongside each mark, make a note of the distance from point 0. (See Figure 92.)

I have now prepared my map to provide me with (1) a clear outline of the course, so

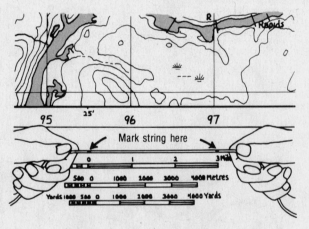

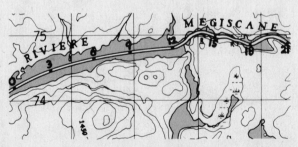

Figure 92

THE WILDERNESS TRIP

I'm never in doubt about where we should be going when I look at my map, and (2) an instant route calculator which tells me at any moment what our total mileage up to that point is, what our daily mileage average has been, and how far we have traveled on that particular day. Before departing, I make an estimate—often subject to revision—of approximately where we will be when we quit paddling each day.

How much mileage should we make on a daily basis to complete our trip in the time allotted? Have we planned too much travel for the group? Will we have a great deal of leisure time? Some of that information can be calculated by looking at the map from the security of the living room. Miscalculations, too, can arise from looking at the map from the security of the living room. Things do change in the wilderness. But with careful study, you will be reasonably well prepared for your trip.

When I use a map in trip planning, I consider whether or not we will be on rivers, lakes, or a combination of both; whether we will be portaging infrequently, frequently, or not at all; and whether we will be traveling with or against the prevailing winds. Next, I must consider the ability and the desires of those with whom I am traveling.

It is difficult to get lost canoeing a single river. It is not difficult, however, to get lost when rivers meander into wide lakes speckled with islands, or when traveling a series of rivers connected by portages. It should be a cardinal rule of the wilderness that no canoe ever ventures forth—on river, lake, portage, or any combination thereof—without a full and complete understanding of maps, compasses, and how to use them singly and together.

If you already have a basic understanding of how to read a topographical map and how to use a compass, it should be relatively simple to combine the two skills into a single navigational system. By using only a map (with the compass on hand merely as reference), it should be possible to ascertain your location within 50 to 100 feet of a recognizable point of reference. The reference point might be a mountain of an unusual shape, a distinct set of small islands, the entrance to a channel, or a clearly defined channel as it branches out of a lake or river.

One aid to knowing where you are at any given moment is to know your approximate rate of travel and the amount of time you have been underway. Basing one's location upon the length of time one has been traveling is not, however, the most accurate system known to canoeists. A brisk head wind may slow your forward speed to $\frac{1}{2}$ mile per hour, or even force you to take shelter in the lee of an island for several hours. A wild tail wind may require that you toss a sea anchor overboard and still blow you along at a brisk clip.

Keeping track of one's location requires a never-ending check against the map, landmarks, and the compass course. Occasionally triangulation from two landmarks is necessary to establish where you are.

Figure 93 is an actual detail of the 1:50,000 map we used on the Megiscane trip. We were proceeding north from (A); we had to work our way through the islands (B). As we emerged at (C), we were hit by a heavy crosswind from the west. Originally I had planned to navigate through the channel at (D), but because of the powerful wind we continued north through the narrower channel at (E). By the time we paddled into the open area (F), the wind had begun to die down. We hugged the shoreline, how-

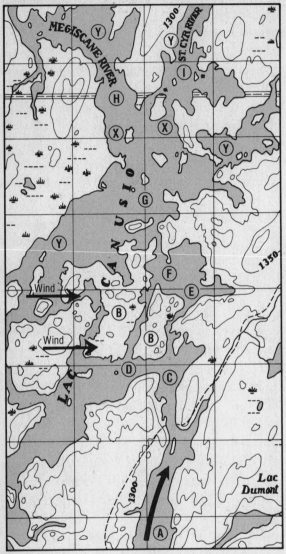

1:50,000

Figure 93

Now, look closely at our dilemma. Remember you are looking at the islands and shore not from the secure elevation of the human eye peering down at a map, but from a canoe scarcely higher than a fish's eyeball. From that elevation all of the shoreline and all of the islands a quarter mile or more away look very much alike.

The map shows two channels flowing to the north, (H) and (I). Anyone could become confused and head up (I) when intending to paddle up (H).

Notice that there is an island at the mouth of each channel, (X) and (X). Notice also that while on the map there is a substantial difference in the size of the islands, this is not nearly so apparent from the canoe level. Unless one paddles around each, they are similar enough in size to be confusing. Once a canoeist has passed the islands, even the open body of water followed by a narrower course can be confusing when fighting those damnable winds.

It is obvious, you say, that once into the water beyond either island you would quickly recognize that you're not where you're supposed to be. Your course is the Megiscane, which swings off to the west by northwest, whereas the other course will lead you up the St. Cyr, following a north by northeasterly route. Obvious, that is, if while you are checking your map against the terrain, you also have a constant eye on your compass.

If you are not careful every foot of the way, in fact, you might even get more mixed up if you got turned around by the winds in the lake and discovered that you could head into any one of four channels radiating out from the center: (Y), (Y), (Y) or (Y).

If I am in the proper channel on the Megiscane, I *must* be traveling at an azimuth of

ever, because the breeze was still quite brisk and troublesome. As we emerged into the open body of water (G), we still fought the frisky winds and clung to the eastern side of every sheltering island we passed. The wind had gradually shoved us farther to the western side of Lac Canusio than I had figured.

approximately 300 degrees. The St. Cyr River flows at a compass bearing of 25 degrees. The channel to the right is on an azimuth of approximately 90 degrees, and the channel to the southwest at an angle of approximately 250 degrees. (See Figure 94.)

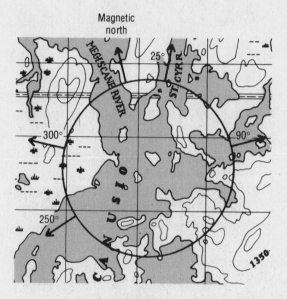

Figure 94

It looks so simple on the map. But paddling across the map from the security of the home is not paddling across the lake in a strong wind that insists on pushing you off course. Hence, the compass becomes a mandatory instrument for determining the true course you should be on.

There are numerous methodologies for adjusting a map and compass to reflect the true direction of travel when there is a difference between north, grid north, and magnetic north. However, most of these are unnecessary if your topographical map has an arrow—usually in the right margin—indicating magnetic north. Every accurate topographical map published in the United States or Canada gives both magnetic and true north, and usually grid north as well. The procedure for determining true direction of travel is simple.

Step one: Place the map on a flat surface. Align the magnetic north arrow on the map with the magnetic north indicated by the compass. Your map is now properly oriented. (See Figure 95.)

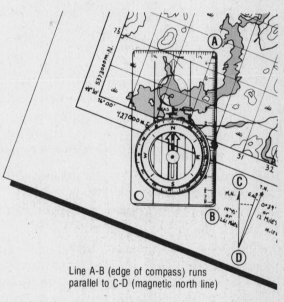

Line A-B (edge of compass) runs parallel to C-D (magnetic north line)

Figure 95

Step two: Without moving the map, place your compass on the map so that you can read the compass bearing, or azimuth, you wish to travel. (See Figure 96.)

No matter how confused you may be by the wind, the clouds, the difficulty of orienting the islands with the map—*you must believe your compass*. There are times in every outdoor experience when every fiber of your mind is screaming that you should be traveling in *this* direction and the damned compass keeps insisting it is *that* direction. The compass is always right. You are wrong.

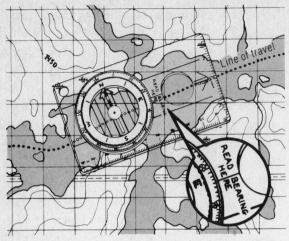

Figure 96

I still recall with a shudder of fright a particularly nasty situation my squad ran into in a war fought a long time ago. It was my job to lead the squad from the CP to an outlying position on the perimeter of the company's defensive position. None of us had been in the area before. We had to scramble down a hillside at dusk, cross an area thick with brush higher than our heads, and move up to the crest of another hill. We moved quietly down the hill. The brush grew thicker, deeper, and higher. Almost elbow to elbow, we struggled through the valley and began to move up the other hill. I glanced at my compass. The compass said we should be moving off to my right front. My own awareness of the terrain—from studying the maps—indicated we should be moving off to our left front. I called the assistant squad leader over.

"Which way is it to the crest?" I asked, staring at my compass.

He pointed to the left. "I think it's that way," he said softly. "It looks like it ought to be."

"Yeah," I nodded, "but the compass says that way."

"Maybe there's something wrong with your compass?"

"Could be. Let's check yours."

His pointed the same way as mine.

"Maybe there could be some iron ore in the ground," I muttered. "You know, that would put a compass off."

"Forget the compass," he said. "I know we're right."

"Okay. Let's get moving."

We edged up the hill. Suddenly, as we neared the top, a voice yelled: "Freeze, you bastards!"

We stopped. Two shots slashed through the air.

"For chrissake, hold your fire," I yelled. "We're from Baker Company."

"What the hell are you doing here?" a voice barked. The voice was followed by a swarthy lieutenant crawling over to us. "You ought to be over there." In the gathering darkness he pointed off to the area to which our compasses originally had told us to go. "You damn near got all your heads blown off," he said.

"We got lost," I said. "My compass jammed."

"Unjam it," he hissed. "Unjam it."

As we paddled, the winds blowing up whitecaps on Lac Canusio, I *knew* we should be heading into the direction of the St. Cyr. That, my instincts said, is the proper direction. But my compass insisted on another course. We followed the compass.

Occasionally, when canoeing through confusing lake country, I'll mark in the morning some of the bearings I'll be paddling later in the day. (See Figure 97.) This technique can be helpful in keeping the canoe oriented without continually stopping to take readings. With preplanned azimuths, you must check the compass

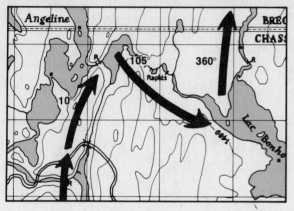

Figure 97

bearing with what the map says the bearing should be in order to determine if you are heading in the right direction.

Sooner or later you'll find yourself in a country where the water stretches on and on, every island looks alike, and it's impossible to distinguish a bay from a through channel. In other words, you're lost. Stop. Don't panic. Take a deep breath or two, and remember that it wasn't long ago that you knew where you were.

Several years ago we had emerged from the Capitachoune River, where getting lost was about as impossible as getting lost on an elevator, into a vast lake region. We were within 10 miles of our take-out point, and for the first time in days we ran into two other people—a couple of fishermen in a powerboat. They were anchored near an island, and as we paddled by we nodded and they waved.

"How's it going?" one of them asked.

"Fine."

"Where you been traveling?"

I told him.

"Going far?"

"No. We're going to end tomorrow."

He asked if we were heading toward the village. I said yes.

"Well," he volunteered, "be careful navigating through the narrows. Hundreds of tiny islands and a lot of marsh."

I looked at my map and wasn't certain where he meant, so I asked him to show me. He pointed to an island and said: "When you round this island, here, you've got to stay well to the south of those islands."

I was confused about where he meant we were to start. He pointed to the island opposite us and then indicated it on the map. I had thought we were a mile or so from the island, but I shrugged and thanked him. In a moment they started up their engine and roared off.

Relocating ourselves on the map, we paddled on. In about an hour we rounded what should have been another island he had indicated, but it wasn't. There should have been a wide channel ahead of us. There was no channel at all, only impassable swamp.

We stopped. I assembled the group and explained that we had been accidentally knocked off our course by a couple of well-intentioned fishermen. Of course, it would have been no great problem to them if they had picked out the wrong island. Traveling at 30 knots, one can correct a mistake in a few minutes that will take an hour or more of back-breaking work by canoe.

"What do we do?"

"Let's go back to where we met them," I said. And back we paddled.

We found the island, pulled in, and stopped on the beach. Now it was a matter of triangulation to establish where we were. Leo and I looked for distinguishing landmarks, not easy to find when the horizon is covered with low rolling hills of almost the same height. We climbed up a slight slope and took another look. Across the way we saw one distinctive peak. To the right there was an unusual-looking bay. Now we could establish where we were by triangulation.

First, I took a reading on the peak. It was exactly 100 degrees. That meant that if I were standing atop the peak taking an azimuth to our island, my direction in degrees would be exactly 180 degrees more than the one from the island to the peak, or 280 degrees. Because the declension on our map between magnetic north and true north was about 15 degrees, I oriented our map with the magnetic north arrow and then drew a line of 280 degrees from the peak. (See Figure 98.)

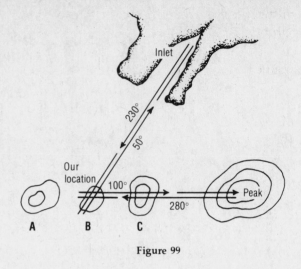

Figure 99

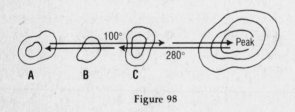

Figure 98

We now knew that we were on one of three islands: A, B, or C. This was a start. Next, I took a compass bearing on the odd inlet we could make out about ¼ mile away. It was 50 degrees. I knew instantly where we were. To double-check, I drew a back azimuth, or added 180 degrees to the reading, and saw where it crossed the line to the high peak. (See Figure 99.)

Now we had no problem proceeding on our way via our map and compass. The island we were on was more than 1 mile from the island the fishermen had thought we were on.

Slight errors in reading a direction usually are of little or no consequence when canoeing rivers. But in lake country or among swamps and islands, accuracy is a critical factor.

An error of 1 degree will amount to slightly less than 100 feet in a mile (92.2 feet, to be specific). If you are off 3 degrees in 3 miles, you will miss your objective by almost 1,000 feet. This is not an alarming problem if the terrain is easily identifiable and if you have landmarks to help you adjust your course as you travel.

If the canoeist must find a specific point and lacks landmarks, he may utilize a technique known as "aiming off." Assume you have carefully checked your map before departing and you must locate an outlet which you cannot sight as you look across a 3-mile-wide lake. It is hidden by trees growing on the water's edge and by a long stretch of swamp.

Locate a landmark. It doesn't matter how slight the landmark is, so long as you know it is actually to the left of the hidden outlet from the lake. When you arrive at the far shore, you know that the outlet is to your right. So you swing right, and there it is.

Otherwise, if you miss the outlet, you have no way of knowing whether to look to the left or the right, and how far wide of the mark you are. (See Figure 100.)

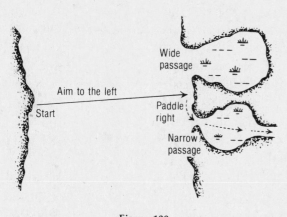

Figure 100

TRAVELING WITH EQUIPMENT

Anticipating trouble is a good way of avoiding trouble. Even when you are canoeing flatwater, it is good sense to see that equipment is properly loaded and lashed in. We were canoeing a wide, easy section of the Delaware on a magnificent October day when a cold front swept across us. The wind, which had been slightly gusty, suddenly turned into a howling tornado, made worse as it funneled up the valley. Within minutes, whitecaps filled choppy water. The fury of the wind increased. It was almost impossible to hold the canoes into the wind to keep from being blown over.

I motioned for all canoes to head for the nearest shore. Two didn't make it. The other three fought wind and waves to help the two which had been blown over by the unexpected fury of the sudden storm. Because they already were near the shore, we got them out without loss of canoes or lives. One canoe did lose a pack with clothing, and the other lost a camera and personal items which had been tucked into a waterproof pack. Unfortunately, because the weather had seemed so pleasant when we began only a couple of hours earlier, and because we were traveling in relatively flat water, none of those in the two canoes upset by the storm had tied equipment down.

When lashing equipment in, attempt to place it so that the weight is centered, with as low a profile as possible. When gear is scattered from end to end of a canoe, the problem of turning is aggravated by the weight at the bow and stern. To cut down wind resistance should you run into gusty weather, avoid stacking equipment higher than the gunwales.

Lash equipment into the canoe securely. If a canoe capsizes in the rapids, water rushing through it can put a tremendous amount of pressure on anything inside. A pack may appear secure when held into the craft with a piece of light cord. But it will take a sturdy rope and solid knots to hold it in when the river is trying its best to rip it out.

When a group of canoes participates in a trip, there must—and I use the word "must" advisedly—be a lead and a sweep canoe. The lead canoe sets the pace, watches for unexpected problems, and sees that the party does not get lost or in trouble. No canoe passes the lead canoe.

The sweep canoe may well be the most important canoe in the party. If anything goes wrong, sweep is in a far better position to know it than lead. No one drops in back of sweep for any reason. If one canoe stops, so does sweep. If a canoe has problems, sweep takes immediate action to help the canoe in trouble. In other words, the sweep team is dependable, experienced, and capable, and has both the knowledge and equipment to make the first move to resolve any difficulty. We always select a strong team for sweep.

Our sweep canoe also carries a red nylon bag marked EMERGENCY—NO FIRST AID. The bag contains the following items:

a sharp hatchet in a sheath
a 100-foot braided nylon rope of ⅜-inch diameter
two carbiners, or snap links, useful for converting a rope to a pulley
an extra compass
matches in a waterproof container
a small flare gun with half a dozen flares
a whistle
a Boy Scout-type pocketknife in a waterproof plastic envelope
a metal mirror

Sweep also carries an extra set of maps in a waterproof case, though these usually are too bulky to put inside the red emergency bag. That bag is *never* tucked away inside anything else. It always is carried in the open and is lashed, by itself, to a thwart. We want to know it is always there and instantly available.

I know there are veterans who will shudder when I say that we load our canoes and secure everything while the canoes are ashore, or partly in the water, then shove them on out. Nonetheless, I recommend this method. Tough hides of aluminum, ABS, or fiberglass may be marred, but never really damaged, when the canoes are hauled into the water. It is far easier to load the canoes properly when the canoeists can work easily around them on shore than

when the canoeists must wade in and out of mud, sand, and water to accomplish the task. A delicate wood and canvas canoe, however, should be loaded in the water. The canvas can be torn too easily on rocks to risk loading the canoe ashore.

Once we are all secure, we shove off, adjusting ourselves as we wish, with the lead setting the course and the pace. Sweep has one last function before pushing out: a final shore check. The sweep team scouts our campsite, checking to make sure no stray cup is left hanging in a tree, no pair of socks still is draped over a branch, no garbage is left behind, no coal is left glowing in the fire area.

When we stop for the night, the need for security continues. When possible, all canoes are brought ashore and turned upside-down side by side like a pod of seals. All paddles, life jackets, loose bailers, and sponges are collected and stuffed under one canoe. As a final precaution, a rope is run through all canoes and tied to a sturdy tree. Should a sudden windstorm arise during the night, we can sleep secure; it won't make off with our canoes.

When in the summer of 1977 we actually took the wilderness canoe trip along the seldom-traveled Megiscane River in northern Quebec, we decided on a route that could carry us 180 miles from the backwoods hamlet of Monet to the frontierlike town of Senneterre. We allotted ourselves fourteen days. A combination of events cost us three noncanoe days. Our alternate plans, which shortened the trip to 120 miles, were put into effect, and we completed the actual distance in eleven travel days. One day we made only 4 miles, and we took a planned day of rest the twelfth and last day of the trip at our alternate take-out point.

It was a canoeist's experience that combined every ingredient one finds in the wilderness—portages, high winds, golden days, lining canoes, running rapids, camping on everything from a wide and sandy beach to a large flat rock that could barely support two tents. Oh, it was a trip!

7

Body Conditioning

Most Americans are neither as vigorous nor as healthy as they sincerely believe they are. We tend to see the sturdy, healthy-looking men and agile, athletic women in TV commercials and magazine ads as reflections of ourselves. Unfortunately, the ads are not a mirror of the average man or woman of any age.

This fact is apparent on weekend canoe-camping trips which Gail and I lead on the Delaware River. We set a moderate pace. We have a favorite two-day downriver course which involves no more than four hours of paddling the first day and roughly five the next. Barring stiff head winds, which can turn even a modest canoe journey into a struggle, we plan around two and a half hours of moderate paddling the first morning, then spend at least an hour for lunch and a study of how to read water, followed by an afternoon of one to one and a half hours of paddling. The second day is divided into a three-hour morning paddle and a two-hour afternoon journey. By the end of the second day most of our guests are genuinely tired. Their muscles ache. Their shoulders are sore. They are glad to come to the end of the trip, sad that such an ex-hilarating experience is over but happy that their muscles can quit working.

Frequently someone will turn to Gail or me and say, "Well, you *should* be in good condition. I would be, too, if I paddled this river as much as you do."

Gail's Monday-to-Friday routine is working as a travel agent in a midtown Manhattan office. Mine also is an office job, and the greatest requirement in terms of physical motion is to operate a manual typewriter.

How, then, is it possible for two office workers to undertake this weekend canoe schedule in substantially better shape than the average guest? The answer is not extraordinary. We keep ourselves fit by exercising. Neither of us is a dedicated jogger who races outdoors each morning and jogs miles through the park or city streets, nor do we bound out of bed on days when the weather is cold, rainy, or snowy and launch into a violent exercise routine in the living room. But we do exercise moderately two or three times on weekdays. The weekends take care of themselves.

If I were to surmise what physical condition you are in at this moment, simply because you are interested in canoeing and canoe-camping, I'd guess you are in better physical shape than the average person of your age and sex, but not in as good physical shape as you believe you are.

It usually comes as some surprise to the beginning canoeist to discover that it takes a moderate amount of muscle power to pick up a canoe paddle, drop it into the water, pull back in a full, driving stroke, lift it out, and repeat that motion for stroke after stroke throughout a day of paddling.

Even one who's never touched a canoe before will recognize that paddling isn't a nonstop motion that goes on hour after hour after hour. There will be many a time when two canoeists will ship their paddles, relax, and gossip in a bright and sunny day, floating along with the current, or simply drifting on a quiet lake. But canoeing from point A to point B requires x number of strokes with x foot-pounds of total force. The more muscle and stamina the two canoeists have, the less difficult it will be for them to cover the distance involved. Indeed, while two canoeists in moderate physical condition may cover the distance in four hours, two in good shape may well make the same trip in three, giving them an extra hour of pleasure when they reach their take-out point or a good hour's advantage in reaching a fine campsite. What a joy it is to sweep up to an empty, excellent campsite and have your tents up and the camp functioning well before another party of canoeists paddles slowly by, jealously staring at your tents, beached canoes, and fire, knowing that they must continue searching for a site for the night.

You must be in good physical condition to enjoy canoeing, whether your goal is to become a downriver racer, a whitewater freak, a leisure daytime once-in-a-while paddler, or a wilderness canoeist.

On our annual one- to two-week Canadian wilderness trips, we take six or eight guests. Before each trip we send a letter to our guests urging that they give some thought to the physical requirements of wilderness travel. Such a letter reads as follows:

We're delighted you'll be canoeing with us for two weeks in Canada. Because you are new to an exhilarating experience of this type, I would like to point out that it is most enjoyable to those in good physical condition. Of course you don't have to have the physique of an Olympic athlete for an exciting journey. But if you haven't done much to keep physically active lately, you may want to consider a personal exercise program for several weeks prior to the start of the trip.

My own suggestion is to work out a program that will concentrate on three things: (1) joint flexibility, (2) muscle tone, and (3) the cardiovascular system. You should be able to do some of each if your daily exercise period is from fifteen to twenty minutes long.

Stretch, touch, bend, and twist exercises flex the joints, stretch the old sedentary bones, and make one as limber as a reed in the wind. To build muscle tone, especially in the arms and upper torso, consider sit-ups, push-ups (for both men and women), pull-ups, or modest weight lifting. As for the cardiovascular system, a final few minutes spent in swimming, bicycling, jogging, or jumping rope should top everything off. I prefer jumping rope because it not only exercises the heart, lungs, and legs, but also puts the arms to work.

For what I consider the most outstanding exercise booklet ever published, pick up *Adult Physical Fitness*, prepared by the President's Council on Physical Fitness, published by the Government Printing Office, Washington, D.C. It costs about 75¢.

If you do not consider yourself in sound physical condition and are *twenty-five years of age or older*, you should review your physical exercise program with your doctor. Just as physical condition is not a matter of age, neither is canoeing a sport with any age limit on it. Mollie spent a week canoeing with us in the Parc de la Verendrye country, paddling as steadily as anyone, doing her full share in hauling gear across every stubborn portage, handling her camp assignments with zest. She went about her work with cheerful gusto. At night around the campfire, hers was the brightest face in the firelight. Of course, Mollie had no excuses; she was only sixty-four. Archer Winsten is a ski columnist and theater critic for the *New York Post*. I've skied with Archer and canoed many a mile with him. He is a big man, easygoing, with a willingness to help others that's a godsend when the day has been long and the going hard. There's no reason why Archer shouldn't lend a helping and capable hand. He's in superb physical condition. Besides, he's only seventy-three.

It is especially important in planning even a one-day canoe trip to have some understanding of the limits of your trip in relation to your physical condition and that of your canoe partner or others accompanying you. The chart below should help evaluate trip plans until time and personal experience dictate otherwise.

Keep in mind that paddling speed the first hour or two is not the same speed you will be paddling after an hour or two. You are not a mechanical device with a set rate of speed which never varies. As the day progresses, you will grow weary and slow down.

Physical condition	Paddling speed (miles per hour)	Lake, no portages, no head winds (miles per day)	Lake, one short portage (miles per day)	Flatwater, river, current 2–3 mph (miles per day)
Fair	2	5–8	3–5	8–12
Good	2½	9–11	7–10	12–15
Very good	3	12–15	11–14	20+

8

Portaging and Lining

The river you have dreamed of traveling by canoe may include a stretch you cannot handle. With some muscle and perseverance, you can get past those rapids or falls dry and in one piece. There are two major methods used to bypass wicked stretches of the river. First, portages.

PORTAGES

In the northeastern United States they still are known as "carries," but generally canoeists refer to them by the more common name, "portage"—or, as it usually is expressed, "damn portage." No one with his sanity intact will attempt to pretend that a portage is a joy. The novice wilderness canoeist must always bear in mind two inexorable facts of nature and portages: (1) The portage always starts with an uphill climb while the river is cascading and roaring on a downstream gradient, and (2) if the portage is long and steep, it always is raining when you reach it.

The biggest problem with a portage is locating it, not always an easy task. In the regions popular with canoe-campers, especially those within state or national reserves, portages generally are indicated on the canoe route maps, and often indicated by highly visible markers from the point where the portage begins.

In wilderness regions seldom traveled by canoeists, portages tend to disappear. Here one must begin exercising judgment on whether or not there ever was a portage around a particular set of rapids. The odds are that at one time there was a portage, even if the rapids are no more than a borderline Grade II. (The heroic ability of the Indians and the old fur traders to whip through rapids was slightly exaggerated by all concerned.)

Search the bank as you approach a potential portage for a slightly worn landing site. This may be no more than a small area where the natural vegetation growing to the water's edge is trampled back in a tiny bay big enough for one or two canoes and enough of a hint of beach to pull the canoe a few inches ashore. But your sharp eye will detect enough of a difference in that one point to suggest that other canoeists have gone inland from there.

The portage probably will begin no more than 100 yards upstream of the rapids. But on which bank? While there is no set rule, I have found that almost all portages on a curve of a river follow the line of least resistance and cut across the inside of the curve. And if there is no curve? If there are exceptionally high banks or cliffs, logic suggests—and the suggestion usually is borne out by ground inspection—that the portage will follow the shore area with the least rise.

While studying your topographical map for a clue, consider also that portages may well cross an island while the river splits and flows around it in two channels filled with drops, souse holes, rocks, and enough whitewater to make walking preferable to being eaten alive by the river. Quickly rule out an island if the map indicates rapids below the confluence of the two branches. If, however, the map indicates a series of rapids on one side of the island and only a single drop on the other, it is likely that early canoeists figured it would be easier to portage around one short set of falls than a long stretch.

Occasionally your own logical suspicions about the location of an old portage will turn out to be right. The only way to determine whether this is so, of course, is to go hiking. Do not strike out blindly. Scout the shoreline thoroughly to see if there is any trace of an old trail. Since the portage is not likely to be more than 200 yards, at the most, from the start of the dangerous water, your search will be somewhat limited. If there is no sign of a portage on one side of the river, and your map does not indicate any reason why it would not be on the other, paddle across and check there, too.

When you find a trail, no matter how faint, check it out. Some canoeists load gear on their backs and start moving equipment on the trip they make to check the trail. I don't. I would rather be certain that I've found the portage and save myself the work of hauling the same gear back to the canoes.

Be cautious enough to check the portage trail all the way to the put-in on the other side. We failed to do this only once. It taught a lesson in not being foolish a second time.

I am well aware that the "proper" way to portage canoes and equipment is for one person to haul the gear, or at least as much of it as can be carried in one load, and another to upend the canoe, put it on his shoulders, and start out. Let me suggest some alternatives.

First, the chances are excellent that because you will be traveling in a 17- or 18-foot canoe, the canoe itself will weigh from 70 to 85 pounds. This is a bulky load for even a husky man. It is an impossible load for the majority of those who canoe. I recommend the two-man canoe carry.

There are several techniques. All involve one person at the bow, the other at the stern. My favorite is to have the bow person place the deck of the canoe on one shoulder, while the stern person either stuffs his head inside the canoe and lets the gunwales rest on both shoulders, or carries the canoe, as the bow does, with the deck resting on one shoulder. Since canoes are hard and shoulders are tender, make a padding from extra sweaters, clothing, or life jackets.

Keep the gear well packed; it is easier to carry when properly fixed in packs. It is not necessary to carry paddles separately. Tie the paddles into the canoes before starting out. Life jackets, if not worn, are also fastened in the canoes.

Organizing gear for a portage should present no problems, but problems will probably arise if the group is large. The most common difficulty is that some are willing to work hard, while others are equally willing to do as little as possible. To avoid it, establish at the outset that on each portage the two paddlers in a canoe are personally responsible for hauling their own gear and canoe across.

On portages of any substantial length, I recommend the leapfrog technique of hauling. First, tote the canoe a few hundred yards. Lay it down. Go back for the gear and haul it up to the canoe. Hoist the canoe back onto your shoulders, move it forward another few hundred yards, then go back and get the gear. This system gives canoeists frequent easy walks so muscles have a chance to relax. It also means that all the gear moves forward at about the same rate, so there is no need to hike back a mile for equipment after the canoes have been carried through.

LINING, PUSHING, AND TUGGING

The map warned us that on our trip down the Megiscane we would enter one stretch with a series of rapids scattered over several miles. I would have bet a genuine silver dollar against a beaver pelt that we would find portages around the three sets. We paddled carefully toward the first set. The right bank was flatter than the left, and as we approached the roaring water I scouted the terrain for a possible put-in point. Twice, within a few hundred yards of the rapids, we saw possible portages and put in to check them out. The north woods were thick, the brush heavy. For an hour we beat our way up and down the bank, scouting for some indication, even ancient blaze marks chopped on trees, that there was a portage. I still am convinced there was, but we could find nothing but trees too dense to bushwhack through.

We assembled about 50 yards from the rapids.

"It looks like we'll have to work our way down the bank," I said.

"You mean line 'em down?"

"Precisely."

We scouted along the rocks and boulders on the shore. The river plunged madly along one bank, a solid series of one Grade-IV set of foaming rapids after the other. However, on the other bank the water eddied and flowed—sometimes easily, sometimes in deep pools—in and out of a mile or more of rocks and boulders, some as big as a two-story house.

In theory it is relatively simple to line canoes down unrunnable water. You use the two painters—one canoeist taking the lead painter, the other the stern—and jockey the empty canoe through the rocks and water as you walk along the bank.

The theory, of course, falls apart almost instantly. First, in any long, rough stretch of boulder-strewn water, there are passages through which the canoe will move easily—but a foot later the canoe is wedged between two rocks. That means someone must go into the water up to his waist to push and haul the canoe over the wedge of rocks.

In any long stretch, the canoe must be empty; the equipment is carried along the bank while the canoe is maneuvered through the water. Portaging the equipment isn't a gentle task. You will slip and slide across rocks one minute, slash your way past brush growing to the water's edge the next, and wade from one rock to another when you cannot find a dry foothold.

While you are struggling to carry the equipment along the bank, it is virtually impossible to shoulder-carry the canoe. It stays in the water as much as possible.

There are times when, as we did on the Megiscane, you will find that lining is the

WILDERNESS CANOEING

most practical way of getting through. But be forewarned: You may not find it quite the gentle experience some "authorities" describe when you are knee-deep in water one minute, high atop a boulder the next, and struggling all the time to jockey the craft in and out of chutes, eddies, still water, and rocks.

Lining works best when the riverbank provides an easy foothold and the set of rapids you want to maneuver your craft through is only a single ledge, too mean to paddle and too short to portage. In this situation, lining saves you the trouble of pulling the canoe out, unloading the gear, carrying the canoe 100 feet, and getting back into the water.

On occasion it is necessary to line a canoe upstream, usually because the water is too swift to paddle against and the canoeist may not be familiar with poling, a technique which sometimes works on an upstream course. It is easier to line upstream using an under-the-keel towing bridle than a tow-

ing painter tied to the top of the deck or to a ring fastened to the stem band.

The towing bridle is made by tying a large loop around the bow or stern, with the rope emerging from under the canoe. A towing bridle fixed in this manner will lift the canoe rather than push it under. This bridle also is used when a canoe must be towed by another craft. (See Figure 101.)

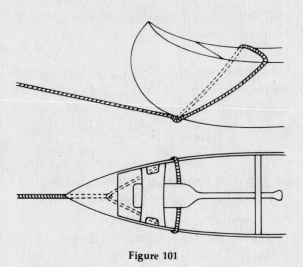

Figure 101

9

Equipment

No two outdoor travelers ever fully agree upon what to take into the wilderness. With sufficient outdoor experience, you can make your own choice of what to take and what to leave home.

Personal equipment can be broken down into the following categories: clothing, personal articles, camp gear, sleeping gear, ditty bag, and recreational materials. The following sections comprise my recommendations for traveling in the northern latitudes, where it can get chilly, if not downright cold, in summer.

CLOTHING

Wide-brimmed hat. This is essential in the rain to keep those drops from running down your forehead and dripping into your eyes. It also is a great help on a bright and sunny day.

Two long-sleeved shirts, one all wool. Wool is nature's answer to keeping warm when wet. All of man's ingenuity has yet to equal the overall utility of the fibers sheared from a sheep's back. Wool is the one material which, even when wet, will help the body hold in heat, acting in much the same way, though not as efficiently, as a wet suit. The all-wool shirt is critical. Both of the shirts I take are wool. One is a lightweight wool fabric; the other is a heavier shirt, almost the equivalent of a jacket.

Long sleeves help to protect the body from the mosquitoes which come swarming out in the morning and evening. Mosquitoes have long awls which can slip between the fibers and into your skin, but the wool will provide some protection. A lightweight cotton or cotton-polyester shirt offers virtually no protection from insect bites.

Two pairs of pants, one all wool, the other whatever you like. The wool pants should be of a sturdy, tight weave. Shaggy wool or a loose weave will gather all of the burrs, twigs, and other hitchhikers that exist in the underbrush. A firm weave will shed them. Those most useful of all pants, jeans, are highly acceptable when the weather is warm and dry.

Thermal long johns. Those made of wool or a wool-blend fabric are best. They will provide that extra margin of comfort if you are paddling in cold, wet weather. Long johns also may be used to supplement other garments. Long-john drawers worn under jeans in inhospitable weather give you almost the equivalent of wool pants. Make certain your jeans are not so tight that they will prove uncomfortable when stretched over thermal underwear. A long-john top worn under a lightweight shirt will provide the same protection as a wool shirt.

Windbreaker. A light nylon windbreaker or a windbreaker of 60–40 material is always handy. The 60-40 material is made from synthetic fibers mixed with cotton, then treated with a water repellent. Artificial fibers do not hold water-repellent sprays. Cotton will. The artificial fibers are stronger than cotton. Mix the two and you save the better qualities of each.

Warm all-wool sweater or a down vest. The sweater should be a tight weave. Untreated natural grease wool has excellent water repellency. Such sweaters, however, tend to be expensive and difficult to find. Down vests are a popular replacement for the wool sweater. Down is much warmer, ounce for ounce, than wool; and a down vest can be packaged into an amazingly small stuff sack, whereas the wool sweater is a bulky item. For use in a wet climate, Fiberfill II, Hollofil II, or PolarGuard vests are as good as down and considerably less expensive. When wet, down packs into clumps. The artificial fill material, however, does not lose its loft when wet. If soaked, it can be wrung out and worn immediately and still provide some warmth.

Four pairs of underwear.

One fishnet undershirt. Take a tip from skiers and backpackers. Both will wear fishnet— one to keep warm, the other to keep cool. Worn by itself or under a thin shirt, the fishnet will allow moisture to evaporate from the body, cooling you off on a miser-ably hot day. Worn under a T-shirt plus an outer shirt or under a long-john top, the net provides air space around the skin to aid in keeping warm.

Four pairs of socks, two of them all wool. The wool socks should be heavy wool such as Ragg wool socks, not the thin and skimpy things that pass for sturdy wool because the manufacturer, using a bulky weave, has made them look thicker than they are. These thick and bulky wool socks will be extremely valuable when your feet are wet in the canoe, as they certainly will be on cold and rainy days.

If you canoe with tennis shoes or sneakers, make certain the shoes are large enough to be worn comfortably over heavy socks. Some canoeists favor wet-suit booties to keep the feet warm when the weather isn't. Another trick for keeping your feet reasonably warm and dry is to slip a pair of light plastic or thin rubber overshoes into your pack for the days when you've got to add something to keep your toes from freezing. A nice dry pair of wool socks slipped onto your feet when you crawl into an icy sleeping bag at night are invaluable for keeping your feet warm.

Gloves, all wool. The heavyweight 100-percent-wool Ragg mitten is excellent. If you suffer from cold hands, you might consider the hand-knitted, oiled, natural-gray-wool Dachstein mitts. These are preshrunk to a thickness which makes them highly water repellent and totally windproof, but they are thick and heavy.

Sneakers. These are essential for canoeing in any kind of weather except ice and snow. You will appreciate having them on your feet when you have to step into rough water to shove your canoe off a rock, crawl down a bank while lining the canoe, or walk on the sharp stones and gravel under the water. Do *not* wear plastic shoes, slippers, thongs, sandals, or any other shoes that cannot be tied firmly. Your shoes must remain on your feet when you are in fast water, stepping in mud, or scrambling up steep slopes.

Hiking boots. These are useful around camp when your sneakers are drying. They also are far sturdier than sneakers for hiking a rough, bush-covered, rock-strewn portage. They are excellent if you wish to do some trail exploring and need tough shoes to protect your feet. The hiking boots should not be the heavy boots favored by novice backpackers or veteran high-altitude mountaineers. Wear a light hiking boot that is more comfortable and easier to walk in. The Vibram lug sole and heel are especially valuable to the canoeist who must contend with a lot of mud.

When leather hiking shoes get wet, dry them slowly in the air. Do not prop them close to the fire. Heat will shrink the leather and make it brittle. Sneakers should not be propped close to the fire to dry, either, as they can become scorched or burned. If they should be damaged, place a piece of birch bark inside to cover the hole.

Cap. A light, close-fitting wool cap is more useful in keeping warm night and day than you might realize. Covering the head with a wool cap serves the same purpose as covering the extremities with gloves and socks; it conserves body heat otherwise lost to the rain and chill. Don't presume that a wool hat is important only during the day. Do you recall all those old-fashioned pictures of people dressed in long nightgowns and *nightcaps* for sleeping in houses built gen-

erations before central heating? They knew they could be a lot more comfortable in bed if their heads were covered. Do likewise.

Rain gear. Want an argument? Speak up in favor of one kind of rain gear as opposed to another; every other canoeist you meet will gladly explain what is wrong with your choice.

I've tried several combinations and have settled for a top-of-the-line rain suit—pants and jacket. Nothing less. Let me cite the disadvantages of some other choices.

As every poncho wearer and ex-poncho wearer knows, when it rains, water seeps in the two sides of the poncho. Water also trickles down the opening where the sides snap around the wrists. In addition, ponchos catch the wind. This is fine when the sky is blue and the wind is behind you. When the sky is leaden and the wind is in your face, the wind-catching propensity of the poncho is an insufferable burden. Ponchos also pose a danger for the whitewater canoeist who capsizes and ends up in the swift water of the rapids. The large and bulky garment can entangle the swimmer, adding greatly to the danger of drowning. However, I do recommend that every canoeist bring a poncho. Not to wear, but to toss over the gear in the canoe and for use around camp.

The Cagoule looks very much like a knee-length nightgown with long sleeves and a hood. It is an improvement over the poncho in resistance to seepage from rain. Like the poncho, its great disadvantages are that it can entangle you if you go for an unexpected dip and that its fullness catches the wind.

Leave the knee-length cheap plastic raincoat at home. It has some advantages in design over the Cagoule because it fits closer, but if it gets caught on any snag or branch or rock, you end up wearing a garment in tatters.

The knee-length sou'wester, or heavy raincoat supposedly worn by sailors, is not as good as a Cagoule, and just as problematical in a surprise swim.

A waterproof parka, if it is a good one, is fine. Rain chaps may protect the legs, but they don't do much in the way of keeping the derriere dry. When rain splashes onto the canoe seat, you'll appreciate having some kind of garment to cover the whole fanny.

The only way to prove that the cheap rain suits, ponchos, or other garments are really no good is to subject them to a test. If you really think you got a great bargain at the huge discount sporting goods store, put on your budget-priced outfit when you get home, then go into the bathroom, turn on the cold shower, and stand under it for a half hour. Then take the outfit back and get a refund.

Cheap rain suits tear easily, leak, absorb water, wear out quickly, and have assorted other debilitating characteristics which make them either useless or foolish for the wilderness. Sturdy rain suits stand up to all the abuse you can subject them to and still serve you well. The better-made garments are lined, or made out of a material which helps get rid of the body moisture which quickly collects inside a rain suit. Even if the rain suit holds in body sweat, the perspiration is substantially warmer than the cold rain hammering at you on the outside.

Meanwhile, you must remember that there is no substitute on a cold and rainy day for a pair of wool pants and a wool shirt under the rain gear to help keep you warm. A pure down vest is not as practical for additional warmth as a wool sweater or a vest filled with the better synthetics, since wet down loses some of its bulk.

Bathing suit. Optional. Skinny-dipping is less confining. Use your own judgment.

Hiking shorts. Optional. On hot days you may prefer shorts to long pants. If you do, be careful of serious sunburn on the exposed upper thighs, for you will be sitting with the legs directly exposed to the sun all day.

———————————

———————————

These last two items are things which you would not feel comfortable without, and which I did not mention. Or substitutes which you are convinced make more sense than my suggestions. You may be right.

PERSONAL ARTICLES

This selection is dictated largely by your own toilet habits and desires. Keep the number of articles down to a minimum.

Toothbrush and toothpaste. If traveling light, keep the toothpaste tube a small one and break the handle off the toothbrush.

Chapstick. Almost any kind of lip salve will do. Lips can get chapped when exposed to the elements day after day.

Sunscreen lotion. A small bottle of this will prove especially helpful for those sensitive to sunburn. Several brands are sold in drugstores. Ask your pharmacist for a recommendation, or pick up a bottle of Class 5 Glacier Cream at a camp store.

Small towel or large washcloth.

Soap in a plastic container. My preference is a soap which contains cold cream. It helps prevent chapped hands and face.

Personal toilet articles. Take a few items which you deem important to your appearance or ego. Don't overdo it. Avoid carrying anything in glass bottles. Glass breaks. Repackage it in small plastic bottles. Even after-shave lotion or perfumes should be put into small plastic containers.

Sunglasses. These are especially helpful in the early morning or late afternoon when the sun is in your eyes, bouncing off the water ahead of the canoe and making it almost impossible for you to read the water. Polaroid lenses are the best for cutting down glare on water.

Insect repellent. Liquid goes much further than spray and takes up less room in your already overcrowded pack. I recommend any of these three: Cutter's, expensive and almost odorless; Off, highly effective and readily available; Old Woodman's Fly Dope, an old-fashioned oil-base dope you rub on. The pungent smell of Old Woodman's not only chases away the mosquitoes, no-see-ums, and blackflies, but also your best friends. Nevertheless, it is my favorite.

If you wear glasses—an elastic eyeglass holder. They are available at drugstores or optical shops. Also—an extra pair of glasses.

Fingernail clipper.

CAMP GEAR

Flashlight. The disposable miniature lights are nice to take on picnics. The wilderness is not a picnic. Take a light that can be of service in a night emergency or even when you may have to beat your way through several hundred yards of bush, undergrowth, and trees. The standard two-cell D-battery light is basic. Start your trip with absolutely fresh batteries, plus one extra set of batteries and one extra bulb. Every light for use in a wilderness setting should have a clip or ring by which it can be attached to your belt or a chain when not in use. Putting a light down while you do something else with your hands is a good way of losing it.

While the two best-known flashlight batteries are carbon-zinc and alkaline, you should be acquainted with the newest lithium-cell batteries. These have twice the voltage of standard flashlight cells and last substantially longer. An alkaline cell, which is about four times as expensive as a carbon-zinc cell, will last ten times as long as the latter. The lithium cell, which is about twice as expensive as the alkaline, will last three or four times longer than the alkaline. However, because a single lithium cell has twice the working voltage (2.7 volts) of the other two (1.3 volts), the price of one lithium battery is comparable in terms of hours of usage and brightness to two alkaline cells. The great advantage of the lithium cell, then, is that you need carry only one lithium battery (weight, 2.8 ounces) to do the work of two alkaline (9.5 ounces) or two zinc-carbon (6.0 ounces) batteries. Another advantage of the lithium batteries is that they will retain their peak brightness for up to 90 percent of their life, whereas both alkaline and carbon-zinc batteries begin fading after a short period of use.

My preference for a flashlight is a three- or four-cell miner's headlamp. The light fastens around the head with an elastic band, while the battery case can be slipped into a back pocket out of the way.

Several high-stearate candles. These are made of a wax which will not melt when tucked deep in a pack lying all day in a canoe exposed to the hot sun. They save the batteries when you're relaxing beside your tent at night. You can fashion an excellent windguard out of a small piece of aluminum foil, or you can protect the flame by placing the candle inside a pot tilted on its side.

Knife. I have rarely seen a person new to the backcountry carry a truly good knife. It is even rarer to find a veteran who does *not* carry the finest knife he can afford. An excellent knife is not a cheap knife. It can be a clasp knife, case knife, or a "hunting" knife in a sheath. The blade need not exceed 4 inches in length. In fact, a blade of 3 inches will serve every need for a canoe-camper. I would suggest a blade made of 440-C stainless steel, which is highly resistant to rust and corrosion, with a hardness on the Rockwell scale of C57–59. This exceptionally hard steel will take and hold a razor-sharp cutting edge. If you are entranced by the prospect of carrying a Swiss Army knife with a multiplicity of gadget blades, buy a Victorinox, the finest made. The Champion model contains twenty-four blades, ranging from a wire stripper to a Phillips screwdriver. Among the manufacturers of very good quality knives are Buck, Gerber, Russell, Case, Henkels, and Kabar. Expect to spend from $20 to $40 for a fine knife.

A disposal cigarette lighter. The disposal lighter popular with smokers also is an excellent replacement for packages and packages of matches. However, each person should also carry a supply of waterproof matches in a waterproof case.

One-quart plastic canteen or bottle. Optional. You may want to have some drinking water in your tent at night. And if you are paddling in water whose potability is suspect, it is comforting to have your own canteen filled with drinkable water.

Personal compass. You can use this in the event that the leader loses his, or you lose the leader.

SLEEPING GEAR
Sleeping bag. A person can suffer all of the arrows of outrageous fortune that the wilderness can hurl upon him—stubborn head winds, impossible portages, insects, rain, burned food—and still maintain his composure if he sleeps well each night. A good sleeping bag is not an absolute guarantee that you will. But a bad sleeping bag is the closest thing to a guarantee that you will not.

Down still is the prime filling to consider for a sleeping bag. The reason is simply that it will provide more loft for less weight than any other material. Unfortunately, top-quality down is expensive, even by today's standard of high prices; it will become even more expensive as the world's source of fine down diminishes and its population of outdoor lovers expands.

Why are you warm in one sleeping bag but freezing in another? The answer lies in that word "loft." The loft, or thickness, keeps you warm by surrounding the body with a layer of dead air. It is the loft that determines whether you will be warm, not the filling. (See the chart on page 100 for minimum comfort ranges.) In addition, down is compressible. Ounce for ounce, it can be squeezed into a smaller ball and spring back to its original shape better than any substance yet discovered for filling sleeping bags or garments.

Filling power is one of the principal factors used in determining the quality of the down. One ounce of fine-quality down will fill at least 550 cubic inches. The best down is from geese raised in cold northern climates. It has a greater filling power than the down from geese raised in southern California, Florida, or Taiwan. As a general rule, the better-quality down is imported from Poland and the People's Republic of China.

Another factor which affects the quality of the down is the amount of feather mixed with the down. In a good bag, the feather content will range from 8 to 11 percent; in garments, the feather content may run as high as 20 percent. It is difficult, if not impossible, to determine the quality of the down by asking the salesclerk, for his source of information is the same as yours—the label and the material supplied by the manufacturer. Protect yourself by knowing the manufacturer.*

A good sleeping bag, regardless of the fill, is made of a tightly woven rip-stop or taffeta-nylon fabric and does not have sewn-through seams. The ultralightweight "summer bags" with sewn-through seams are of value only for camping in an area where the night temperature will not drop below 50-60 degrees.

A fine-quality down bag is not cheap. A three-season bag will cost upwards of $100. A bag effective in midwinter may cost as much as $250. Since canoeists rarely go camping when the temperature drops below zero, a three-season bag should meet your needs.

Now let's turn to bags filled with material other than down. Bags filled with Hollofil II, Fiberfill II, or PolarGuard, all man-made materials, are increasingly popular. At best, these will be about 60 percent as efficient as down; it takes roughly 1½ pounds of man-made material to equal the loft of 1 pound of down. These materials are not as compressible as down, but this factor is not as important to a canoeist as it is to a backpacker.

The man-made fibers have an advantage over down. If you get a down bag wet, it looks like a sad sheet of wet paper towel with lumps inside. If a bag filled with man-made fiber gets wet, it will return almost instantly to its full loft after you wring it out. A thoroughly wet down bag may take several days to dry in normal summer sunshine. A fiber-filled bag will dry in one good sunning. Even if wet, a fiber-filled sleeping bag will provide some warmth.

Another advantage of fiber over down is cost. Good-quality fiber bags will range in price from approximately $50 to $75.

No two people sleep with the same feeling of warmth. One is comfortable with the windows open in midwinter; the other freezes with the windows closed and the thermostat turned up. However, manufacturers tend to agree on the minimum comfort range for bags. The range is expressed in terms of loft. The loft is measured when the bag is zipped shut and lies flat.

When the temperature plunges unexpectedly and your bag is inadequate, you must put on enough clothing to stay warm at night. Remember that you can lose a great amount of heat from your head. The first garment to add is that wool cap. Next, put on your wool socks. Then add whatever else you need. With your head and feet pro-

*Appendix V lists some of the better retail and mail-order stores and some of the outstanding manufacturers of top-quality camping equipment.

Loft (inches)	Minimum comfort range (degrees Fahrenheit)
9	−40
8	−20
7	−10
6½	0–10
6	10–20
5	30
4	40
3	50–60

tected, you may not need as many extra clothes as you anticipated.

Sleeping pad. Since both down and man-made fibers are compressible, the minute you slip into your bag at night you'll feel as though you are lying on the hard, cold ground. And indeed you are. To provide insulation from the ground under you, you will need some kind of pad. An air mattress is fine in warmer climates, but a poor choice in the north country. Each time you breathe or twitch, the air inside the mattress will circulate, mixing the warm layer of air next to the body with the cold layer of air next to the ground. To avoid this problem, use a foam pad. Even great handfuls of dried leaves heaped under the tent will provide more insulation than the air mattress.

My own recommendation is an open-cell polyurethane pad from 1 to 1½ inches thick, depending upon your need for comfort. If you will be traveling in the early spring, late fall, or far enough north where the night temperatures may drop into the freezing zone occasionally even in midsummer, consider a pad that is a combination of 1-inch polyurethane and a layer of ensolite, or closed-cell foam. While ensolite pads can be used alone or in combination with the foam pad, it is more convenient to buy the sandwich type. A ¼-inch ensolite pad will insulate you from the cold. Unfortunately, it won't

protect you from rocks, twigs, and knobs which dig into your sensitive body at night.

To save space and weight, consider a shorty pad, measuring from 36 to 40 inches, or enough to stretch from hips to shoulders.

Better pads come in fabric envelopes. Most envelopes are made of waterproof nylon on one side and cotton on the other; some are all nylon. You can easily slide off the slick nylon pad in the middle of the night. Avoid this by placing several diagonal strips of wide adhesive tape on top.

DITTY BAG

This bag is something every old-time sailor carried. In it goes all those "other things" you will need, or think you will need, on your wilderness canoe voyage.

When that preeminent advocate of light-weight wilderness canoe travel, Nessmuk, wrote a book of superb advice for the amateur outdoorsmen of the last century, he outlined the gear necessary for wilderness travel. Among other things, he wrote:

And don't neglect to take what sailors call a "ditty bag." This may be a little sack of chamois leather about 4 inches wide by 6 inches in length. Mine is before me as I write. Emptying the contents, I find it inventories as follows: A dozen hooks, running in size from small minnow hooks to large Limericks; four lines of six yards each, varying from the finest to a size sufficient for a ten-pound fish; three darning needles and a few common sewing needles; a dozen buttons; sewing silk; thread, and a small ball of strong yarn for darning socks; sticking salve; a bit of shoemaker's wax; beeswax; sinkers; and a very fine file for sharpening hooks. The ditty bag weighs, with contents, 2½ ounces; and it goes in a small buckskin bullet pouch, which I wear almost as constantly as my hat. The pouch has a sheath strongly sewed on the back side of it, where the light hunting knife is always at hand, and it also carries a two-ounce vial of fly medicine, a vial of "pain killer," and two or three gangs of hooks on brass wire snells—of which, more in another place. I can always go down into that pouch for a water-proof match safe, strings, compass, bits of linen and scarlet flannel—for frogging—copper tacks, and other light duffles. It is about as handy a piece of woods-kit as I carry.*

Sitting before me, as I write, is *my* ditty bag. It is a nylon-duck sack, and it is about 6 inches wide and 8 inches in length. I don't keep it dangling from my side but keep it inside my waterproof canoe bag. Its contents include:

a Zeiss eight-power monocular which I find more pleasurable to have along than essential

a small packet of nylon thread and needles

several buttons

a cluster of mixed safety pins, all affixed to one large pin

three medium-size fishhooks and 10 yards of line (sufficient to catch my 10-pound fish—though I confess to not being a fisherman)

a Buck three-blade pocketknife

some matches in a waterproof case

a diamond-dust knife sharpener which comes in the shape of a sharpening steel

a note pad and small pencil

some old 10¢ stamps inside a sealed wrapping of plastic

an extra buckskin shoelace

a wind-up traveling alarm clock

an extra Silva compass

a 1-ounce bottle of rum

some loose change, both Canadian and American

my favorite Suunto compass

At night, the compass is the first thing I take from my pack and place inside my tent, for it is one of the most valuable things I carry on a canoe trip.

RECREATIONAL MATERIALS

Small musical instrument. Harmonicas, mouth harps, and ocarinas can add a musical touch to an evening when there is no need to do anything more exciting than sit by the fire, staring vacantly at the flames.

Something to read. A couple of pocket books dealing with the out-of-doors are excellent. Consider, for example, how expert you will become identifying some of the flora and fauna along your route with a book on mycology, birds, or plants of the region. There are two brief tomes I always carry, sometimes to read aloud, sometimes to read by myself. One is Nessmuk's classic, *Woodcraft,* first published in the late 1800s, now avail-

*Nessmuck [pseud.], *Woodcraft*, (New York: Dover, 1963).

able in modern reprints. The other is by Robert W. Service, the author of such magic verse as "The Call of the Wild," "The Law of the Yukon," "The Shooting of Dan McGrew," "The Cremation of Sam McGee," and others.

A miniature game. Checkers, chess, and/or a deck of cards. There will come a day when you are stormbound. These things help pass the hours while sitting in a tent or under a rain tarp waiting for the wind to die and the weather to clear.

Camera, film, accessories, and a waterproof case. Much can be said about what kind of camera to take into the wilds, including a discussion of lenses, filters, the best type of film to use, and so on. But this is not a lesson in photography. Bring the camera you are used to. Make certain the battery is absolutely fresh. Unless you are a shutter nut, do not bring too many extras. You probably will find that a 35-millimeter camera is the best of all models to carry into the woods. I take 35-, 50-, and 200-millimeter lenses. I use the 35 for general scenic shots, the 50 for people pictures, and the 200 for distance pictures and action shots when canoes are bouncing through the rapids.

A polarizing filter is valuable for reducing water glare. You can broaden your range of useful filters with black and white film. A yellow filter is excellent for separating the tones of green in the woods. A red filter can produce dramatic effects.

I carry my camera and film in a waterproof plastic pouch inside a teardrop backpack. An even more secure method is to acquire an Army surplus ammunition box. For a few dollars you can buy one that will hold your camera and extra film. Make certain the rubber gasket seal is in good shape. Test the box before you try it on a trip. Drop it in a tub of water and weight it down. No air bubbles? Fine.

The ammunition-box system permits quick access to your camera when you see that one picture you simply must shoot. Stow the box under a seat. It should be secured to the seat or a thwart with a cord. If the box floats in an upset, swift water may sweep it out of sight in minutes.

A super-8 movie camera. Good movies require more planning than good stills. Figure out how you can tell a story with your camera, and shoot accordingly. If you have any doubts about planning a story that will hold everyone's interest while they sit in a living room hundreds of miles from where the action took place, spend a few hours reading any of the dozens of booklets designed to help the amateur producer.

I strongly recommend against bringing guns or radios on a wilderness trip.

FISHING GEAR

I wouldn't presume to tell a fisherman what to bring on a canoe trip. Let me mention, however, that on our northern Canadian wilderness journeys—when we paddle through areas that can be reached only by canoe, float plane, or helicopter—even I have managed to haul in a husky 7- or 8-pound walleye or northern pike. I've seen fighting bass and sturdy trout carried proudly into camp by those who suffer under the illusion that they are true Izaak Waltons of the wilderness when, in truth, they catch them because this is the country where even the novice can bring the big ones ashore.

EQUIPMENT

TENTS AND SHELTERS

There are tents and there are tents. Big ones, small ones, tiny ones, tall ones, low ones, good ones, and bad ones. Some bush-country travelers pride themselves on using a poncho as a shelter, while others would not be caught in anything less than a $200 shelter that can withstand a 75-mile-per-hour gale in a violent storm, weighs less than 10 pounds, and can sleep three husky adults with room for all of their duffle.

Certainly, on a fair night with the stars sparkling in a brilliant array against a velvet sky and a warm breeze blowing across the lake, any tent will do. But on a night when the wind is howling and the rain coming down in sheets, a cheap tent proves worthless in protecting you and your gear against the fury of a storm.

My choice is a double-wall nylon mountain tent with a built-in floor and a mosquito netting which can be zipped shut. I do not recommend canvas. First, canvas tents are heavy and bulky. Second, they tend to leak like dripping faucets in the rain whenever something touches them from the inside. Nor do I recommend the single-wall coated-nylon tents. These may be light, easy to assemble, and pleasant for sleeping when all of the flaps can be left open so that the breezes can waft out the moisture which collects inside from breathing and perspiration. But on a stormy night when the flaps must be closed to keep out the elements, these tents become cold and clammy. Every gust of wind will send the moisture which collects on the inside spattering down like a shower.

A double-wall mountain tent is made out of two units. The first is the tent itself. It has a waterproof floor which extends partway up the sides to keep groundwater and dampness from penetrating the inside of the tent. The sides of the tent are made of porous nylon, so moisture exhaled by sleeping bodies will easily pass through into the night air. Because moisture can pass out, rain can drip through. The solution is the waterproof fly which fits like a cap over the tent. There is a space of 2 or 3 inches between the fly and the walls of the tent. Double-wall tents are warmer on cold nights and cooler on hot days than conventional single-wall tents.

A new material now being used for both outdoor clothing and tents is known by the trade name Gore-Tex. The manufacturer claims that Gore-Tex will permit body moisture to escape but will not permit rain to penetrate. I have not used any Gore-Tex equipment, but reports indicate that it lives up to the manufacturer's claims.

Avoid the temptation to drag along a very large shelter. It may be more comfortable for night housing, but you may have difficulty finding a clearing large enough in which to pitch it.

Under no circumstances should you take an untried tent into the bush. Test it before you use it. Erect it in the backyard. Turn a hose on it. Make certain the seams do not leak and there are no cuts or tears in the tent material. Leakage is most likely to occur around the seams. Leaky seams can be easily fixed with liquid seam sealer.

Double-wall mountain tents are made in two basic styles: the pop-up, or external skeleton suspension system, and the internal pole system. If the elaborate external suspension system of the latter type is damaged, the tent is all but useless. If you lose, damage, or break a pole of a pole tent, you can fashion a substitute as quickly as you can shape a sapling to the proper size.

While external suspension system tents

can be erected as easily on solid rock as on the ground, it also is possible to pitch a pole tent on a solid slab.

First, anchor the tent with a rock at each inside corner. Then erect the front and rear poles and fasten the guy cords to large rocks. Then put the fly over the tent, again using rocks to anchor the four corner guy ropes.

In addition to tents, we carry a tarp. Tarps are useful on those days when you come ashore in the rain seeking a quick shelter. Ours is a 10-foot-square tarp of long staple cotton. It was an expensive item when I acquired it a decade ago and is still serviceable and strong and highly water-resistant. The coated-nylon tarps widely available today are cheaper and even more serviceable.

I use two 50-foot lengths of nylon parachute cord to sling the tarp to four trees. Thread one rope into one corner grommet and out the opposite grommet. The second rope is placed parallel to the first on the opposite side of the tarp, with the second rope also threaded into the grommet at one corner and out the grommet at the other. The ropes should be tied with half-hitches to one pair of trees, and adjustable tautline hitches to a second pair of trees. This hitch is excellent for adjusting the tension of the tarp.

A tarp must have an extra patch in the center, because once pitched, it will sag in the middle. Correct the problem by cutting a long sapling and using it as a center pole. The pole makes the tarp pyramidal, so that rain will not collect in the center and collapse the whole affair in a great splash.

You can build a small fire under the protective overhang of the tarp, but be certain the tarp is high enough above the fire so that it will not burn. When the tarp becomes coated with soot and smoke from the fire, keep it from soiling other equipment by storing it in its own plastic bag.

KITCHEN EQUIPMENT

Equipping the kitchen is, like everything else in canoe-camping, a matter of having enough of the right kind of items to make camping pleasurable without overloading yourselves with unnecessary gadgets. The following items are included in our kitchen equipment.

Pots and pans. We carry a set of nesting aluminum pots. The largest has a capacity of at least 1 pint of liquid for each member of the group. The Sigg cooking set is excellent. The handles lock securely when erect. The lids may be used as plates or frying pans. The Sigg lids fit snugly atop the pots, making them difficult to remove when hot. We solve this problem by putting the lids on upside down, making it a simple maneuver to remove them with sturdy aluminum pot tongs or a quick grab with a hand protected by a glove or a piece of cloth.

A pot of hot water with the lid upside-down makes an excellent warming tray for the cooked food you may wish to put aside temporarily while finishing up other goodies for the meal.

We also carry one sturdy aluminum frying pan.

Kitchen necessities. These include a wire whisk, a spatula, a dipper, a can opener, a large serving spoon, a 1-liter plastic bottle (used for mixing powdered milk), and an enamel 8-ounce measuring cup.

Cleaning necessities. These include a couple of both plastic and copper pot scrubbers, biodegradable laundry bar soap (never any detergents), and a scouring pad. We are meticulous about cleaning the insides of the pots but merely rinse off the outsides, leaving them heavy with soot accumulated from the fire. A black pot is much more efficient in absorbing the heat from the fire than a shiny surface, which looks attractive but reflects the heat. We drop the cleaning items into a plastic bag which, in turn, we store inside the smallest of the nesting pots after they are cleaned and packed.

Eating utensils. Included for each person are a stainless-steel knife, fork, and spoon set; one sturdy plastic bowl (melamine); and a stainless-steel Sierra cup. I cannot sing the praises of that Sierra cup loudly enough. The one I carry today has been traveling in the wilderness with me for more than a dozen years. Remember, however, when using a Sierra cup for measuring, that the Sierra container holds 10 ounces, while a regular cup holds only 8.

Stove. We never travel without one lightweight mountaineering stove; depending upon the trip and group, we may carry two. A stove will vary from a nice thing to have along—on a violently rainy morning when it's much easier to light a stove than to build a fire—to a necessity—when the authorities prohibit wood fires because of unusually dry weather or a lack of burnable wood in the camp area.

Outdoor stoves, depending on the type, burn gasoline, kerosine, butane, propane, or alcohol. Each type of stove has its merits. However, the most popular for rugged wilderness use are the stoves which burn white gasoline. They are extremely efficient, simple to operate, and burn under almost every conceivable type of weather from subzero to cloudbursts.

Of the various gasoline models, we carry the Optimus 111B. The stove is only 4 inches high; it is 7 inches square and weighs 56 ounces, somewhat heavier than other gasoline models. It will convert a quart of tepid water at room temperature to boiling water in five to six minutes and will burn for at least two hours on one pint of gasoline. Two other efficient gasoline stoves are the Phoebus 625 and the MSR gasoline stove. Of the tiny gasoline stoves, useful for a couple or a small group, I find three models excellent: the SVEA 123R, a self-cleaning model; the Optimus 8R or the newer Optimus 99; and the Phoebus 725. Expect to spend at least $50 for an MSR or Optimus 111B. The smaller stoves will retail for about $25.

On our Megiscane trip we carried one Optimus 111B. On several days, when the temperature hovered around 50 degrees and cold drizzle and occasional outbursts of rain made us miserable, we whipped out our stove when we stopped for lunch. Within minutes we had a boiling pot of water for tea, hot chocolate, instant coffee, or hot soup. Once we used it for a complete dinner. Within one hour the single stove produced a deliciously aromatic and tasty one-pot meal.

If you plan to carry two burners, I strongly recommend *against* a two-burner stove. In any two-burner stove, the heating units are so close together that it is difficult, if not impossible, to use two large pots at the same time with maximum efficiency. One always is shoved halfway off the burner. Take two individual stoves and there is no such problem.

Alcohol burns clean, but it is expensive and produces much less heat for the weight of fuel than gasoline. Propane and butane are extremely convenient and burn without fuss or muss. However, butane is not as efficient as gasoline and may not ignite properly when the temperature drops below 32 degrees Fahrenheit. Propane will burn at much lower temperatures than butane. You do not know when a propane cartridge is empty, however, until the flame goes out. And you must carry all of the spent cartridges with you.

Kerosine is not quite as efficient as gasoline. It may be more practical, however, if you intend to canoe remote waterways outside North America where kerosine often is more readily available than white gasoline.

Lantern. A single-mantle Coleman gasoline lantern is as much a part of our camping equipment for a large group as soap, pots, and flashlights. Because we do not carry butane cartridges for stoves and do carry Coleman or Blazo gasoline, a gasoline lantern eliminates the need for two kinds of fuel.

Gasoline. It is no problem to carry in the wilderness.

A reasonably large funnel. You would be well advised to use this when pouring gasoline so the gas won't spatter as you fill the lantern and stove reservoirs.

Lantern repair kit. Coleman makes an excellent unit which fits like a waterproof lid onto the bottom of the lantern. Inside are spare mantles, a lantern repair wrench, and an extra generator.

Aluminum foil. Although aluminum foil has limited uses in the wilderness, a sheet comes in handy if you break the Pyrex-glass bulb of your gasoline lantern. A field expedient can be fashioned by wrapping a sheet of aluminum foil, in the shape of the glass,

around three-fourths of the lantern. The opening is wide enough to permit a bright light to shine upon the camp, yet small enough to prevent the wind from blowing the flame out.

Shelter tarp. The tarp is stored in a tough plastic bag when not in use.

Folding shovel. In addition to coming in handy for camp chores, this tool is useful for digging a canoe trailer out of the sand when it bogs down on dirt roads en route to the put-in point.

An extra poncho. Spread it out as a tablecloth at mealtime, and cover kitchen and community gear with it at night. Also, toss some branches under it, so you'll be sure to have dry kindling for starting a fire in the morning.

COMMUNITY GEAR

Toilet paper. Figure on one-third of a roll per person per week. Use sparingly.

Tent repair kit. The contents of the kit are nylon patching material, available from most outdoor equipment stores; several extra nylon cords for guy ropes; a tube of seam sealer; and a handful of 10-inch light-metal tent pegs. If you run short of the tent pegs, chop a few from branches.

General repair kit. The contents include a small pair of pliers, two screwdrivers (one regular, one Phillips), a small assortment of tacks and nails, a sewing awl, a 6-foot strand of wire, and a small file.

Canoe repair kit. Take a fiberglass repair kit, available from auto supply stores, hardware stores, and sporting goods stores. It should include polyester resin for field repairs. Another useful repair item is a package of the new claylike epoxy that is packaged as two materials of different colors. When the two materials are blended, they form a single piece of doughy material which is excellent for filling holes. The kit should also include silver furnace-duct tape or heavy-gauge plastic canoe repair tape, a tube of waterproof silicone caulking, and an assortment of metal screws and bolts.

The emergency–no first aid kit. It includes a hatchet.

PACKING

I use a simple system for keeping track of everything, so I know where an item is when it is needed instead of discovering it twenty-four hours after the emergency has passed. It's called "The Gordon Bag System." It works.

Each of the repair kits is a nylon-duck bag of a different color. I use bags just large enough for each set of items, usually about 6 inches by 12 inches. I attach a strip of adhesive tape to the outside of each bag and clearly label them TENT REPAIRS, GENERAL REPAIRS, CANOE REPAIRS, EMERGENCY—NO FIRST AID, and EXTRAS.

I store all of these bags inside one waterproof, rubberized U.S. Army sleeping-bag cover, a sturdy bag about as large as a laundry bag. I place a strip of adhesive tape on the outside of the large bag and mark it with indelible ink, CAMP UTILITY. On a weekend trip, the CAMP UTILITY bag may be carried in a canoe as is. On a lengthy wilderness trip I may place it inside a large Duluth pack for easy carrying on tough portages. If so, the Duluth pack is also labeled CAMP UTILITY.

I use an identical rubberized U.S. Army waterproof bag to store all kitchen items. On a piece of adhesive tape on the outside

is the label KITCHEN UTILITY. I store everything connected with the kitchen, from cups to stoves (except gasoline and the lantern, which are carried separately), in this one large bag. To keep everything orderly, I keep the cups and bowls; knives, forks, and spoons; pots and pans; "table" tarp; and the small kitchen items in individual plastic bags. I always carry extra plastic bags—inside another plastic bag.

There are considerable advantages to using the Gordon Bag System. Since each set of similar items is put inside its own small bag and all the related small bags are packed into one large bag, there are only two major bags—one for KITCHEN UTILITY and one for CAMP UTILITY. (See Figure 102.) (There is, in addition, a secondary bag labeled FOOD UTILITY that contains staple foods only; see Chapter 11, page 111, for a description of its contents.) You always know where they are and what they contain. They are easy to carry in a canoe. When you put ashore in the late afternoon, you can bring the two bags ashore within minutes to set up camp.

Figure 102

10

Emergencies and Field Medicine

There is a dangerous element to canoeing, as indeed there is to every active sport. Canoe accidents are complicated by the fact that they occur in an unfamiliar medium.

DROWNING AND HYPOTHERMIA

Canoeists must be prepared to resolve the complexity of handling canoe accidents. In any water accident, all good first aid rules must be subordinated to one overriding possibility: *drowning*. There is no time to determine, when a person is overboard and hurt, how badly the person is injured, or how delicately he must be treated, so long as the danger of drowning is present. That danger must be eliminated before any other steps can be undertaken to help a victim.

After less than five minutes without oxygen, the brain begins to slip beyond the point of no return. Thus, when there is the danger of a drowning, artificial respiration must be started as quickly as possible. If it takes two or three minutes to reach a victim in the water, and another two or three minutes to reach shore to begin normal artificial-respiration procedures, death is apt to win that race to save a life.

Learn, before it is necessary, how to give mouth-to-mouth resuscitation while lean-ing over a canoe and holding an unconscious victim afloat in the water. Let someone else worry about paddling ashore.

Only within the past few years has *hypothermia*, or the lowering of body temperature through natural or artificial means, been recognized as the critical factor in deaths long attributed to "exposure."

Hypothermia is a special danger around water, because water is so effective in robbing the body of heat. The danger is present when the craft capsizes and the canoeist suffers the indignity of an unwanted bath, or when a canoeist is paddling all day in a cold, driving rain. Prevent it. Unless appropriately dressed, avoid canoeing when the water temperature drops below 50 degrees. If you canoe in cold spring months, either acquire a wet suit or dress in layers of wool: woolen long johns, woolen pants, woolen shirt, woolen socks, woolen jacket; and, if you need more warmth, replace your down vest with an Aran wool sweater.

The only treatment for a person suffering the violent, uncontrollable chills and shivering of hypothermia is to restore warmth. Quickly. During World War II, fliers hauled from the icy North Atlantic waters were stripped, dried, and put in bed with one or two companions whose body heat would help restore theirs. Do not warm the extremities if the torso itself is not warmed, because this will lower the inner ("core") temperature.

In his excellent booklet, *Mountaineering Medicine*, Dr. Fred Darvill warns that since "metabolic abnormalities are common after significant hypothermia, hospitalization should be effected as soon as possible."

FIRST AID

Basic first aid training is as essential for the canoeist as any item he takes with him on the water. Courses given by the American Red Cross are the best sources of first aid information. The wilderness traveler, however, must be prepared to go beyond the mere basics. He should acquire some skills in the practice of medicine, such as administering antibiotics, morphine, and other prescription medication, or reducing a dislocation.

Elementary first aid is concerned only with alleviating a patient's anguish or preventing further injury during the hour or so it may take to get him to competent medical treatment. Hours become days when deep in the bush. Under such circumstances, immediate medical treatment probably will be more beneficial than harmful.

THE FIRST AID KIT

A well-stocked first aid kit and an acceptable first aid text are as important as food and drink. Among the texts I recommend are the following:

Mountaineering Medicine, Fred Darvill, M.D., available through Skagit Mountain Rescue Unit, Inc., Box 2, Mount Vernon, Washington 98273 ($1.00)

Medicine for Mountaineering, James A. Wilkerson (ed.), Mountaineers, P.O. Box 122, Seattle, Washington 98111

Emergency Care, R.H. Kennedy, M.D., W.B. Saunders Co., W. Washington Square, Philadelphia, Pennsylvania 19105

Polar Manual, E.E. Hedblom, M.D., U.S. Naval Medical School, Bethesda, Maryland 20014

On a wilderness trip, I carry the following first aid items:

adhesive tape, both narrow and broad
various Band-Aids
adhesive butterfly dressings
sterile gauze pads, 2 inches by 2 inches
3-inch Ace bandage
Cutter snakebite kit
moleskin
sunscreen ointment (for those who forget theirs)
rectal thermometer
tweezers
small pair of bandage scissors
single-edge razor blades
tube of sterile Vaseline (especially for covering burns)
small tube of toothache medicine
Pepto Bismol (repackaged in plastic bottle)
5-grain aspirin
throat lozenges
needle
roll of 1-inch sterile gauze bandage
cotton swab sticks (wrapped in plastic)
fingernail clippers
several safety pins
small tube of antibiotic ointment
small magnifying glass (invaluable in digging for difficult-to-locate slivers, locating foreign particles in the eye, etc.)

In addition, there are prescription drugs which may prove critically necessary in the wilderness. These include the following:

a broad-range antibiotic such as tetracycline or ampicillin to treat infections

an antihistamine such as Teldrin spansules or Benadryl for allergic reaction to insect bites, colds, hives, or hay fever

sleeping pills (such as Dalmane)

a sedative (such as meprobamate) for hysteria or general nervous reaction

an antiexhaustion pill (Dexedrine) to be used only if it is absolutely necessary to postpone needed rest

drugs for severe pain (codeine, morphine)

Pontocaine or 10-percent hydrocortisone for use directly in the eye (for snowblindness)

paregoric or Lomotil tabs for diarrhea

Neosporin ophthalmic ointment for eye infections

It is imperative that, in obtaining these prescription drugs, you explain fully to your physician why you are acquiring them and discuss with the doctor how and under what circumstances they should be administered.

A first aid kit should be distinctive and clearly marked so that it is easily recognizable. Mark the kit with reflector tape to aid in finding it at night. Preferably, the kit should be kept by the same person in the same place at all times. On the trail this means in the same pocket of the same pack; in camp, in the same place in the same tent. In the canoe, keep the kit in one easily accessible place.

Don't make the mistake of hiding or locking up the first aid kit when children are present. You may not be able to find it or get it open when the emergency for which you brought it arises. Store it out of the reach of children, making certain that all bottles have lids which are difficult or impossible for the little ones to remove. Above all, teach youngsters that this is an emergency kit which they must always leave alone.

While most first aid kits are metal boxes, I prefer a plastic or leather kit because metal rusts.

11

Enjoy, Enjoy

We ate until we were as stuffed as Thanksgiving turkeys, savoring every last drop of a memorable meal served to half a dozen starving canoeists. Since early morning we had braved rapids, portages, and long stretches of shimmering blue water to reach this crescent of beach where we had set up our camp. The wilderness decor added to the glory of the dinner. The reflected fire of a setting sun set the lake aflame. The endless forest that carpeted the land stopped only at the very edge of the water. Empty canoes lay silent on the shore. From time to time the eerie laugh of a loon echoed across the lake. The smell of wood smoke mingled with the aroma of fresh coffee.

When we travel the wilderness we operate on the gastronomical theory that every meal, including all snacks, should be memorable.

CAMP CUISINE

Preparing excellent meals is not difficult. You need not be skilled in haute cuisine to make campfire biscuits. You do not need to carry two heavy volumes of Julia Child in order to produce a superb meal. What you do need is an understanding of how important good food is—to you and everyone else involved. You must recognize the particular requirements for good nutrition imposed by the strenuous activity of canoeing. Let me quote, in part, from Bunnelle and Sarvis, coauthors of the excellent Sierra Club Totebook, *Cooking for Camp and Trail.*

Active people require a high protein diet. Protein and fat digest slowly and should be present in all meals. A breakfast including a protein and some fat will alleviate the hunger that comes all too soon after a breakfast only of carbohydrates, or only fruit and cereal. Keep down the sugar and starch content of your meals. Such foods are filling but not satisfying, and while a little candy is useful for quick energy snacks, protein foods provide a higher level of energy.

Carefully planned diets contain sufficient quantities of vitamins and minerals for most people, but because cooking destroys vitamin C, supplements of that are advisable for any trip more than a few days long. If there is any question about the nutritional content of your canned or dried foods, add vitamin and mineral supplements. Take whole-grained cereals, fresh meats, nuts, vegetables, and few if any highly refined foods.

...Canoeists and skiers need high calorie, high protein diets—more so than provided by most of the "organic vegetarian" diets currently popular, especially with young people. If you are into a vegetarian diet be sure it contains at least 65 grams of high quality protein for every 3,000 calories, the number of calories an active sportsman probably needs. Soy is an excellent source of vegetable protein, and soy flour can be used in many ways. Other beans, peas, lentils, and brown rice are good but less complete sources, and therefore should not be relied upon entirely.

Milk, eggs, and cheese contain high quality protein and should be included in any vegetarian diet.*

You can eat any foods on a weekend canoe jaunt that you would eat at home. Keep in mind that the meals will be prepared over an open fire or on a camp stove, not the home gas or electric range. If you forget anything, you can't pull open the nearest drawer and take it out. Fresh meats and perishables can be packed into a portable ice chest and will keep in good condition for up to forty-eight hours.

On our weekend trips we use a Coleman camp ice chest which fits between the gunwales of a 17-foot Grumman. To avoid carrying ice, however, we use a much simpler expedient. All the meat is first frozen rock-hard in the home freezer. The frozen meat is carefully wrapped in plastic bags and plopped into the ice chest, along with chilled fresh vegetables, fresh eggs, and luncheon meats and cheeses. We have found that the frozen meat keeps everything else properly cool. We remove frozen chickens several hours before they are to be cooked, so that they will be fully thawed when the fire has burned itself to a usable bed of hot, hot coals.

When a trip stretches into days and weeks, fresh food is out. We build long-distance menus around freeze-dried, dehydrated, and canned foods; both precooked and uncooked legumes such as peas, beans, and lentils; rice; and the whole range of pastas, from kosher noodles to Italian macaroni. The simplest of all foods to prepare in the wilderness are the prepackaged freeze-dried camp meals. It takes but a few moments to reconstitute them.

I have several objections to the prepackaged instant meals. They range in flavor from bland to tasteless; they are high on starches and low on proteins; the labels overestimate the number of meals per package; and they are expensive. If you construct your own menu instead of using prepackaged meals, you will find any number of delightful advantages: a greater variety of foods, an excellent nutritional balance, and superbly flavored dishes. Would you settle for less?

Menu planning should be a combination of adventure and convention. Certainly include those foods and dishes you like and often prepare, but also try something new and unusual. Prowl the shelves of the supermarket for ideas. Ever had a "campfire cheesecake"? Pick up a package of instant cheesecake mix at the supermarket and turn it into an instant hit at the close of a camp meal. When blueberries are ripe, gather them by the handful and add to the cheesecake mix before it jells for a mouth-watering dessert. Use the frying pan for a cake tin.

*Hasse Bunnelle and Shirley Sarvis, *Cooking for Camp and Trail*, Sierra Club Books, San Francisco, p. 12.

ENJOY, ENJOY

BREAKFAST.   We build breakfasts around cereal, hot or cold; a protein dish; and something extra. Two of our favorite hot cereals are instant oatmeal, made by adding boiling water to the cereal, and Cream of Wheat mixed with raisins. Among the cold cereals are Familia, various granola and granola-style cereals, and occasionally Grape Nuts or Cheerios. To improve the nutritional value of the commercial granolas, add 1 teaspoon of wheat germ per serving.

Protein needs are satisfied with eggs and/or some type of breakfast meat. On short trips, fresh eggs are no problem. On longer trips, buy freeze-dried or dehydrated eggs. The freeze-dried egg is much more flavorful than the dehydrated; it is also more expensive. Egg mixes come in a number of varieties, such as "western" style or egg with "bacon bits." When any other ingredient is added, the amount of egg decreases sharply and the overall cost per ounce of egg increases sharply. Therefore, buy only the egg powder and add your own extras. Not only does this cost less, but it will taste better. Canned bacon, Spam or similar canned pork meat, or hard salami are all excellent sources of meat protein.

The "extra" something may range from the packaged instant hash browns purchased at the supermarket to "fruit compote." The compote is simply a package of mixed dried fruits—either mix your own or buy a carton of any popular brand—emptied into a pot. Add enough water to cover. Simmer for fifteen minutes. The liquid is especially tasty when poured over a dry cereal. For a super dinner dessert, add ½ cup of sugar to the 12 ounces of mixed fruits and simmer for at least fifteen minutes.

Keep your breakfasts simple to prepare. Pancakes and French toast are tasty at home, but almost impossibly difficult to cook in the wilderness; it takes an incredibly long time to feed eight or ten hungry campers when each dish has to be prepared separately. Eggs, whether fresh or powdered, should be prepared as one massive pot of scrambled eggs. This eliminates the burden of cooking eight or ten different egg dishes for eight or ten canoeists.

LUNCH.   Our lunches include such foods as cheese, salami, gorp, deviled meat, tuna fish, peanut butter and jelly, candy, and cold drinks (Tang, Kool-Aid, powdered lemonade, or instant ice tea).

Gorp is the modern outdoor equivalent of that ancient standby, pemmican. The original pemmican was made of pounded meat mixed with fat and dried berries and wrapped in a hide bag. Gorp is concocted from a mixture of nuts, beans, fruits, and candies and wrapped in a plastic bag. The recipe for my favorite gorp is: one-fourth soybeans, one-fourth mixed nuts, one-eighth raisins or currants, one-eighth peanuts, one-eighth M & M candies, one-eighth Cheerios, and one-eighth other good things (minced dried apple, minced dried banana, minced dried pineapple, sunflower seeds, or whatever strikes my fancy at the moment). Vary the amounts of the different ingredients according to your own tastes. Any gorp mixture, however, should be high in both protein and fat (i.e., oil contained in the nuts), with a touch of sweet and fruit.

The gorp can be carried as a mixture on canoe trips, or it can be run through a food grinder and ground into a mixture which can be molded like sausage meat. It is excellent for nibbling during the day.

DINNER.   Dinner always begins with soup.

After strenuous exertion on a long day, especially in hot weather, the body loses a substantial amount of fluid. Drinking soup helps to restore the body's fluid balance. All of our soups are the dehydrated varieties available at every grocery store. I favor Swiss Knorr soups; they are tastier and available in much greater variety than the better-known national brands. When shopping for soups, look for specialty brands popular in different regions of the United States, as well as "ethnic" soups available in Italian, German, Chinese, and Japanese neighborhoods, among others. All soups do not have to be served hot. Many soups are meant to be served cold, among them the delicious fruit soups popular in the northern European countries.

Walk through a large supermarket and peer closely in the corners for an astounding variety of starch foods. Everyone knows about macaroni. It comes with cheese. It also can be served with margarine and sprinkled with garlic powder and dehydrated parsley flakes. Spaghetti can be served with or without a meat sauce, and its other sauce possibilities are limited only by your ability to modify cookbook recipes for campfire use. Dehydrated mashed potatoes are available, of course, but also look at the other potato possibilities, such as au gratin or scalloped. Even if the recipe says "bake," you can prepare potatoes by slowly simmering them in a covered pot over a low fire or your camp stove.

Rice is available in an even greater variety of forms than potatoes. Beans are a campfire food older than recorded history. Unless they are precooked, beans are better left for meals where you have plenty of time to let them simmer until they are tender. Noodles come in a variety of sizes and shapes and take about the same length of time to cook as the various pastas.

Couscous is a popular dish in North African lands. It looks like finely ground wheat and can be served instead of potatoes. It is delicious and can be prepared in a matter of minutes. Kasha is similar to couscous, although it is a little more time-consuming to prepare. Lentils, like beans, can be added to soups and stews, used as the main ingredient in one-pot meals, or prepared as a separate and wonderfully tasty dish.

Meat, fish, and fowl are available in canned, freeze-dried, dehydrated, smoked, or salted form. Canned meats are the best-known, but freeze-dried are the most convenient for the wilderness. Freeze-dried meat is substantially lighter than canned and is simple to use. However, it also is the most expensive, and it occupies about the same space as the equivalent in canned meat. Cook freeze-dried meats as briefly as possible. Overcooked reconstituted meat becomes tough and chewy.

Canned meat can be prepared in an endless variety of ways. It is surprising, for example, how many stews and meat dishes can be prepared from that old standby, corned beef. When doctored with wine, spices, sauces, and imagination, corned beef tastes like anything but corned beef.

Every dinner should include a dessert. Puddings are always welcome. Take a variety of flavors. Instant desserts which can be prepared from cold milk are obviously less of a problem than those which must be cooked. Freeze-dried ice cream, Jell-O, some especially exotic or unusual dried fruit, instant cheesecake, Fig Newtons, even a small box of chocolates—all are candidates for that pleasant after-dinner sweet.

We carry two alcoholic beverages: wine

and brandy. On a lengthy trip we carry enough wine so that we may use some in cooking and serve a well-filled Sierra cup at dinner every second or third night. The brandy makes an excellent occasional after-dinner social drink, and also is welcome after the difficult task of rescuing people, gear, and canoe in a capsize.

QUANTITIES

The following tables will help you to plan a sufficient supply of food for your trip.

Breakfast

Food	Ounces per person per day	Calories	Comments
Dried fruits	1.5	110	Excellent when eaten dry, mixed with cereal, or simmered.
Cereals: compact cold cereals such as various granolas, Familia, Grape Nuts, etc.	1.5	150–180	Avoid presugared cereals, or cereals with high sugar content. Sugars add bulk without adding nutritional value.
Instant hot cereals: Quaker Oats, Wheatena, Cream of Wheat, etc.	1.5	150	Some are prepared by simply adding hot water; others must be boiled for a minute or two. Cereals with such extras as raisins, fruits, or flavorings are especially popular. If the cereal does not contain any, add them yourself.

(*Note*: Cereals commercially packaged into individual servings usually contain portions too small for husky camp appetites. Figure on one and one-half packages per person.)

Food	Ounces per person per day	Calories	Comments
Bacon, Spam	1.4	250–300	For long trips buy the canned varieties. Use the grease for cooking.
Boneless ham or shoulder	1.4	160	Take precooked only.
Eggs	two per person	170	Whether fresh, freeze-dried, or dehydrated, eggs are a breakfast staple.
Potatoes, dehydrated and prepackaged	1.0	150–200	Available in supermarkets; exceptionally popular.
Pancake mixes	2.0	200	Popular, but drags out a breakfast. Reserve for days when you'll be in camp.

Lunch

Food	Ounces per person per day	Calories	Comments
Crackers, such as RyKrisp	1.5	175	Keep well and are excellent with peanut butter and jelly.
Firm "German" or Westphalian pumpernickel	1.5	100	Also keeps well, but is more likely to be crushed than firm crackers.
Various dry salamis and bolognas	1.5	120–150	Many varieties keep well without refrigeration.
Cheeses	1.5	170	Look for hard cheeses (such as Monterey Jack, Swiss, or provolone) or those canned cheeses which do not need refrigeration. On shorter trips try the canned French cheeses such as Brie and Camembert. Avoid cheeses with unusual and strong flavors.

Lunch (Continued)

Food	Ounces per person per day	Calories	Comments
Tuna fish	1.5	125	Canned tuna can be served as is, or mixed with mayonnaise or sandwich spread.
Deviled meats	1.5	Varies	Sample at home; some types are quite spicy.
Gorp	1.0	220	Use salted nuts or salted soybeans when mixing gorp, especially in hot weather.
Nuts, various	1.0	175	
Peanut butter	1.0	200	A luncheon favorite.
Jelly	0.3	80	To add a touch of something special to the peanut butter.
Candy	0.5	75	Avoid candy that melts.
Dried fruits	1.3	100	Raisins and apples are the most popular.
Powdered drink mixes, including instant ice coffee and tea.	Varies		The label will give you the approximate amount per cupful.

Dinner

Food	Ounces per person per day	Calories	Comments
Soup, dehydrated	Varies	Check on label	Packaged soups specify the servings in either 6- or 8-ounce amounts. Figure on 12 liquid ounces per person.
Sauces and gravy mixes	Varies	Check on label	Usually a package makes an 8-ounce cupful. Popular with almost every starch dish from mashed potatoes to couscous.
Meat, fresh—steak, boneless	5.0	250	A fine main course the first night in camp.
Fowl, fresh—chicken, turkey	16.0	140	Chickens broil in about 40 minutes; turkey takes much longer. Also best the first night at your put-in.
Canned corned beef Canned roast beef	3.0	200	For large groups, buy the meat in No. 10 cans. Quantities and servings are usually clearly specified and accurate.
Canned ham, boneless	3.0	230	
Canned chicken, turkey	3.0	220	
Canned tuna	3.0	250	
Freeze-dried beef, chops, patties	1.0	130	
Pasta, noodles	3.0	300	
Precooked rice	2.0	200	
Dehydrated mashed potatoes		160	Servings specified on the label are about 50% less than hungry adults will eat in camp.
Dehydrated potato dishes, such as au gratin or scalloped		210	
Couscous, kasha	1.6	160	Serve with a gravy mix.
Desserts: Jell-O, instant pudding, instant cheesecake, etc.			Number of servings listed on the package.

ENJOY, ENJOY

Staples

Item	Ounces per person per day	Calories	Comments
Coffee, instant	0.15	0	
Tea, instant	0.15	0	
Tea bags	1½ bags	0	
Hot chocolate mix	1.0	150	
Nonfat dry milk		100	Buy in prepackaged one-quart envelopes; figure on 1½ quarts per day per four people.
Flour or biscuit mix			The box will indicate the number of biscuits its contents will make; judge accordingly. Mixes also can be used for thickening instead of ordinary flour.
Sugar	1.0	100	A bottle of 500 tablets of sweetener equivalent to 500 teaspoons of sugar will substantially reduce the amount of sugar bulk you must carry.
Artificial sweetener			
Dehydrated soup greens	0.1		For enriching many dishes.
Dehydrated onion flakes	0.1		For enriching many dishes.
Dried mushrooms	0.15		Buy dried Chinese mushrooms.
Margarine	1.0	230	Read the label; some require no refrigeration and will keep for several weeks.
Condiments			Based upon your own preference and specific recipes.
Salt			
Pepper			
Basil			
Thyme			
Oregano			
Chili powder			
Curry powder			
Ginger, powdered			
Tarragon			
Cloves			
Red pepper			
Sesame seed			
Chervil			
Parsley			
Bouillon cubes			
Garlic or garlic powder			
Rosemary			
Cumin			
Marjoram			
Cinnamon			
Maple flavoring			Useful if you make your own syrup out of sugar.

Two unusually useful books will help you to figure out the quantities of food necessary for any group on any trip. *Food for Knapsackers and Other Trail Travelers*, a Sierra Club Totebook by Hasse Bunnelle, is especially helpful. It includes a chart which itemizes quantities per person per day. The other useful book is Edwin P. Drew's *The Complete Light-Pack Camping and Trail-Foods Cookbook*, published by McGraw-Hill Paperbacks. He provides information. You work out the necessary quantities. Drew also provides recipes for preparing dried, dehydrated, and precooked trail and camp foods at home.

SHOPPING HINTS

Shopping and packing for any canoe trip, from a weekend to a week or longer, is relatively painless if you adopt a careful system—and follow it. The shopping plan resolves itself into a series of logical steps.

First, plan the menu, every food for every meal. For a long trip, plan at least one extra full day's meals for a twenty-four-hour emergency layover.

Break the meal down into quantities.

Write down, in appropriate columns, the food, the number of meals, and the quantity you will need.

Now you are ready to go shopping. Take friends. Make it an enjoyable occasion.

Don't stint on your purchases. It is better to have a shade too much at each meal than to end every meal dissatisfied with the amounts.

Repack the supplies you have bought. Transfer all liquids and all foods which come in glass containers to plastic bottles. Do not take glass into the wilderness—not even the brandy and wine bottles. Either repackage greasy foods into plastic containers or wrap each individual plastic tub in a plastic bag.

Toss out all packaging, and repack all dry foods in *double* plastic bags. Remember, however, to clip out the directions and include them with the repackaged food. You will be astounded at the volume and excess weight you have disposed of when you repackage dry foods.

Pack all spices into individual small plastic bags or the containers from 35-millimeter film. Write the name in *indelible* ink on each separate package. We spent the last four days on one wilderness canoe trip guessing at the various spices, because someone accidentally kicked the spice bag into a pool of water. The bag came up dripping. The spices were secure and dry in their individual packages, but the nonwaterproof-ink labels marking each spice turned into illegible blobs.

Put each breakfast into its own white plastic bag. Mark the breakfast B—MONDAY—DAY 1, B—TUESDAY—DAY 2, B—WEDNESDAY—DAY 3, etc. Do the same with each lunch and dinner.

Each day's meals can be placed in one sturdy nylon stuff bag; or, all the breakfasts can be placed in one bag, all the lunches in another, and all the dinners in a third. On shorter trips we place each day's complete menu in its own stuff bag. Then we put a piece of adhesive tape on the outside of the bag and mark it, for example, MONDAY, 1; TUESDAY, 2; WEDNESDAY, 3. On trips extending a week or longer, we put all the breakfasts in one bag, all the lunches in another, and all the dinners in a third.

As you can see, either system not only is efficient but also assures you, in packing, that you have every meal complete, the meals for every day complete, and the food for the entire trip complete. The few hours it takes to prepack at home will save hours in camp.

What about the items you use for almost every meal, day in and day out? You could divide these into small amounts, with the proper amount in each day's food bag. But I favor the use of a *food utility bag*. In this bag we place coffee, tea, hot chocolate mix, spices, sugar, salt, and pepper, along with extra containers of salt and pepper. Include a jar of mustard in a leak-proof plastic bottle. A ruptured mustard jar creates a very special kind of havoc.

Avoid finding yourself knee-deep in food bags on a major trip. Consolidate the various food bags into two or three large Duluth packs. To save the confusion of opening every pack at every stop to find what you are looking for, clearly label the packs on the outside as to contents with a strip of adhesive tape and indelible ink.

MENUS

Written menus are a tremendous help, especially in larger groups when camp assignments are rotated and different canoeists are cooks on different days. The menu should include complete instructions for preparing special dishes. Make enough copies so there is one complete set in each main food bag, plus several in the food utility bag.

The following is a sample of a written menu, the one used on the Megiscane River trip. All quantities are based on eight per meal. Our group consisted of equal numbers of adult men and women. If the group members were all men, we would have increased the quantities by about 10 percent. If the group had consisted of male teenagers, we would have increased quantities by 20 percent.

Menu: Canada—Megiscane River Trip, August 7–20, 1977
(*Note: Unless otherwise noted, all quantities are based upon the recommended amounts in the preceding charts for 8 adult canoeists.*)

MONDAY, DAY 1

LUNCH: Cheese wedges, crackers, peanut butter and jelly, candy, drink.

(*Note: We generally kept lunch simple to avoid major cooking projects.*)

DINNER: Soup, creamed tuna fish with ginger on noodles, wine, pudding, drink.

Make a cream sauce of 6 T butter, $\frac{1}{3}$ c flour, 3 c milk, 2 t ground ginger, 1 oz Chinese dried mushrooms (presoak mushrooms 10 minutes in $\frac{1}{2}$ c water and add the water to the sauce), 2 lb canned tuna, 1 t salt, $\frac{1}{4}$ t pepper. Cook noodles *al dente*. Drain. Serve tuna over noodles.

*(**Note:** While the amount of tuna for eight would figure out at 24 ounces, according to the table on page 117, we fudged and made it 32 ounces. We also figured 3 instead of 2 ounces of noodles per person. This was a slight mistake; we had noodles left over. All milk on this and subsequent meals was prepared from powdered skim milk. The soup was dehydrated Swiss Knorr oxtail. A soupçon of red wine was added to the soup. "Drink" always means coffee, tea, hot chocolate, or, at lunch, a fruit-flavored drink.)*

TUESDAY, DAY 2

BREAKFAST: Scrambled eggs, hot cereal, fruit compote, drink.

*(**Note:** We prepared the scrambled eggs from fresh eggs, the last fresh eggs of the trip. The hot cereal was Quick Quaker Oats in individual packages. We made the fruit compote by simmering a package of Libby's mixed dried fruits for 15 minutes.)*

LUNCH: Salami slices, gorp, candy, drink.

DINNER: Soup, campfire ham, mashed potatoes, yams, hot biscuits, wine, pudding, drink.

Mix together ham juices with 1 c white wine, $\frac{1}{2}$ c guava jelly, 1 T ground ginger. Pierce ham with cloves. Place ham in large pot, pour mixture over it, and heat thoroughly on low heat. Baste frequently with the sauce. When ham is thoroughly heated, remove ham. Make paste with flour and 1 c water, add to pan juices, and simmer to thicken.

*(**Note:** Again, we fudged a little and used 3 ounces of canned ham per person. The soup was a filling Knorr minestrone. The yams were canned in syrup. Very good. We made hot biscuits simply by adding milk to Bisquick until the flour was a thick consistency and then dropping tablespoons full of dough onto a very lightly greased frying pan. First we browned the bottoms, then tilted the frying pan toward the fire and built up the fire. The reflected heat browned the tops.)*

WEDNESDAY, DAY 3

BREAKFAST: Cold cereal, crispy potatoes, bacon, drink.

*(**Note:** The cold cereal was Familia. The potatoes were supermarket dehydrated hash browns which make up into a tantalizing and crisp potato over the campfire. Bacon was canned.)*

LUNCH: Deviled meat with crackers, peanut butter and jelly, candy, drink.

*(**Note:** The deviled meat was canned. The crackers were Triscuits instead of the usual RyKrisp.)*

DINNER: Soup, spaghetti with hearty meat sauce, cheesecake, drink.

Mix together in a large pot three 12-oz cans corned beef, 3 oz margarine, 5 T onion flakes, ½ t basil, 1 t garlic powder, one 12-oz can tomato paste, 1 T oregano, 1 oz dried mushrooms. Stir together well and add sufficient water to make a thick sauce. Simmer 30 minutes. Add more water if necessary. Boil spaghetti *al dente*.

(*Note: The soup was a vegetable soup. We used 3 ounces of spaghetti per person, more than usual. There was too much. The cheesecake was an instant cheesecake from the supermarket.*)

THURSDAY, DAY 4

BREAKFAST: Cold cereal, *huevos rancheros*, pumpernickel, drink.

Huevos rancheros are relatively uncomplicated. First, make scrambled eggs. Make a sauce by cooking together several strips of bacon cut into 1-in pieces, a 6-oz can of tomato paste mixed with 1½ cans of water, and a 4-oz jar of taco or *jalapeño* sauce. Sprinkle the sauce with garlic powder. Add crushed red pepper to taste. To serve, place egg on a slice of pumpernickel and cover with sauce. Be careful about making the sauce too hot for ordinary mortals.

(*Note: Cold cereal was a granola.*)

LUNCH: Cheese wedges, gorp, crackers, candy, drink.

(*Note: The cheese varied for different lunches. Occasionally we mixed two types of cheese for the same meal.*)

DINNER: Soup, turkey and rice, crackers, pudding, drink.

In a large kettle combine turkey, 2 oz onion flakes, 2 oz mixed dried soup greens, 1 oz dried mushrooms, 3 c water, 1 t salt, 1 t pepper, 1 t tarragon, three bouillon cubes, 1 T butter. Heat and then let stand 20 minutes. Reheat if necessary before serving. Cook rice. Serve turkey over rice.

(*Note: The turkey was freeze-dried and reconstituted per package directions before cooking. To hold down costs, all freeze-dried meats were purchased in No. 10 cans. We used instant rice.*)

FRIDAY, DAY 5

BREAKFAST: Hot cereal, bacon, eggs, drink.

(*Note: The bacon was the remainder of the bacon in the can opened the day before. Eggs were scrambled.*)

LUNCH: Macaroni and cheese, crackers, candy, drink.

*(**Note:** Actually, this was a hot lunch thrown in for a day when we might really have needed a hot lunch. We did not eat it on this day but substituted another cold lunch. The macaroni-and-cheese mix was the well-known Kraft brand from the corner supermarket.)*

DINNER: Soup, Korean beef with mushrooms, noodles, crackers, pudding, drink.

Reconstitute beef. Reconstitute 4 oz crumbled Chinese mushrooms and 2 T onions in enough water to cover. Mix beef and mushrooms. Add to large pot with 2 T margarine. Brown over medium heat. Add ½ t garlic powder, 1 t ginger, 2 T sesame seeds, ¼ t crushed red pepper, 8 T soy sauce, and 1 c water. Simmer 5 minutes. If too dry, add more water. Prepare noodles *al dente*. Heap beef atop noodles.

SATURDAY, DAY 6

BREAKFAST: Scrambled eggs with mushrooms, potato latkes, drink.

*(**Note:** Latkes? These are potato pancakes. The dehydrated mix is available in most supermarkets. They are much easier to prepare and keep hot than pancakes. The scrambled eggs were varied by adding a large handful of presoaked Chinese mushrooms. No cereal, and everyone complained.)*

LUNCH: Salami wedges, peanut butter and jelly, candy, crackers, raisins, drink.

DINNER: Soup, turkey curry with chutney, sambals, couscous, wine, drink.

Reconstitute turkey. In separate pot, mix 1 T hot curry powder, 1 T coriander, 4 oz margarine, 1 qt milk, and ½ c flour. Mix well and simmer for a few minutes. Add turkey and simmer briefly. Serve with separate cups filled respectively with raisins, chopped walnuts, shredded coconut, minced dates, and banana flakes.

To prepare couscous, make bouillon with 3 pt water and 3 T onion flakes. Bring to a boil. Add couscous. Boil 2 minutes. Mix thoroughly. Set aside for 15 minutes before serving.

*(**Note:** This curry is mildly spiced. You may want to add more curry powder. The curry was served on a special occasion. It had been raining all day, and we were tired and cold. As we rounded a bend in the river, there—in the middle of the wilderness, totally unexpected—was a big, lavish hunting lodge. As we later learned, it had been built out of material flown in by helicopter. The lodge was completely equipped. Scattered around outside were thousands of dollars worth of canoes, aluminum dories, power pumps, axes, and assorted pieces of equipment useful to hunters and fishermen in the wilderness. The lodge, however, was locked. We found an open window, got inside, and spent the night there—cooking on a fancy butane*

ENJOY, ENJOY

stove and enjoying the warmth of a fireplace. We left the lodge spotlessly clean, replenished the wood supply in the box by the great wood range, thanked the unknown occupants for our use of their facilities, and left some money to pay for our stay. We dined in splendor seated on two long benches paralleling a huge wooden table, while the rain beat a steady tattoo on the roof.)

SUNDAY, DAY 7

BREAKFAST: Cold cereal, broiled Spam, fruit compote, drink.

LUNCH: Tuna fish with mix, crackers, gorp, candy, drink.

(Note: Mixing tuna fish with Hellmann's sandwich spread enhances its flavor.)

DINNER: Soup, freeze-dried beef patties *au poivre*, au gratin potatoes, biscuits, cheesecake, wine.

Reconstitute patties. Cover generously with crushed whole peppercorns and let stand ½ hour. Sauté rare. Put aside. To the pan juices add 5 T brandy, 6 T margarine, 1½ c wine, 2 T onion flakes, 2 c beef bouillon. Simmer until reduced by one-third. Put patties back in, warm briefly, and serve with sauce.

(Note: The au gratin potatoes were the instant variety available at the corner store. We cooked them over medium heat in a tightly closed pan, although the directions call for baking. We made the biscuits, as usual, from Bisquick and milk. The cheesecake was loaded with freshly picked blueberries.)

MONDAY, DAY 8

BREAKFAST: *Oeufs aux fines herbes* with hollandaise sauce, bacon, drink.

(Note: There's a wilderness dish fit for a gourmet. The oeufs are scrambled eggs mixed with 1 t tarragon, 1 T parsley flakes, and 1 T onion flakes. Knorr provided the powdered hollandaise sauce; follow the directions. Serve each group member a couple of strips of bacon, topped with scrambled egg, topped with sauce.)

LUNCH: Salami wedges, dried apples, mixed nuts, drink, candy.

DINNER: Soup, trail stew, lentil pilaf, pudding, drink.

Reconstitute beef, corn, carrots, green beans. Mix with 2 T dehydrated bell pepper, 2 T onion flakes, 1 T marjoram, ½ t crushed hot peppers. Add sufficient liquid to cover. Simmer for 10 minutes.

(Note: The beef, corn, carrots, and green beans were all freeze-dried. Lentil pilaf is a supermarket item, easy to prepare and delicious. It can serve as a side dish, or a main dish if mixed with sausages, chunks of ham, or salami wedges.)

TUESDAY, DAY 9

BREAKFAST: Cold cereal, home fries, fruit compote, drink.

(*Note: This breakfast tasted good, but it should have had a higher protein content.*)

LUNCH: Cheese wedges, crackers, peanut butter and jelly, candy, drink.

DINNER: Soup, chili, crackers, mixed fruits, drink.

Precook beans. In separate pot, mix one 12-oz can tomato paste, 4 T onion flakes, ½ t garlic powder, 1 t basil or oregano, 1 T cumin, 2 T chili powder, three cans corned beef, salt and pepper, and enough water to make a thick sauce. Simmer 10 minutes. Add to bean pot and simmer another 10 minutes. Add more water if necessary.

Prepare the mixed fruit from a 12-oz package of mixed dried fruits, ½ c sugar, and enough water to cover. Simmer for 15 minutes.

(*Note: Buy the precooked beans to save a few hours of parboiling. This is not a spicy chili, so keep the chili powder handy for those who want it to taste more authentic.*)

WEDNESDAY, DAY 10

BREAKFAST: Scrambled eggs with mushrooms, hot cereal, drink.

LUNCH: Deviled meat, crackers, gorp, drink, candy.

DINNER: Soup, curried beef patties, couscous, wine, pudding, drink.

Reconstitute beef patties. Mix together 1½ c water, 1 T flour, 2 T raisins, ¼ c almonds, 2 bouillon cubes, 5 T minced onion, ¼ t garlic powder, 3 T margarine, 3 t curry powder, 1 t ginger powder. Simmer 5 minutes. Add beef patties. Continue simmering another 10 minutes.

(*Note: Couscous goes well with most curry-type dinners.*)

THURSDAY, DAY 11

BREAKFAST: Cold cereal, latkes, bacon, dried fruit, drink.

(*Note: Raining like hell. Camped on sliver of beach. Nearest firewood 200 yards away through 6-foot-high wall of brush. Cooked everything under a tent fly on the single Optimus stove.*)

LUNCH: Tuna fish with spread, crackers, peanut butter and jelly, candy, drink.

(*Note: We didn't have peanut butter and jelly yesterday and everyone yelled.*)

DINNER: Soup, Spanish rice*, crackers, pudding, wine, drink.

*Mix together 2½ qt water, three cans corned beef, one 12-oz can tomato paste, ¼ c onion flakes, 1 T bell pepper flakes, ½ t garlic powder, 2 T parsley flakes, 4 oz margarine. Simmer briefly. Add instant rice and ½ c wine. Simmer another 10 minutes.

FRIDAY, DAY 12

BREAKFAST: Scrambled eggs, hash browns, apple-raisin compote, drink.

Apple-raisin compote is a quick dish: Mix dried apples with a handful of raisins, place in a pot with enough water to cover (add sugar, if you must), and simmer 10 minutes.

LUNCH: Salami, gorp, candy, drink.

DINNER: Soup, hunter stew, mashed potatoes, gravy, pudding, drink.

Mix together in 1 qt water: 4 T onion flakes, 1 c dehydrated soup greens, 1 t garlic powder, ½ T oregano, 1 T bell pepper flakes, ½ t rosemary, 3 oz dried mushrooms, 1 t ginger powder, 4 T margarine. Simmer 10 minutes. Add three cans corned beef. Simmer another 10 minutes. Add more water if necessary.

(*Note: Instant mashed potatoes are easy to prepare. They are more palatable if served with a gravy.*)

SATURDAY, DAY 13

BREAKFAST: Hot cereal, broiled Spam, hot biscuits, drink.

(*Note: Because this was scheduled to be our last in-camp meal, we decided to take it easy and have biscuits. We enjoyed a leisurely meal before packing up and loading our canoes and ourselves on a truck for the last few miles into Senneterre. A bus took us from Senneterre back to Montreal. Total miles canoed: 120; total meals: 36; total calories: about 300,000.*)

LUNCH: Leftovers, if necessary.

DINNER: Soup, mashed potatoes, drink.

(*Note: These were planned as emergency meals. The soup was to be chicken noodle, with added cans of chicken for a thick, tasty, one-pot main dish. In addition, we carried enough cereal, peanut butter, soup, Spam, and corned beef for another full day.*)

On five days we also added to our supplies with fresh-caught, mouth-watering northern pike, walleye, and trout. The trout weighed in at around 3 pounds. The walleye and pike were about 7 pounds each.

The usual method of preparation was to fillet the fish, dice the meat, and add it to the day's soup, making a very good chowder. However, we also lightly pan-fried fillets as an addition to several dinners and some breakfasts.

In bear country, prepare fish reasonably far from camp. A paddle blade makes an excellent "table" for the filleting operation. Be sure to rinse off the blade well before bringing it back to camp, so the odor won't attract a hungry and curious bear during the night.

12

Making Camp

Locating a campsite in the wilderness usually is a matter of where, not when. It is relatively easy to canoe-camp in state and national forests and parks, or Canadian provincial parks, where canoe routes are marked and campsites are maintained. It is much more difficult to make camp when you are deep in the bush and totally dependent upon your ability to make do with whatever clearing is available

In the backwoods, begin looking early in the afternoon. On lakes, keep an eye out for beach areas on inlets that face the prevailing wind. Be mindful, however, that if you are camped in the path of the prevailing wind you also are camped in the path of the prevailing storm patterns; when the weather is foul, the result can be a disaster.

Where you have the choice, pick a site open to the breeze and well above the water level. A brisk evening wind will sweep an open area clear of insects. Camping close to the water or in thick brush is like setting a feast before every hungry blackfly and mosquito in the country.

Before you start pitching camp, give a few minutes' thought to where facilities will be. The first and most important is the kitchen area. Can you find a spot where you can

erect the shelter tarp between trees if necessary? Is the ground reasonably solid, so the cooks can work without churning up the soil into mud?

As soon as you locate the kitchen area, unload all food and community packs and bring them over. Then put the tents up. Once the tents are secure, the work details can get under way. If each member of your group has a specific chore, pleasant camping is a matter of meshing the parts into a harmonizing whole. If you camp on the theory that "everyone will pitch in," you will quickly observe that not everyone does. Some do; others ignore all work at hand.

Pick a spot where the fire will create no damage and leave as small a permanent scar as possible. Where you can, dig a fire pit— or at least a shallow depression—for the campfire. Pile the dirt to one side. When you break camp, scatter the burned wood. Cover the fire pit with the dirt you saved. It is important to leave the area spotless and to erase all scars of the camp's existence. Fire-blackened stones and an abandoned fire ring are among the most unsightly camp scars.

Starting a fire should be a painless task. Rain should not deter the fire crew. Gather birch bark as a starter. The oil in the bark will burn even when wet. If there is no bark, hunt for dripping resin in pine trees. Gather a blob. It will burn like solid turpentine.

Atop the starter, pile several handfuls of tiny, tiny dead twigs. The larger the pile of starter twigs, the quicker the fire will burn. Over the smaller twigs, make a stack of twigs as big as your finger. Pile them in a crisscross or wigwam fashion to allow air in. Add a few branches as large as your thumb along with about a dozen twigs. Start the fire using a pocket lighter.

The woodpile nearby should contain brush ranging from logs as big as your arm to branches as small as your thumb. It is almost totally unnecessary to chop wood. Small sticks can be broken across the knee. Larger pieces can be placed against a stone and stamped on. If you must break up larger branches, find a forked tree, insert one end of the branch in the fork and push the branch until it cracks into convenient lengths. Leave the hatchet in the EMER-GENCY—NO FIRST AID bag until you really need it.

Half of camping is cookery. As that noble purveyor of woodland lore in the nineteenth century, Horace Kephart, wrote in his classic, *The Book of Camping & Woodcraft*:

> Half of cookery is the fire thereof. It is quite impossible to prepare a good meal over a higgledy-piggledy heap of smoking chunks, or over a fierce blaze, or over a great bed of coals that will warp cast iron and melt everything else. One must have a small fire, free from smoke and flame, with coals or dry twigs in reserve; there must be some way of regulating the heat;

and there must be some sort of rampart around the fire on which pots and pans will perch level and at the right elevation, and perhaps a frame from which kettles can be suspended. It is a very simple matter to build the fire aright in the first place.

When merely making a "one-night stand" in summer, start a small cooking fire the moment you stop for camping and put your kettle on. Then you will have coals and boiling water ready when you begin cooking, and the rest is easy—supper will be ready within twenty minutes.*

To make a fireplace, find two large rocks, preferably flat on two sides. The rocks should be at least 1 foot across. With these rocks, build two parallel walls 2 to 3 feet long and not more than 18 inches apart. Place a cooking grill atop the rocks, making certain it sits level and solid. The grill should not be more than 18 inches above the surface of the ground. Build the fire under the grill. The rock walls will hold the heat in. If the wind is brisk, find a large flat rock big enough to place over the opening facing into the wind as a deflector to keep the breeze from blowing the heat out from under the pots.

After you begin to cook, make certain there is fire under the appropriate pot or kettle. If the fire shifts, either push it back with fresh twigs kept on hand for that purpose, or shift the cooking pot. On a campfire, the heat is constantly shifting, growing, and dying. Keep the fire only strong enough for cooking, never roaring so high that the flames drive the cooks away from the food, which then boils over or burns to a crisp.

On one lengthy trip we forgot our cooking grill. No matter. Each time we set up camp

*Horace Kephart, *The Book of Camping & Woodcraft*, Field and Stream (1905): 115.

we scoured the area for several large, flat rocks, less than ½-inch thick. Two or three such rocks laid atop the two side walls of rock formed an excellent stove top. In many ways we found the all-rock stove more satisfactory than the grill fire, because the flat rock top would hold the heat and distribute it evenly. We placed pots over the open spaces between the flat rocks for fast heating.

As one group completes work on the fire, others haul in firewood and bark. Bring plenty. Downed wood is dry and burns far more quickly than freshly chopped logs. Keep the woodpile well to one side of the fire. Clear an area alongside the fire for the cooks. This space is sacrosanct. It belongs to the cooks alone. Bring into the cook area the food for the meal, the kitchen utility bag, and all other items useful to the cooks. Before beginning any meal, the cooks should double-check the menu and make certain that all the food for the meal, and all the accessories, are at hand.

Cleaning after a meal should be done at camp, never in the river or lake. A good technique is to put two pots of water on heat, one for washing and one for rinsing. Wash all food particles off the pots, pans, dishes, and flatware.

Dishes and kitchenware need not be towel dried at night if they can as easily be air dried. After the final meal, stow all food and gear in the appropriate packs. Bring all of the packs together and protect them by tossing the dining poncho over the top. Place the pots and pans on top of the poncho if you are worried about hungry raccoons, bears, or other varmints. The theory is that if a bear does come snooping for food, the first time he pushes on the poncho the pots and pans will come tumbling down and the noise will frighten him off.

Once a young brown bear did visit our camp and pull a food sack out from under the poncho. He was frightened off by the noise of the falling pots and pans and ran awkwardly out of the camp–hauling the bag in his mouth. We found the bag a few hours later. Fortunately he had only smashed it apart and eaten the peanuts and candy. The rest of the food was untouched.

Bodily functions should be performed well away from camp. Keep the community folding shovel and a roll of toilet paper carefully wrapped inside a plastic bag in the kitchen area. Use them both. It takes only an extra moment to toss a spadeful of dirt over one's private contribution to the wilderness manure. In any area, no matter how remote, remember that others will almost surely camp in the same general location after you. There is nothing more unwelcome than to set up a tent only to find human excrement, toilet paper, and sanitary napkins scattered about.

If there was no time to do so in the morning, hang up sleeping pads and sleeping bags to air, fluff them well after airing, and toss them into the tents before the evening dew falls. If you aired them in the morning sun, unroll, fluff, and place them in the tents at least an hour before retiring. If you do so, they will regain their full loft before you crawl wearily in for the night.

The first essential for a comfortable night's sleep is a level site. It's worth the extra ten or twenty minutes of scouting around to find a place comfortably flat and large enough to accommodate your tent. If you must camp on a slope, pitch your tent so that you sleep with your head uphill. Pitch the tent with its longitudinal axis parallel to the prevailing wind. If a brisk breeze springs up, your tent may flap like a frustrated rooster trying to take off, but it will shed the greatest strain of the wind. A tent pitched sideways to a brisk breeze is a candidate for ripped guy lines, torn seams, and/or total collapse.

Vigorous "old-timers" talk lovingly about how comfortable it is to roll your canoe on its side and slip underneath for a night's sleep. You can use a canoe as a makeshift shelter, improved if you have a poncho or tarp to use with it. However, it is not very pleasant or comfortable. If you have any doubts, try it.

Some canoeists haul canoes ashore at camp and use them as tables or chairs, a practice I frown upon. I shudder at the memory of a lightweight gasoline stove burning merrily away atop a canoe converted to a table. One accidental bump and blazing gasoline could have spread across the canoe. A canoe is a canoe is a canoe.

Garbage disposal can be summed up in the words of a Sierra Club instruction: "Take nothing but pictures. Leave nothing but footprints."

In heavily traveled areas, edible, animal-attracting garbage should be burned or packed into plastic bags and taken with you in the appropriate "garbage scow." In areas where canoeists are infrequent, edible biodegradable leftovers may be carried well away from camp and scattered in the underbrush. Burn the burnables. Bag every trace of aluminum foil you scratch out of the fire after burning the burnables, for aluminum will hang around for centuries, spoiling the scenery. Flatten the cans and put them in your mobile garbage sack. Bring burned-out flashlight batteries. Empty propane or butane cylinders for the ride back home.

If you merely dig a garbage pit and bury everything, you have *not* cleaned up. Animals, attracted by the odors, will dig up the pit. Rain may soak the pit, causing a "pot hole." Cans and garbage will eventually emerge to the surface, or the pit will wash away, creating a source of erosion.

13

Animals and Other Things that Creep, Crawl, Bite, and Sting

Myths die hard. Even veteran hunters recount as Gospel stories of sudden attacks by wild animals upon innocent humans. On rare occasions a news report is flashed on page one detailing in full gore how a bear attacked and killed a sleeping camper.

Unless an animal is rabid, neither in the city nor in the wilderness will it attack without some provocation. Wolves may sound ferocious howling in the moonlight. But they do not race in packs after a helpless person lost in the snow. Bears do not come charging out of the brush to attack a camper. Bobcats, cougars, mountain lions, badgers, raccoons, skunks, rabbits, field mice, bats, owls, hawks, and all their cousins are equally reluctant to do battle with humans in the wild.

Only a few rules are necessary for the wilderness canoe-camper to avoid trouble with animals. They are as follows:

(1) Never fire a gun at a big game animal. Wounded, an animal may lash out with understandable ferocity. What happens if you see a dangerous animal approaching? Usually nothing, except that you and the animal both will back off. A shrill blast on a whis-tle, or the banging of pots, is highly effective in encouraging the animal to back off. On all of our wilderness trips, every member of the party carries a police whistle on a lanyard hanging around his neck.

(2) Do not keep food inside a tent or sleeping bag. I am aware of only one fully verifiable case in this century in the continental United States in which a bear "attacked" a sleeping camper without provocation, and there is substantial evidence that the camper—a woman in a sleeping bag in an open area that was known bear country—had candy bars in bed with her. Wilderness logic suggests the bear was attracted by the smell of the chocolate and was after it, not the sleeper's life.

(3) Even around highly used campsites where wild animals seem "tame," do not hand-feed or attempt to pet them.

(4) Give all baby animals a wide berth. Admire them from a distance. Under no circumstances come between a mother and her young. Nothing will provoke a female to violence more

quickly than a threat, or apparent threat, to her young.

(5) Big beasts can be bad-tempered. Startled, they may attack rather than yield. Approach moose or elk with a telephoto lens.

(6) Avoid startling animals when walking through their home territory. Talk loudly, blow a whistle from time to time, or fasten to your belt a small bell whose tinkle announces your presence with every step you take.

(7) Use common sense. In the wilderness you are the guest in the home of many wild animals. Even if the animals don't like you, they will tolerate your presence—unless you do something foolish. Don't yield to the sudden desire to throw a stone at one, or attempt to track a dangerous animal so you can get a close-up with your Instamatic.

Avoiding trouble with the creepies, crawlies, and bities of the wilderness is quite another matter. You cannot avoid getting bitten and stung by insects. But there is much you can do to minimize the insect problem.

Start with clothing. Thin clothing offers virtually no protection against a hungry mosquito. Its bloodsucking lance can easily pierce a cotton shirt. Heavier and bulkier clothing will provide more protection.

Try various insect repellents. Because of the mysteries of body chemistry, some repellents which are highly effective on one person are much less effective on another. While spray cans are very useful for misting the entire body, they also are the most bulky and expensive repellents. Where space is a problem, buy the liquid, not the spray.

Once you are heavily coated with repellent, forego the civilized folly of frequent washing. Instead, simply add more repellent from time to time. The oily types which build up a protective layer are most effectively applied in this way.

When possible, avoid insects. Camp in open areas. And, in the name of all that is holy to the body free of lumps and itches, know when the mosquitoes and blackflies are the thickest in the area you hope to travel. Blackflies are less numerous later in the summer. Early spring travel is almost impossible in large areas of the Northeast and Canada. By mid-August the summer heat has burned off the clouds of blackflies that plague mid-May canoeists.

In tick country, rub repellent around your cuffs and shirt collar, inside your pants, around the belt seam, and on your socks, as well as on your exposed skin.

Such items as heavy gloves and mosquito netting over your face are uncomfortable but effective. However, you must lift the face veil to eat. And every hungry blackfly and mosquito is aware of this Achilles' heel in your armor.

Campfire smudge has some repellent effect on mosquitoes, but it also is uncomfortable. I have long heard rumors that Indians would burn certain plants whose odor would repel insects. However, I've not been able to find anyone, not even Indians I've spoken to, who can verify this story or identify any plants whose burning odor is effective as a repellent. On the other hand, I'm absolutely certain this is forgotten fact, not foolish legend.

Use very hot water to relieve the itch of mosquito bites. Cover the bites with water as hot as your skin can withstand for five minutes. I have no idea why this procedure

ANIMALS AND OTHER THINGS THAT CREEP, CRAWL, BITE, AND STING

is effective, but it is remarkably successful in eliminating the itch for up to eight hours.

The simplest way to remove ticks is to cover them with oil or Vaseline. This will seal the pores through which they breathe, and in about half an hour the ticks can be removed—head and all. A quicker but trickier method is to apply heat to the tick, using a hot pin or burning cigarette to tickle its rump. After five or ten minutes the tick can be removed with tweezers. Treat the bite with antibiotic ointment. Unless you develop Rocky Mountain spotted fever from an infected tick, you have little to worry about. Should you develop the fever, it does respond to antibiotics. Untreated, it can be fatal.

After surviving animals, protecting himself against blackflies, and relieving the itch of mosquito bites with hot water, the intrepid canoeist faces one other major hazard: poison plants. The most frequent source of trouble is poison ivy. Stinging nettle and poison sumac are also dangerous.

If you do not recognize poison ivy, you will inevitably become its victim. Some people have a lifelong immunity to poison ivy, while others are so sensitive that they will erupt with weeping sores almost at the sight of it. Those with a present immunity may become sensitive to poison ivy, and those sensitive may suddenly develop an unexplained immunity.

The first defense against poison ivy, stinging nettle, and poison sumac is to learn to identify and avoid them.

There are many "accepted" treatments for both poison ivy and the much rarer poison sumac. Wash the affected spot thoroughly, then cover with either laundry soap or the proprietary drugs available through any pharmacy. Serious cases should be treated by a doctor. The newest home and camp treatment is hot, hot water, applied every few hours. It is as effective in relieving poison ivy or poison sumac irritation as it is in relieving mosquito bites.

Stinging nettle is not a long-term problem. An old wives' treatment is to rub the afflicted area with butter. Ice or cold water will relieve nettle itch. The sting from nettles usually disappears within an hour or two.

The growing tendency to seek the "natural health" contained in "natural foods" has led an increasing number of food faddists, especially younger people, to search the woods and swamps for edible plants, roots, and fungi. There are some plants which can cause anything from a minor stomach upset and dizziness to death. Unless you have a thorough understanding of whatever it is you plan to pick and eat—don't.

Wasps and bees are attracted by odors, especially those from sugars in anything from candy bars to jelly. They also find some perfumes and after-shave lotions attractive.

If you react to stinging bites, the best antidote is an antihistamine. For wilderness travel you'll need a more powerful antihistamine than you can buy off the shelf at the corner drugstore. If you develop unusual reactions to insect bites, talk to your family physician before you head into the bush.

14

Keeping Dry

Water, water everywhere
And storm clouds filled the sky.
Water, water everywhere
But all the gear stayed dry.

　　　　—With appropriate apologies

There is no more comforting thought on a stormy day in an open canoe than that your gear is safe and dry. At the opposite end of the spectrum, it is a sad and bitter feeling to know that everything aboard is wet, and getting wetter.

No canoe is 100-percent secure against the possibility of capsizing in strong rapids. Barring such a disaster, however, every canoe should be at least $99\frac{44}{100}$-percent immune to the unhappy prospect of getting gear wet, either from rain or an upset.

Three elements are involved in keeping equipment dry. One is the quality of the outer pack. The second is how your equipment is stored inside the pack. The third is how everything is handled in the canoe.

THE PACK

There are as many opinions among wilderness canoeists on how to select the appropriate pack as there are different types of packs on the market. There are those who advocate with all the vehemence of religious zealots the merits of the famous Adirondack pack baskets. There are the worthies who insist no pack should ever grace a canoe except the big Duluth packs. Some canoeists of more recent vintage swear by the modern canoe bag, a barracks-type bag with a waterproof nylon-duck outer bag and an inner bag of heavy vinyl. Others place their faith in the backpacker's pack and frame system.

No matter what pack you select, there are some important elements to consider in determining its fitness to go in your canoe. First, the outer fabric should be a sturdy material, preferably nylon duck coated to make it waterproof. Most better backpacks, whether soft bags with interior supports or packs with frames, meet this requirement. Duluth packs, however, are made of a heavy canvas duck. The material swells when wet and forms a highly water-resistant barrier, but the fabric is not waterproof. Ideally, canoe packs should have shoulder straps to simplify the job of carrying them on a portage.

Except for specialized canoe bags, packs have seams which leak. The packs are closed by drawstrings or zippers, which also leak. Thus, it is imperative to provide a waterproof inner lining to keep your gear dry. This can be accomplished quickly by placing a strong plastic garbage bag inside, and stuffing everything into the garbage bag. However, the plastic inner bag must be strong enough to stand up under day-to-day use. The 3-mil plastic garbage bags are the lightest weight you should consider. Even more practical are the heavier plastic bags, ranging in thickness up to 6 mils. These are used commercially; unfortunately, they are not always readily available to canoeists.

For double protection, use two inner linings. Fasten each one separately, and carry extra bags to replace those that are damaged or torn after long use. Divide your equipment into separate groups and put each group inside its own plastic bag before slipping everything into the pack.

The military-surplus waterproof sleeping-bag covers are a substantial improvement over plastic garbage bags. Stuff them loosely so that you can double over the tops and tie them tight.

Experiment at home to see if your pack is waterproof. Toss your loaded pack into the tub and turn the shower on full force. Roll the pack around occasionally. With the shower still blasting, put in the plug and let the tub slowly fill with water. After the tub is full, turn off the shower and let the pack bob around by itself for a while. Drain tub. Remove pack. Open up. Everything still dry? Don't think this is a tough test. Consider what happens if a canoe capsizes in whitewater.

If you carry your sleeping bag in a separate bag, it too must be waterproof. Some sleeping-bag stuff bags are made from waterproof fabric, but even these will leak at the seams and around the top. Use an inner lining of heavy-duty plastic garbage bags to ensure a dry sleeping bag.

Waterproof canoe bags may be purchased commercially. The better ones are made of a barracks-type outer bag of nylon duck with a heavy-gauge inner plastic bag. A less practical bag is a heavy-gauge plastic liner with a light outer nylon envelope. The two bags seal with a hollow rod. The most obvious drawback of the latter bag is its lack of carrying straps.

The rubberized U.S. military cargo bag, about 30 × 18 × 10 inches, is a superior waterproof canoe bag. It is so good, in fact, that a number of inferior commerical versions are now being marketed.

Even the most waterproof of packs may develop minute pinhole leaks or stretched seams. Take care to keep the packs off the wet deck. Toss in some heavy branches and put the bags on them. Lash everything securely so the canoe and gear will remain together in the event of a capsize. It is difficult enough to rescue canoeists and canoes without chasing after gear and equipment that has been swept into the foaming water.

There are some excellent canoe cover kits available through retail outlets and canoe manufacturers. These come in two basic designs. One design covers the canoe entirely except for cockpit openings for bow and stern paddlers. The other covers the canoe from directly behind the bow paddler to just forward of the stern paddler. Covers are affixed outside the gunwales by special fasteners attached to the canoe. This is fine if you are modifying your own canoe, but expensive and impractical for a rental canoe.

A field expedient to keep rain off the gear can be fashioned by tossing that extra poncho over the canoe when the storm clouds begin to glower. Hang the edges of the poncho over the outwales. It's simple enough to secure the poncho with rocks or heavy branches. This won't work in the wildest winds. When the winds are strong, you'll be safer and more comfortable by paddling as quickly as possible to get into the lee of some island or shoreline until the wind subsides.

15

Repairs

Aluminum canoes can be repaired fairly easily in the field with the proper repair supplies. A minor hole can be covered with duct tape. If the hole does not involve a seam, use a dab of claylike epoxy compound to fill the hole. Make certain some of the compound is spread larger than the hole both on the inside and outside, then covered with duct tape. On seams and around rivets I recommend the silicone–rubber caulking compound; it remains flexible and will not crack loose from the constant banging against obstructions in rock gardens and shallow water.

Tape alone is effective on canoes made from any material. I've never actually seen a hole punched in an ABS craft, although I've seen them almost doubled around rocks when broached in swift rapids, only to spring back to their proper shape with nothing more to show than a wrinkled skin. Major dents and bends in an aluminum canoe respond equally well to a pair of heavy boots or the rock-and-wood method. When hammering out dents, make certain the outside is cushioned by a muddy or sandy bank.

In the case of permanent repairs, aluminum canoes should have a patch riveted over the hole. Aluminum can be welded, but this operation should be performed only by a skilled aluminum-aircraft welder. The chief drawback to welding is that the metal next to the weld may lose its temper and become brittle. Grumman sells complete patching kits with full instructions.

Kevlar and fiberglass canoes can be fixed with fiberglass mending kits. The damaged area should be scraped and the fiberglass applied directly to the break. In the field, use a polyester resin with some extra peroxide hardener for quick setting. Use epoxy resin when time is not a factor. It takes several days to cure, but it is considerably stronger than the polyester resin.

Wrinkles can be removed from ABS canoes by warming the area to between 225 and 250 degrees. Since different manufacturers use different sandwich layers of ABS, it is best to contact the maker for specific instructions on removing wrinkles or repairing holes.

Fiberglass-coated cedar canoes can be repaired by the same methods used for Kevlar and all fiberglass canoes.

Although wood and canvas canoes are becoming a rarity, the *American Red Cross Canoeing Manual* goes into considerable detail on how to repair them. Both Chestnut and Old Town canoe factories sell everything needed for anything from a minor repair job to a major restoration.

A broken paddle shaft can be rejoined by gluing the two broken ends together with epoxy and wrapping the shaft with several layers of fiberglass. Work the fiberglass well above and below the break. Repaired paddles should be carried only as reserve paddles.

To prevent the tip of a wooden blade from splintering, apply a guard of fiberglass soaked in epoxy resin 1 to 2 inches around the bottom. Some models now are made with fiberglass protective caps over the tips. Metal caps can be applied, but care must be taken to ensure that the minute nail holes are sealed so that water cannot penetrate the interior wood.

Even minor cuts and scratches on wooden paddles should be treated promptly to prevent the wood from becoming water-soaked. Sand lightly and spray with a polyurethane or marine spar varnish. Veteran paddlers usually sand the varnish from the lower third of the shaft and from the grip, then soak the wood in linseed oil. On a long wilderness trip, the bare wooden sections can be covered occasionally with any type of grease or even margarine to avoid water logging.

Except those torn apart or crushed beyond all hope of salvage by a wild set of rapids, I have never seen a damaged canoe or paddle that could not be fixed in the wilderness by using duct tape, hauling out the fiberglass repair kit, or digging into the repair bag for a screw, bolt, or piece of wire—and some ingenuity.

16

Knots

No canoe is fully equipped without a painter, a good rope that can be used in emergencies or for tying a canoe when putting in. But a good rope is valuable for more than serving as a painter. It can be used to lash equipment, as a temporary clothesline in camp, for hauling gear up a cliff, to make an emergency stretcher, to anchor a canoe to the roof of a car, and for dozens of other assorted tasks. A sensible length of rope for the canoeist is about 30 feet, long enough for most situations yet not so long as to be difficult to handle. While $\frac{1}{4}$-inch rope will serve virtually every important need, I prefer a $\frac{3}{8}$-inch rope because it is more comfortable in the hands for lining or hauling heavy loads.

Hemp, manila, or sisal ropes are no longer favored by canoeists. Select a rope of man-made fiber. Some are made of a loose weave which floats. Select a rope with breaking strength rated at least 1,500 pounds for general use. (For the rope in your emergency rescue kit, choose one with a breaking strength of at least 2,500 pounds; keep in mind that if it is used for pulling a swamped canoe out of the rapids, the load on the canoe may well exceed 1 ton.)

Man-made fibers are virtually rot-proof;

considering how often a canoe rope is wet, this is an important factor. Some rope is made with a built-in ability to "stretch" under a heavy load, a virtue for the technical rock climber, who may need the give in a fall—but a liability for the canoeist who may need the rope to haul a broached canoe out of the rapids. If a rope with high stretch breaks, it can whip back with the stinging force of a giant rubber band.

Do acquire basic proficiency in tying some elemental knots.

Tie two ropes together with a sheet bend or fisherman's knot. (See Figure 103.) The fisherman's knot tends to jam under heavy loads. In using a sheet bend, especially with nylon or Dacron rope, tie it with extra-long ends and take a hitch or two on the standing parts.

When making a rope fast in a hurry, and where a long strain is not expected, use two half hitches. (See Figure 104.) This is a good knot for tying a canoe ashore, or for one end of a camp clothesline.

A clove hitch is good when the strain is temporary. (See Figure 105.) Use it for tying the other end of a clothesline, or for a camp tarp shelter.

When you need to put extra pressure on

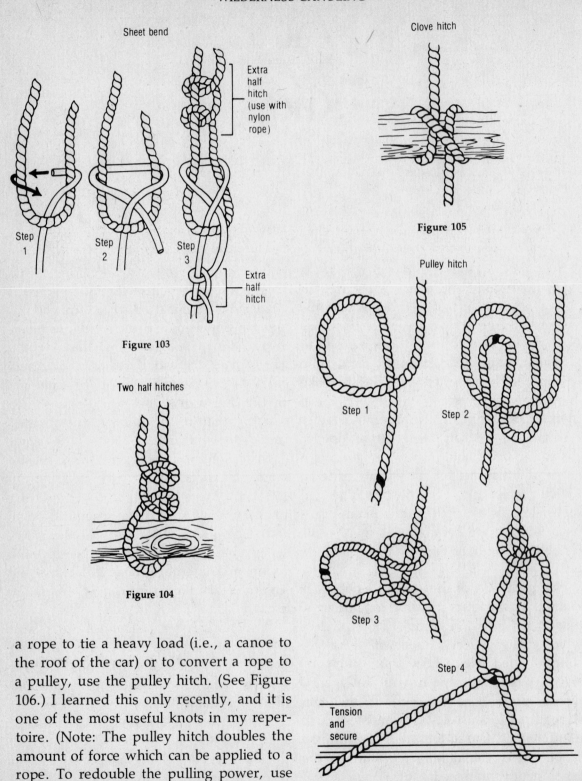

Sheet bend

Extra half hitch (use with nylon rope)

Step 1

Step 2

Step 3

Extra half hitch

Figure 103

Clove hitch

Figure 105

Two half hitches

Figure 104

Pulley hitch

Step 1

Step 2

Step 3

Step 4

Tension and secure

Figure 106

a rope to tie a heavy load (i.e., a canoe to the roof of the car) or to convert a rope to a pulley, use the pulley hitch. (See Figure 106.) I learned this only recently, and it is one of the most useful knots in my repertoire. (Note: The pulley hitch doubles the amount of force which can be applied to a rope. To redouble the pulling power, use a double pulley hitch.)

KNOTS

For tying a nonslip loop at the end of a rope, use a bowline. (See Figure 107.)

For a nonslip double loop in the middle of a rope, use the bowline on a bight. (See Figure 108.)

For a knot that can be used to adjust tension on a rope such as a main guy line to a tent, make a taut-line hitch. (See Figure 109.) This is an adjustable knot.

Bowline on a bight

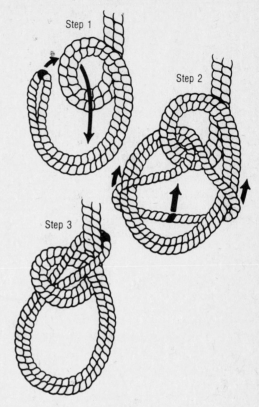

Bowline

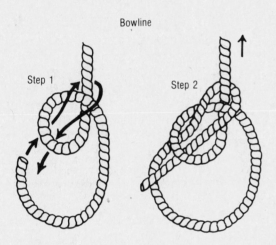

Figure 107

Figure 108

Taut-line hitch

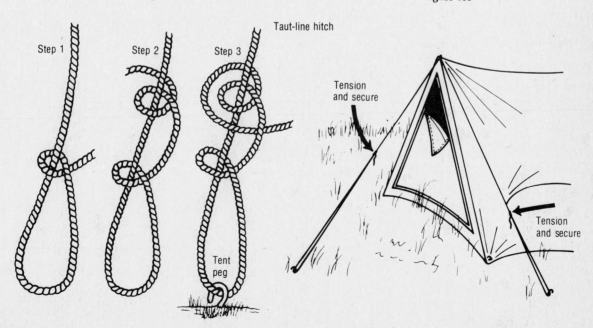

Figure 109

For hauling a canoe, use a bowline; attach it as illustrated in Figure 101, page 92.

It's easy to drag a bundle of wood into camp using a timber hitch. (See Figure 110.)

Timber hitch

Figure 110

When using nylon or Dacron, remember that the rope is slippery. Make long free ends for a knot, then loop the free ends around the standing end with half hitches or overhands to secure the knot.

To keep the ends of nylon or Dacron rope from unraveling, you no longer need to learn how to whip them. Instead, take a match and melt the ends. Be careful—nylon burns at a very high temperature. As quickly as the end of the rope begins to melt, use an old rag to "wipe" it clean, pulling the end into a thin strand rather than letting it form a solid knot larger than the rope itself. (See Figure 111.)

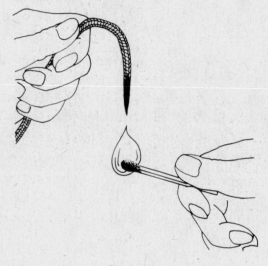

Figure 111

17

Pets

Ideally, dogs belong in the country. Even many city-dwelling dog owners agree, and I'm among them. Whenever I head for the country, I want to take my dog along to enjoy the freedom, the smells, the openness of the out-of-doors. Taking a dog canoeing and camping poses problems. You must understand them before you will be at ease with a dog out-of-doors.

There are the numerous little annoyances. Where will the dog sleep? Will he drive you up the walls of the tent if he trots in and out with muddy feet, shaking leaves and brush on the tent floor? How about canine first aid? What about the dog's food? Will the dog sit quietly in the canoe if he sees something intriguing on a nearby shore? These are problems to mull over at your leisure before you make the go or no-go decision about the family pet.

Should you take your dog canoeing? Think about it carefully. If you do, begin with an easy, short trip to gain an idea of how you and the dog will get along once you're waterborne.

Even before you decide to take your dog, you must know that he will be permitted where you are going. If you will be stopping at campsites on the way, will the dog be welcome? If you will use a public campsite as your base, will he be permitted? Campsites, both public and private, which admit dogs usually have quite strict requirements: (1) that the animal must be on a leash at all times and (2), though not as rigidly enforced, that you have in your possession proof of current rabies inoculation. Lacking such proof, are you prepared for what could happen to your dog if he should happen to take a nip out of some unsuspecting hand thrust toward his upturned head? If there is any suspicion that he may have rabies, his head may be summarily removed from his body and shipped to a laboratory for study to determine if, indeed, the dog did have rabies. Additionally, some states require a health certificate signed by a veterinarian. A health certificate and proof of rabies inoculation are mandatory before entering Canada. Mexico requires not only both certifications but also approval in advance by a Mexican consul. Try not to lose the documents in some remote river. When you return to the United States, both documents are necessary to get your dog back home.

When traveling with a dog, be especially careful to see that he wears some sort of identification tag at all times. Even the most placid dog may become nervous and leap from a car, run out of an open doorway, or disappear from camp while chasing an imaginary rabbit into the woods. A metal name tag securely fastened to his collar or identification tattooed in his ear could be the only means you'll have of ever seeing him again.

A dog's food requirements are as important in camp as at home. If possible, he should be maintained on his regular feed, because a sudden change of diet can upset his digestion. Canoeing with a dog can pose enough problems without adding a touch of diarrhea. If you must change his feed, do so gradually at home to acclimate the animal to a camp diet. I recommend dry foods. They do not spoil and are high in nutritional value.

Preconditioning a dog is as important as preconditioning for the adult canoeist. Our dog, Amber, usually behaves with model rectitude in a canoe. Ashore may be a different matter. She's excited by the woods and wilds. She loves to race around. This is all to the good, except for the fact that she's a genuine apartment dog who would rather curl up and sleep on the couch than even go for a gentle jog with her master. Once in the wilds she will tire easily, get sore-footed, and become a stodgy mass of 35 pounds of unhappy dog—unless she's in condition.

We had a difficult time on a weekend canoe trip with Amber the first time we took her. Now we try to keep her in much better physical condition at all times. A couple of weeks before a trip, I take her out for a short jog twice daily and spend some time with her each morning in the park along the river.

Before the actual start of a trip, do not feed or water your dog for several hours. En route, give him plenty of time to empty his bladder and bowels. Exercise him at each stop. If you stay overnight at a motel, it is wise to call ahead and see if your intended lodging place will accept animals. The American Automobile Association provides a free *Camping and Trailering* directory for its members which lists those lodgings with restrictions on pets. Woodall Publishing Company (500 Hyacinth Place, Highland Park, Illinois 60035) and Gaines Dog Research Center (250 North St., White Plains, New York 10605) sell publications which list restrictions on pets at hotels, motels, campgrounds, and trailer parks.

Railroads and airlines do carry pets. Regulations vary widely, so check early with the local ticket office.

Even the most amiable pet may become snappish on the road. As the Gaines people so aptly note:

When the family goes camping, normally well-adjusted dogs can become quite excitable. To help make the adjustment, a family dog on a trip needs reassurances from the people he knows and loves. A friendly nod, an occasional petting, a familiar toy or blanket, sufficient food and water, and frequent roadside stops are all helpful. Strangers, especially children, should be kept at a distance if the dog appears upset. When a dog is nervous, a child's playful poking can provoke even the gentlest animal into growling or snapping.*

Animal first aid usually consists of treat-

*Touring with Towser, Gaines Dog Research Center, White Plains, N.Y.

ing skin cut or torn in a collision with another dog, an occasional confrontation with a wild animal, or an accident. Wash the affected area with soap and water, and treat with an antibiotic ointment if it is in an area the dog cannot lick. Only a veterinarian is qualified to treat serious wounds and broken bones. In the extremely unlikely event that the dog is bitten by a poisonous snake, treat the bite as you would snake bite in a human.

Ticks are a constant problem. Examine the dog every night, from nose tip to wagging tail. Remove ticks by first coating the insect with cooking, machine, or castor oil. Keep it well covered for at least a half hour. The oil will shut off the insect's oxygen supply and kill it or cause it to loosen its head, which is buried in the animal's hide. Carefully work the tick loose with a pair of sterilized tweezers.

A city dog, out of foolish curiosity, may tangle with a skunk or a porcupine. The first sign of a porcupine quill usually is a wild howl as the dog races around in agony. First, catch the dog. Quills are held in place by thousands of minute, reverse barbs. Usually they can be jerked out by hand or a pair of pliers. Quills in the mouth sometimes may be pushed all the way through the skin, and worked out. In serious cases, take the animal to a vet. Do not let the barbs work their way into the body.

I know of no way to rid a dog of the noxious, heavy odor that marks his meeting with a skunk. Douse him with vinegar or tomato juice, if available. Wash him with detergent or laundry soap. Throw him out of the canoe regularly and let him soak himself thoroughly. Until you can bear the odor, try leashing him downwind from camp.

A pair of scissors is invaluable for cutting away hair that becomes painfully matted from burrs in and around the ears and feet. Keep a careful watch for any change in bowel movements, either diarrhea or constipation. These may be caused by a sudden change of diet or from the dog's finding a carcass of an animal in the brush and gnawing on a bite or two from it.

Be especially cautious about letting your dog run loose when ashore. In most farm and backcountry areas a peace officer may shoot any dog that is not chained. Most loose dogs have an insatiable desire to chase sheep, pigs, colts, fawns, and similar animals, and even to kill them. Yes—your dog, too.

If you must keep your dog chained in camp while you're off racing through an exciting set of rapids, keep him on a light chain leash, never a leather leash or rope. In a strange environment he may chew through a leather strap or rope and disappear.

Even though every dog is a natural swimmer there always is a need to be safety conscious with an animal in a canoe. If your dog is a rugged, outdoor breed that enjoys dashing into ice-filled water, you obviously have less need to worry about what would happen in a capsize than if your pet is a soft, city dog with limited physical ability to withstand a dangerous situation. Sudden strain can kill a dog by precipitating a heart attack even as it can a person.

Here are a few pointers to remember:

Should your dog wear a life preserver? If he faces any danger of drowning—absolutely. Dog life jackets are available commercially. A dog panier with a small inflated plastic beach ball stuffed in each pocket is equally effective as a personal flotation device for your animal. Or, you can do as we do and devise a life jacket simply by strapping a horse collar PFD to your dog. If you do, however, make certain that in an upset the makeshift life jacket will hold firmly to the area just back of the head, and will not slip to his rear quarters.

Finally, consider carefully how your dog will react if there is a capsize even in Class II rapids, and whether he ought to be aboard or put ashore so he can trot along the bank and follow your progress. I consider it stupid to put a dog in a canoe racing through Class III rapids, though I have seen it done.

If you're uncertain whether you and your dog are prepared to put up with the difficulties you will encounter when out-of-doors together, leave him behind. He may be lonely boarded in a kennel, but he'll be safe and secure. If you take him, you will learn much of a dog's great love for his master or mistress, his willingness to share the delights and miseries of your adventure, his instinct to protect the camp from the strange sounds of the night. You and your dog will have shared the ultimate companionship found only in the wilderness.

PART III

Appendixes

Appendix I

Canoeing Organizations

The greater your interest in canoeing, the more likely you will want to seek others to share the experience of everything from wilderness canoe trips to running whitewater. Your best opportunity to locate canoe and kayak enthusiasts is through two organizations.

The American Canoe Association has headquarters at 4260 E. Evans Ave., Denver, Colorado 80222. Annual membership fees are as follows: governing member, $10; sustaining member, $14; junior member (for those under 18), $6. Membership includes a subscription to the bimonthly magazine, *Canoe*.

American Whitewater Affiliation, Box 321, Concord, New Hampshire 03301, charges a club membership fee of $10. Subscription to the bimonthly journal, *American Whitewater*, costs $5.

The ACA's publication, *Canoe*, is a general-interest magazine devoted to all phases of kayaking and canoeing, from how to repair a broken thwart to news of major races. *American Whitewater* focuses on whitewater canoeing and kayaking. Both are excellent publications.

Clubs affiliated both with the ACA and AWA are located throughout the United States. Lists of clubs, including contacts and addresses, are included in this appendix. Club officers change frequently. However, if you are interested in a club in your area, contact the name given or contact either the ACA or AWA.

APPENDIX I

AMERICAN CANOE ASSOCIATION AFFILIATES

Alaska

Alaska Whitewater Assn.
Bill Kenyon
Glenn Allen, AK 99588

Krik Kanoers
Ed Swanson
Box 14 Columbia
Anchorage, AK 99504

California

American Guides Assn.
P.O. Box B
Woodland, CA 95695

Cakara
E. R. Leach
675 Overhill Drive
Redding, CA 96001

Feather River Kayak Club
Mike Schneller
1773 Broadway St.
Marysville, CA 95901

Haystackers Whitewater Canoe
Tom Johnson
P.O. Box 675
Kernville, CA 93238

Loma Prieta Paddlers
Don Burnham
1374 Colinton Way
Sunnyvale, CA 94087

Marin Canoe Club
Richard M. Brown
P.O. Box 3023
San Rafael, CA 94902

Powell Boating UC Berkeley
Charles Martin
5499 Claremont Ave.
Oakland, CA 94618

Sierra Club T.S.
Charles Smith
1760 Walnut St.
Berkeley, CA 94709

So. Cal. Canoe Assn.
Marvin A. Cornett
3966 S. Menlo Ave.
Los Angeles, CA 90037

Valley Canoe Club
Bob Blackstone
10363 Calvin Ave.
Los Angeles, CA 90025

Westlake Canoe Club
Bill Bragg
3427 Gloria
Newbury Park, CA 91320

YMCA Whitewater Club
Richard Hambley
640 N. Center St.
Stockton, CA 95202

Colorado

Fibark, Inc.
John L. Carr
Box 762
Salida, CO 81201

Colorado Whitewater Assn.
Deane Hall
4260 E. Evans Ave.
Denver, CO 80222

Connecticut

Amston Lake Canoe Club
Robert G. Dickinson
Deepwood Drive
Amston, CT 06231

Columbia Canoe Club
Mrs. Wm. J. Murphy
Lake Road
Columbia, CT 06237

Waterford Canoe Club
Ralph G. Clark
Box 111
Waterford, CT 06385

Delaware

Wilmington Trail Club
George M. Lecierca
324 Spaulding Rd.
Wilmington, DE 19803

District of Columbia

Potomac Boat Club
Jerry Welbourn
3530 Water St., N.W.
Washington, DC 20007

Washington Canoe Club
John T. Brosius
3700 K St., N.W.
Washington, DC 20007

Florida

Citrus County Kayak Club
Jack Rademaker
Route 1, Box 415
Floral City, FL 32636

Everglades Canoe Club
Charles Graves
239 N.E. 20th St.
Delray Beach, FL 33440

Florida Sport Paddling Club
Phil A. Rhodes
133 Hickory Lane
Seffner, FL 33584

Seminole Canoe & Yacht Club
Noble Enge
5653 Windermere Drive
Jacksonville, FL 32211

Georgia

Explorer Post 49
Doug Woodward
1506 Brawley Circle
Atlanta, GA 30313

Georgia Canoeing Assn.
Wm. D. Crowley, Jr.
P.O. Box 7023
Atlanta, GA 30309

Hawaii

Hawaii Kayak Club
Virginia Moore
407 D. Keariani St.
Kailea, HI 69734

International Hawaiian Canoe Assn.
A. E. Minvielle
1638-A Kona
Honolulu, HI 96814

Idaho

American Indian Center Canoe Club
Roger Hazelwood
115 N. Walnut
Boise, ID 83702

Illinois

American Youth Hostels
3712 N. Clark St.
Chicago, IL 60613

CANOEING ORGANIZATIONS

Belleville Whitewater Club
Linda Seaman
3 Oakwood
Belleville, IL 62223

Caterpillar Canoe Club
Henry Schwemlein
314 W. Arnold Rd.
Sandwich, IL 60548

Chicago Whitewater Assn.
Barb Press
10912 Liberty Grove Drive
Willow Springs, IL 60480

Le Brigade Illinois
Jim Strid
451 S. St. Mary's Rd.
Libertyville, IL 60048

Lincoln Park Boat Club
Frank Dallos
2737 N. Hampden Court
Chicago, IL 60614

Mackinaw Canoe Club
Perry Foltz
120 Circle Drive
East Peoria, IL 61611

Prairie Club Canoeists
Warren Lahners
517 Miller Rd.
Barrington, IL 60010

Prairie State Canoeists
Mrs. H. Reidinger
5055 N. Kildare Ave.
Chicago, IL 60630

Sauk Valley Canoe Club
John Whitver
R.R. 2
Morrison, IL 61270

Sierra Club Canoeists
Randy Fort
625 W. Barry
Chicago, IL 60657

St. Charles Canoe Club
Jim Doberstein
1074 Cherry Lane
Lombard, IL 60148

Tippecanoers
Stanton Warburton
1270 W. Green St.
Decatur, IL 62521

University of Chicago Whitewater Club
Bruce Campbell
933 E. 56th St.
Chicago, IL 60637

Indiana

Bloomington Canoe & Kayak Club
Ned Bleuer
2221 Maxwell
Bloomington, IN 47401

Connersville Canoe Club
Arlington Hudson
R.R. 3
Connersville, IN 47331

Elkhart YMCA Canoe Club
James Trader
229 W. Franklin St.
Elkhart, IN 46514

Hoosier Canoe Club
Dave Ellis
5641 N. Delaware
Indianapolis, IN 46220

Kekionga Voyageurs
Jack Crance
1517 Werling Rd.
New Haven, IN 46774

Paddle Pushers Canoe Club
Edward Scholf
2506 Rainbow Drive
Lafayette, IN 47904

Prairie Club Canoeists
Charles Stewart
364 Rose Ellen Drive
Crown Point, IN 46307

St. Joe Valley Canoe & Kayak Club
Ruskin Oldfather
R.R. 2, Box 451
Goshen, IN 46526

Sugar Creek Paddlers
Maxine Rady
R.R. 8
Crawfordsville, IN 47933

Whitewater Valley Canoe Club
Chuck Taylor
1032 Cliff St.
Brookville, IN 47012

Wild American Paddlers
Bob Frederick
R.R. 7, Box 66D
Greenfield, IN 46140

Kentucky

Blue Grass Pack & Paddle Club
Richard Tileston
216 Inverness Drive
Lexington, KY 40503

Kentucky Canoe Assn.
Joe Medley
2006 Marilee Drive
Louisville, KY 40272

Louisville Paddle Club
Harry Hardin
Route 1
Smithfield, KY 40068

Viking Canoe Club
Joe Venhoff
3108 Rockaway Drive
Louisville, KY 40216

Maine

Penobscot Paddle & Chowder Assn.
William F. Stearns
Box 121
Stillwater, ME 04489

Maryland

Baltimore Kayak Club
Al Karasa
1099 Tollgate
Belair, MD 21014

Monocacy Canoe Club
127 S. Bentz St.
Frederick, MD 21701

St. Mary's College of Maryland
John A. Spangler
St. Mary's City, MD 20686

Massachusetts

AMC Berkshire
Forrest House
Knollwood Drive
East Longmeadow, MA 01028

Cochituate Canoe Club
Guy Newhall
99 Dudley Rd.
Cochituate, MA 01760

Foxboro Camp Canoe Club
Paul F. Neely
32 Taunton St.
Bellingham, MA 02019

Lake Chaogg Canoe Club
William R. Graham
P.O. Box 512
Webster, MA 01570

MIT Whitewater Club
James Aiglin
R 6432, MIT
Cambridge, MA 02139

APPENDIX I

Northeast Sports & Recreation Assn.
Chas. Cicciarella
2 Fairmont Terrace
Wakefield, MA 01880

Nor'east Voyageurs
R. A. Paulson
West Street
Kingston, MA 02360

Waupanog Paddlers
James Clear
13 Borden St.
North Seituate, MA 02060

Westfield River Whitewater Canoe
Merritt Andrews
90 W. Silver St.
Westfield, MA 01085

Michigan

Kalamazoo Down Streamers
James Tootle
6820 Evergreen
Kalamazoo, MI 49002

Lansing Canoe Club
Darwin Gilbert
6101 Norburn Way
Lansing, MI 48910

Lower Michigan Paddling Council
Edward Woods
8266 Patton
Detroit, MI 48228

Michigan Canoe Race Assn.
Al Robinson
4735 Hillcrest
Trenton, MI 48183

Michigan Trailfinders Club
David M. Groenleer
2630 Rockhill, N.E.
Grand Rapids, MI 49505

Niles Kayak Club
Mrs. William Smoke
Route 1, Box 83
Buchanan, MI 49107

Minnesota

Minnesota Canoe Assn., Inc.
Box 14177
Union Station
Minneapolis, MN 55414

Missouri

CMA College Outing Club
Dr. O. Hawksley
Biology Dept.
Warrensburg, MO 64093

Meramec River Canoe Club
Al Beletz
3636 Oxford Blvd.
Maplewood, MO 63143

Ozark Wilderness Waterways
Box 8165
Kansas City, MO 64112

Nebraska

Ft. Kearney Canoeists
Ward Schrack
2623 Avenue D
Kearney, NB 68847

Nevada

Basic High Canoe Club
John Shannon
751 Palo Verde Drive
Henderson, NV 89015

New Hampshire

Androscoggin Canoe & Kayak
John Wilson
Lancaster, NH 03584

Ledyard Canoe Club
Christopher Daniel
Robinson Hall
Hanover, NH 03755

Mad Pemi Canoe Club
Dennis Keating
93 Realty
Campton, NH 03223

New Jersey

KCC—New York
Ed Alexander
6 Winslow Ave.
East Brunswick, NJ 08816

Knickerbocker Canoe Club
Frank Principe, Jr.
1263 River Rd.
Edgewater, NJ 07020

Mohawk Canoe Club
Charles Schrey
11 Thomas St.
High Bridge, NJ 08829

Murray Hill Canoe Club
William J. Schreibeis
c/o Bell Labs
600 Mountain Ave.
Murray Hill, NJ 07974

Neversink Canoe Sailing Society
William Reed
Oak Tree Lane
Rumson, NJ 07760

NY-NJ River Conference
52 W. Union Ave.
Bound Brook, NJ 08805

Red Dragon Canoe Club
221 Edgewater Ave.
Edgewater Park, NJ 08010

Wanda Canoe Club
Clyde Britt
47 Summit St.
Ridgefield Park, NJ 07660

New Mexico

Albuquerque Whitewater Club
Glenn Fowler
804 Warm Sands Dr. S.E.
Albuquerque, NM 87112

New York

AYH—New York
Jim Naven
6 Cardinal Court
West Nyack, NY 10994

Adirondack Mountain Club
Doug Smith
769 John Glenn Rd.
Webster, NY 14580

AMC—NY Canoe Comm.
John Niers
Midland S., Box 1956
Syosset, NY 11791

Inwood Canoe Club
Stephen Kelly
509 W. 212th St.
New York, NY 10036

KCC—Cooperstown
Agnes Jones
Riverbrink
Cooperstown, NY 13326

CANOEING ORGANIZATIONS

KA NA WA KE Canoe Club
Harold J. Gray
26 Pickwick Rd.
Dewitt, NY 13214

Niagara Gorge Kayak Club
Michael J. McGee
147 Lancaster Ave.
Buffalo, NY 14322

Otterkill Canoe Club
Lee Aubel
5 Yankee Main Lane
Goshen, NY 10924

Sebago Canoe Club
Al Musial
9622 Avenue M
Brooklyn, NY 11236

Sierra Club Canoe Comm.
Ed Mernyk
5 Lakeview Ave.
North Tarrytown, NY 10591

TASCA
P.O. Box 41
Oakland Gardens, NY 11364

Wellsville Down-River Paddlers
Leray Dodson
Proctor Road
Wellsville, NY 14895

Yonkers Canoe Club
Joe Beczak
360 Edwards Place
Yonkers, NY 10701

North Carolina

Carolina Canoe Club
Bob Moyer
121 Turner St.
Elkin, NC 20621

Ohio

AYH—Columbus
Charles H. Pace
565 Old Farm Rd.
Columbus, OH 43213

Dayton Canoe Club, Inc.
Wm. P. Morman
1020 Riverside Drive
Dayton, OH 45405

Keel-Haulers Canoe Club
John A. Kobak
2929 W. River Rd.
Elyria, OH 44035

Warner & Swasey Canoe Club
Wayne McRobie
406 Millave S.W.
New Philadelphia, OH 44663

Oklahoma

OK Canoers
B. L. Smith
3112 Chaucer Drive
Village, OK 73120

Tulsa Canoe & Camping Club
Jean Estep
5810 E. 30 Place
Tulsa, OK 74114

Oregon

Lower Columbia Canoe Club
Route 1, Box 134E
Scappoose, OR 97056

Mary Kayak Club
Rob Blickensderfer
830 N.W. 23rd, No. 17
Corvallis, OR 97330

Oregon Kayak & Canoe Club
Rod Kiel
P.O. Box 692
Portland, OR 97207

Pennsylvania

Allegheny Canoe Club
Walter J. Pilewski
131 Park Ave.
Franklin, PA 16323

AMC Delaware Valley
Donald M. Demarest
306 Crestview Circle
Media, PA 19063

American Youth Hostels
Philip H. Mason
6300 5th Ave.
Pittsburgh, PA 15232

ATH—Delaware Valley
Fred Rosen
4714 York Rd.
Philadelphia, PA 19141

AYH—Pittsburgh
George Robertson
6300 5th Ave.
Pittsburgh, PA 15232

Henscreek Canoe Club
Roger Hager
R.D. 5, Box 356
Johnstown, PA 15905

Buck Ridge Ski Club
William Wright
1728 Earlington Rd.
Havertown, PA 19083

Bucknell Outing Club
Ray Charles
Box C-1610-Bucknell U.
Lewisburg, PA 17837

Delaware Canoe Club
William Woodring
14 S. 14th St.
Easton, PA 18042

Endless Mtn. Voyageurs
Louis Hopt
285 Shorthill Rd.
Clarks Green, PA 18411

Explorer Post 65
N. Hosking
22 Caralpa Place
Pittsburgh, PA 15228

Fox Chapel Canoe Club
Bill Henderson
610 Squaw Run Rd.
Pittsburgh, PA 15238

Indiana U Outing Club
David Cox
Chemistry IUP
Indiana, PA 15701

Kishacoquillas Canoe & Rafting
c/o Wilderness
P.O. Box 97
Ohiopyle, PA 15470

Mohawk Canoe Club
Charles Lopinto
6 Canary Rd.
Levittown, PA 19057

North Hills YMCA WW
Tim Hawthorn
1130 Sandlewood Lane
Pittsburgh, PA 15237

APPENDIX I

Oil Creek Valley Canoe Club
Ray W. Gerard
214 N. 1st St.
Titusville, PA 16354

Paoli Troop I BSA
Douglas Hoffman
432 Strafford Ave.
Wayne, PA 19087

Penn Hills WW Canoe Club
James Catello
12200 Garland Drive
Pittsburgh, PA 15235

Penn State Outing Club
John Sweet
118 S. Buckhout St.
State College, PA 16801

Philadelphia Canoe Club
Dr. Paul Liebman
4900 Ridge Ave.
Philadelphia, PA 19128

Post 42 BSA
James Oro
Route 2
Palmerton, PA 19053

Scudder Falls WW Club
Dave Benham
795 River Rd.
Yardley, PA 19067

Shenango Valley Canoe Club
E. K. Holloway
863 Bechtal Ave.
Sharon, PA 16146

Sylvan Canoe Club
Don Hoecker
132 Arch St.
Verona, PA 15147

Wildwater Boating Club
Robert Martin
Lock Box 179
Bellefonte, PA 16823

Williamsport YMCA Canoe Club
John L. Houser
343 W. 4th St.
Williamsport, PA 17701

South Carolina

Sierra Club Canoe Comm.
Gordon Howard
P.O. Box 163
Clemson, SC 29631

Tennessee

Bluff City Canoe Club
Lawrence Migllore
P.O. Box 4523
Memphis, TN 38104

Carbide Canoe Club
Herbert Pomerance
104 Ulena Lane
Oak Ridge, TN 37830

Chota Canoe Club
A. Murray Evans
3811 Woodhill Place
Knoxville, TN 37919

East Tennessee WW Club
Reid K. Gryder
P.O. Box 3074
Oak Ridge, TN 37830

Tennessee Valley Canoe Club
Ralph L. Suggs
Box 11125
Chattanooga, TN 37401

U. of Tenn. Hiking & Canoe Club
William R. Krueger
Route 6
Concord, TN 37730

Texas

Boy Scout 51 & Post 151
Tom Sloan
2008 Bedford
Midland, TX 79701

Heart of Texas Canoe Club
Bob Burleson
Box 844
Temple, TX 76501

Houston Canoe Club
Harold Walls
3116 Broadway
Houston, TX 77017

Utah

Wasatch Mtn. Club
J. C. Giddings
904 Military Drive
Salt Lake City, UT 84108

Virginia

Appalachian Transit Authority
G. Hechtman
11453 Washington Plaza
Reston, VA 22070

Blue Ridge Voyagers
Ralph Smith
8119 Hilcrest
Manassas, VA 22110

Canoe Cruisers Assn.
John Sessler
1623 Seneca Ave.
McLean, VA 22101

Coastal Canoeists, Inc.
Tom Frink
319 65th St.
Newport News, VA 23607

Shenandoah River Canoe Club
Ray Stocklinski
Box 1423
Front Royal, VA 22630

Washington

Paddle Trails Canoe Club
Ev Woodard
Box 86
Ashford, WA 98304

Seattle Canoe Club
Ted Houk
6019 51 N.E.
Seattle, WA 98115

Spokane Canoe Club
Norm Krebbs
N. 10804 Nelson
Spokane, WA 99218

Tri-C Camping Assn.
Craig Jorgenson
17404 8th Ave.
Seattle, WA 98155

Washington Kayak Club
James Aaker
Box 24264
Seattle, WA 98124

West Virginia

West Virginia WW Assn.
Ward Eister
Route 1, Box 87
Ravenswood, WV 26164

Wisconsin

Wolf River Canoe Club
Wolf River Lodge
White Lake, WI 51491

CANOEING ORGANIZATIONS

AMERICAN WHITEWATER AFFILIATION ORGANIZATIONS

Alabama

**North Alabama
River-Runners Assoc.**
Ron Coe
8120 Hickory Hill Lane
Huntsville, AL 35802

Alaska

Knik Kanoers & Kayakers
Ed Swanson
3014 Columbia
Anchorage, AK 99504

Arizona

Dry Wash Canoe & Kayak Club
Ron Ehmsen, ECG 348
Dept. of Chem. & Bio Eng.
Arizona State University
Tempe, AZ 85281

Arkansas

The Bow & Stern
Joel S. Freund
1408 Rockwood Trail
Fayetteville, AR 72701

California

Southern California Canoe Assoc.
Ron Ceurvorst
3906 S. Menlo Ave.
Los Angeles, CA 90037

**LERC Voyageurs Canoe & Kayak
Club**
Leon Hannah
12814 Arminta St.
North Hollywood, CA 91605

Lorien Canoe Club
J. A. Rose
P.O. Box 1238
Vista, CA 92083

Chasm Outing Club
P.O. Box 5622
Orange, CA 92667

Lera Canoe Club
Harold Black
200 Almond Ave.
Los Altos, CA 94022

**Sierra Club
Loma Prieta Paddlers**
Joe Kilner
185 Loucks Ave.
Los Altos, CA 94022

Idlewild Yacht Club
Bob Symon, Rep.
800 Market St.
San Francisco, CA 94102

Outdoor Adventures
Robt. J. Volpert
688 Sutter St.
San Francisco, CA 94102

**Sierra Club River Touring
Bay Chapter**
Norman Glickman
62 Hancock St.
San Francisco, CA 94114

Tomales Bay Kayak Club
Mike Eschenbach
P.O. Box 468
Point Reyes Station, CA 94956

The Great Outdoors Trading Co.
109 Second St.
Sausalito, CA 94965

Mother Lode Whitewater Experience
Pacific High School
Ken Brunges
581 Continental Drive
San Jose, CA 95111

**American Youth Hostels
Santa Clara Valley Club**
R. C. Stevens
5493 Blossom Wood Ave.
San Jose, CA 95124

YMCA of San Joaquin County
640 N. Center St.
Stockton, CA 95202

The Confluence
Box 76
Vallecito, CA 95251

Alpine West
Tom Lovering
1021 R St.
Sacramento, CA 95814

Colorado

Colorado White Water Assoc.
4260 E. Evans Ave.
Denver, CO 80222

Whitewater Expeditions
Tom Anderson
P.O. Box 9541
Colorado Springs, CO 80932

Colorado Rivers
Preston B. Ellsworth
P.O. Box 1386
Durango, CO 81301

Aspen Kayak School
P.O. Box 1520
Aspen, CO 81611

Connecticut

**Appalachian Mt. Club
Connecticut Chapter**
David Sinish, Chmn. WW Comm.
20 Dyer Ave.
Collinsville, CT 06059

Main Stream Canoes
Joe & Jack Casey
Route 44
Barkhamsted, CT 06059

Great World
W. B. Haskell, Jr.
250 Farms Village Rd.
West Simsbury, CT 06092

Good Earth, Inc.
Dan Kogut
539 Broad St.
Meriden, CT 06450

OGRCC Family Paddlers
20 Arcadia Rd.
Old Greenwich, CT 06870

Delaware

Wilmington Trail Club
Fred Pickett, Canoe Chmn.
Inverness Circle, Apt. M-9
Newcastle, DE 19720

Florida

Indian Prairie Farm
Ramone S. Eaton
Route 1, Box 1319
Anthony, FL 32617

APPENDIX I

Georgia

Georgia Canoeing Association
W. D. Crowley, Jr.
Box 7023
Atlanta, GA 30309

Idaho

Idaho Alpine Club
Pat Leonard
460 N. Ridge
Idaho Falls, ID 83401

Illinois

Northern Prairie Outfitters
Randy Hendee
206 N.W. Highway
Fox River Grove, IL 60021

Chicago Whitewater Assoc.
Pamela Allen
5460 S. Ridgewood Court
Chicago, IL 60629

Belleville Whitewater Club
Linda Seaman, Rep.
No. 3 Oakwood
Belleville, IL 62223

Indiana

Hoosier Canoe Club
Rusten Smith
824 Aumen East Drive
Carmel, IN 46032

St. Joe Valley Canoe & Kayak Club YMCA
200 E. Jackson Blvd.
Elkhard, IN 46514

Tukumu Club
952 Riverside Drive
South Bend, IN 46616

Kekionga Voyageurs
E. Heinz Wahl
1818 Kensington Blvd.
Ft. Wayne, IN 46805

Kentucky

The Viking Canoe Club
Ken Wentworth
5117 W. Pages Lane
Pleasure Ridge Park, KY 40258

SAGE—School of Outdoors
209 E. High St.
Lexington, KY 40507

Four Rivers Canoe Club
Brad & Betty Arterburn
523 Alben Barkley Drive
Paducah, KY 42001

Louisiana

Bayou Haystackers
Susie Latham
624 Moss St.
New Orleans, LA 70119

Maine

Saco Bound Canoe & Kayak
Ned McSherry
Fryeburg, ME 04037

Bates Outing Club
Steve Rhodes
Box 580, Bates College
Lewiston, ME 04240

Mattawamkeag Wilderness Park
Robt. Kelly, Park Mgr.
P.O. Box 104
Mattawamkeag, ME 04459

Sunrise County Canoe Exped.
Marty Brown
Cathance Lake
Grove, ME 04638

Maryland

Terrapin Trail Club
Box 18, Student Union Bldg.
U. of Maryland
College Park, MD 20742

Potomac Paddlers
Sea Scout 489
Jim Hill
18505 Kingshill Rd.
Germantown, MD 20767

Baltimore Kayak Club
Al Karasa
1099 Tollgate Rd.
Belair, MD 21014

Monocacy Canoe Club
Box 1083
Frederick, MD 21701

Mason-Dixon Canoe Cruisers
Ron Shanholtz
222 Pheasant Tr.
Hagerstown, MD 21740

Massachusetts

Hampshire College Outdoors Program
Eric M. Evans
Amherst, MA 01002

Experiment with Travel Inc.
Box 2452
281 Franklin St.
Springfield, MA 01101

Michigan

Raw Strength & Courage Kayakers
Jerry Gluck
2185 Mershon Drive
Ann Arbor, MI 48103

Minnesota

BIG Water Associates
Andy Westerhaus
1905 River Hills Drive
Burnsville, MN 55337

Cascaders Canoe & Kayak Club
Stephen Parsons
3128 W. Calhoun Blvd.
Minneapolis, MN 55416

Mississippi

Msubee Canoe Club
P.O. Box 3317
Mississippi State, MS 39762

Missouri

Arnold Whitewater Assoc.
John J. Schuh, Pres.
490 Pine Court
Arnold, MO 63010

Meramee River Canoe Club
Earl G. Biffle
26 Lake Rd.
Fenton, MO 63026

Central Missouri State University Outing Club
Dr. O. Hawksley, Rep.
Warrensburg, MO 64093

Ozark Wilderness Waterways
George Chase
4941 Laramie Lane
Kansas City, MO 64129

CANOEING ORGANIZATIONS

Ozark Cruisers
Robt. A. McKelvey
#1 Blue Acres Tr. Ct.
Columbia, MO 65201

University of Missouri
Chris Wilhelm
Wilderness Adventures Comm.
18 Read Hall
Columbia, MO 65201

Montana

Montana Kayak Club
Doug Abelin
Box 2
Brady, MT 59416

New Hampshire

Ledyard Canoe Club
Steve Ruhle
Robinson Hall
Hanover, NH 03755

Nulhegan Paddle Co.
David Hawkins
Box 381
North Stratford, NH 03590

New Jersey

Murray Hill Canoe Club
Carol Maclennan
Bell Labs, Rm. 1 E-436
Murray Hill, NJ 07974

Mohawk Canoe Club
Dartery Lewis
455 W. State St.
Trenton, NJ 08618

Rutgers University Outdoor Club
Rutgers University
New Brunswick, NJ 08903

New Mexico

Rio Grande River Runners
Buck Cully
2210 Central Ave., SE
Albuquerque, NM 87106

New York

Appalachian Mountain Club
  New York Chapter
Helen Chapman
R.F.D. 1, Box 573
Princeton, NJ 08540

Kayak and Canoe Club of New York
Ed Alexander, Rep.
6 Winslow Ave.
East Brunswick, NJ 08816

Adirondack Mountain Club
  Schenectady Chapter
Betty Lou Bailey
Schuyler 16, Netherlands Village
Schenectady, NY 12308

Wild River Canoe Supplies
Wm. Machonis
Ludingtonville Road
Holmes, NY 12531

Adirondack White Water
E. Hixson, M.D.
103 Riverside Dr.
Saranac Lake, NY 12983

Colgate Outing Club
c/o Recreation Office
Colgate University
Hamilton, NY 13346

Niagara Gorge Kayak Club
Doug Bushnell
41 17th St.
Buffalo, NY 14213

Adirondack Mountain Club
  Genesee Valley Chapter
John A. Robertson, Jr.
581 Lake Rd.
Webster, NY 14580

North Carolina

Carolina Canoe Club
Tom Erikson
Box 9011
Greensboro, NC 27408

Nantahala Outdoor Center
Payson Kennedy
Star Route, Box 68
Bryson City, NC 28713

River Transit Authority
Amber Alley
Chapel Hill, NC 27514
      and
700 W. Market
Greensboro, NC 27402

Venture Program
John B. Griffin
Cone Univ. Ctr. UNCC
Charlotte, NC 28223

Ohio

Columbus Council, AYH
Joe Feiertag
1421 Inglis Ave.
Columbus, OH 43212

Toledo Area Canoe & Kayak
John Dunn
5837 Elden St.
Sylvania, OH 43560

Pack & Paddle
Ronald J. Morgan
4082 Erie St.
Willoughby, OH 44094

Keel-Haulers Canoe Club
John A. Kobak, Rep.
1649 Allen Drive
Westlake, OH 44145

Wilderness Adventures
Charles Comer
256 Forrer Blvd.
Dayton, OH 45419

Oregon

Oregon Rafting Club
Joe Chappell
Route 1, Box 300
Hubbard, OR 97032

Oregon Kayak & Canoe Club
Box 692
Portland, OR 97205

Northwest Outward Bound School
3200 Judkins Rd.
Eugene, OR 97403

Sundance Expeditions, Inc.
665 Hunt Lane
Grants Pass, OR 97526

Wilderness Waterways
Bryce Whitmore
12260 Galice Rd.
Merlin, OR 97532

Pennsylvania

Sylvan Canoe Club
132 Arch St.
Verona, PA 15147

Pittsburgh Council, AYH
6300 Fifth Ave.
Pittsburgh, PA 15213

Canoe, Kayak & Sailing Craft
Douglass Ettinger
701 Wood St.
Wilkinsburg, PA 15221

North Allegheny River Rats
Tim Hawthorne
1130 Sandalwood Lane
Pittsburgh, PA 15237

Mountain Streams & Trails
Outfitters
Ralph W. McCarty
Box 106
Ohiopyle, PA 15470

Slippery Rock State College
L. H. Heddleston, Dir.
Student Activities & Recreation
Slippery Rock, PA 16057

Oil City Canoe
Route 62 N. Rd. 2
Oil City, PA 16301

Allegheny Canoe Club
Walter Pilewski
755 W. Spring St.
Titusville, PA 16354

Penn State Outing Club
John R. Sweet
118 S. Buckhout St.
State College, PA 16801

Wildwater Boating Club
Robert L. Martin
Lock Box 179
Bellefonte, PA 16823

Conewago Canoe Club
George F. Figdore
2267 Willow Rd.
York, PA 17404

Allentown Hiking Club
Bill Bevan
124 S. 16th St.
Allentown, PA 18102

Appalachian Trail Outfitters
29 S. Main St.
Doylestown, PA 18901

Philadelphia Canoe Club
Dr. David Knight
4900 Ridge Ave.
Philadelphia, PA 19128

Buck Ridge Ski Club
Louis F. Metzger
986 Anders Rd.
Lansdale, PA 19446

Rhode Island

Rhode Island Whitewater Club
Rist Bonnefond
10 Pond St.
Wakefield, RI 02879

Summit Shop
Christopher Hardee
185 Wayland Ave.
Providence, RI 02906

South Carolina

Palmetto Kayakers
Russell Jones
210 Irene St.
North Augusta, SC 29381

Carolina Paddlers
Jim Parker
112 Pine St.
Walterboro, SC 29488

Savannah River Paddlers
Explorer Ship 121 & Sea Scout 404
Jim Hill
1211 Woodbine Rd.
Aiken, SC 29801

Tennessee

Tenn-Tucky Lake Canoe-Camping
Club
Calvin Philips, Jr.
Route 1, Box 23-A
Tennessee Ridge, TN 37178

Tennessee Scenic Rivers Assoc.
Box 3104
Nashville, TN 37219

Sewanee Ski & Outing Club
Hugh Caldwell
University of the South
Sewanee, TN 37375

Tennessee Valley Canoe Club
Geo. M. Marterre
Box 11125
Chattanooga, TN 37401

Footsloggers
P.O. Box 3865 CRS
2220 N. Roan St.
Johnson City, TN 37601

Carbide Canoe Club
Herbert Pomerance
104 Ulena Lane
Oak Ridge, TN 37830

E. Tenn. WW Club
Tom Berg
Box 3074
Oak Ridge, TN 37830

Chota Canoe Club
Box 8270 University Sta.
Knoxville, TN 37916

Bluff City Canoe Club
P.O. Box 4523
Memphis, TN 38111

Texas

Down River Club—Dallas
Paul W. McCarty
1412 Oak Lea
Irving, TX 75061

Texas Explorers Club
Bob Burleson, Rep.
Box 844
Temple, TX 76501

Explorer Post 425
A. B. Millett
708 Mercedes
Ft. Worth, TX 76126

Kayaks Limited
Myra J. Obenhaus, Pres.
11527 Lynda Dr.
Houston, TX 77038

Trinity Univ. Canoe Club
Major Sharpe McCollough
Box 180, 715 Stadium Drive
San Antonio, TX 78284

Texas Whitewater Association
Thomas B. Cowden
P.O. Box 5264
Austin, TX 78763

Explorer Post 151
Tom Sloan, Scoutmaster
2008 Bedford
Midland, TX 79701

Vermont

Marlboro College Outdoor Program
Malcom Moore
Marlboro, VT 05344

CANOEING ORGANIZATIONS

Northern Vermont Canoe Cruisers
Edwin Amidon, Jr.
Box 254
Shelburne, VT 05482

Virginia

Canoe Cruisers Assoc.
John Sessler
1623 Seneca Ave.
McLean, VA 22101

Blue Ridge Voyageurs
Ralph T. Smith
8119 Hillerest Drive
Manassas, VA 22110

Coastal Canoeists, Inc.
Hope Gross
R.F.D. 4, Mockingbird Lane
Spotsylvania, VA 22553

Explorer Post 999
R. Steve Thomas, Jr.
3509 N. Colonial Drive
Hopewell, VA 23860

Washington

U of W Canoe Club
Jean M. Dewart, Pres.
IMA Bldg.
University of Washington
Seattle, WA 98105

The Tacoma Mountaineers
Kayak & Canoe Comm.
Bob Hammond
3512 Crystal Spring
Tacoma, WA 98466

Whitewater-Northwest Kayak Club
Box 1081
Spokane, WA 99201

West Virginia

West Virginia Wildwater Assoc.
Idair Smookler
2737 Daniels Ave.
South Charleston, WV 25303

White Water Canoe Club
Mt. Lair Recreation Ctr.
West Virginia University
Morgantown, WV 26506

Wisconsin

Sierra Club
John Muir Chapter
Howard Kietzke
7541 S. 31st St.
Franklin, WI 53132

Wild Rivers Club
Steve Kaufman
4901 36th Ave., Apt. 206
Kenosha, WI 53140

Wisconsin Hoofers Outing Club
Wisconsin Union Directorate
800 Langdon St.
Madison, WI 53706

Wolf River Canoe Club
R. Charles Steed
Wolf River Lodge
White Lake, WI 54491

Wyoming

Croaking Toad Boat Works
Game Hill Ranch
Bondurant, WY 82922

Western Wyoming Kayak Club
Donald L. Hahn
General Delivery
Wilson, WY 83014

Canada

B. C. Kayak & Canoe Club
c/o Dave Steenes
1247A Cambie Rd.
Richmond, B. C., Canada

Canot-Kayak-Camping L'Aval
Jacques Cassista
1600 Rue St.-Denis Ste.-Foy
Quebec, Canada

Edmonton Whitewater Paddlers
P.O. Box 4117 S. Edmonton P.O.
Edmonton, Alberta
Canada T6E-4S8

North West Voyageurs
10922 88th Ave.
Edmonton, Alberta
Canada

Australia

Indooroopilly Canoe Club
Box 36, Indooroopilly
Queensland, Australia

New Zealand

Gisborne Canoe & Tramping Club, Inc.
Tony Geard
Box 289
Gisborne, New Zealand

Palmerston North Canoe Club, Inc.
Box 1126
Palmerston North, New Zealand

Spain

Alberche Kayak Club
Jesus Trujillo Morla
Calle Camarena, 110, 7B
Madrid 24, Spain

Switzerland

Kanu Club Zurich
Otto Kosma
8008 Zurich Dufour Str. 3
Switzerland

Appendix II

United States Canoeing Information Sources

There are canoeable rivers and lakes in every section of the United States. Some are remote from all traces of the tension and pollution and strife we call "civilization." Others are as close to our cities as the lake in the heart of New York City's Central Park.

Virtually every state has a department which provides information for canoeists or will help canoeists locate information. Our National Forests and National Parks offer magnificent opportunities for canoeists. Most of the larger Indian reservations welcome visitors as campers and canoeists, though fishing and hunting rights on Indian lands are another matter.

Before undertaking a canoe trip in an unfamiliar area, make advance inquiries. Are you interested in canoeing for an extended period? If so, are campsites available? May you build camp fires during the summer? What fees are charged? If there is a quota system, how do you get a permit? Are permits mandatory whether or not quotas are imposed on the number of canoeists? Are you required to file a travel plan before embarking? Will the authorities automatically institute a search-and-rescue mission if you do not return within a specified time period? If you need help, will you be charged for the cost of any rescue operations? If the waterway leads through private lands, do you need special permission from the landowners? What about fishing rights? Where, and at what cost, can you obtain a fishing permit? Will you run into any problems putting in or taking out at the specific places you propose?

You might also want to find out whether water levels of rivers fluctuate wildly during storms, or how much they are affected by dams which may release water at regular periods daily. Can you make arrangements for water release from dams when the flow is unusually light? Is the water flow regulated to assure good canoeing only on weekends?

UNITED STATES CANOEING INFORMATION SOURCES

Is the water potable? Is there a pollution problem caused by sewage, industrial waste, or chemical discharge? Is it safe to eat the fish?

Are you obligated to check in with either state or federal authorities before undertaking a canoe journey? Must you also report to ranger stations which you may pass en route to your final take-out point?

Find the answers to all of these questions, whether you plan to canoe in the United States, Canada, or any other country. You may have even more questions when you are outside the United States.

There are hundreds of brochures, river guidebooks, and detailed maps of rivers for the United States and Canada. Some are merely sketches adapted from topographical maps; others are so detailed that they will carry you every yard of a trip 50 miles long. Some are based upon careful observation by people who have actually canoed the routes; others are compiled from various sources by authors who may never even have seen the waterway involved. Some use the international rating systems to classify river flow and grade rapids; others use a system unique to that particular river.

However, all do have one thing in common: They will give you some guidance to the route you wish to canoe, or help you locate a river or lake new to your experience. Don't accept every guidebook as gospel. At best they are someone else's interpretation of a river. Before you run someone else's rapids, rate them yourself.

Following are several lists which should be helpful. The first is a state-by-state summary of some brochures, booklets, map guides, and guidebooks (pages 162–167). The list is by no means all-inclusive. Some of the material is excellent. All is useful. Where known, prices have been included. But in an age when today's inflation makes yesterday's prices outmoded, please recognize that what once was free now may carry a price tag, and what once seemed modestly priced now may cost more than you can afford.

The second list is a directory of the National Parks, giving the acreage and mailing address of each park (page 168). Contact the superintendent of each park at the address given.

Third is a list of National Forests (pages 169–171). For information about each National Forest, write to the regional office of the state in which the forest is located.

For general information about Indian reservations, contact the Bureau of Indian Affairs, Washington, D.C. For specific information about policies on a particular reservation, write directly to the reservation.

APPENDIX II

Information Sources

Alaska

Canoe pamphlets are available from the Department of the Interior, Bureau of Land Management, Alaska State Office, 555 Cordova St., Anchorage, AK 99501; and Refuge Manager, Kenai National Moose Range, U.S. Fish and Wildlife Service, Box 500, Kenai, AK 99661.

Wild Rivers of Alaska (Weber, Alaska Northwest Publishing Co.): Westwater Books, Box 365, Boulder City, NV 89005. $8.95.

Alabama

Specific canoe guides are difficult to track down. For general information: Alabama Department of Conservation, Division of Fish and Game, Montgomery, AL 36130.

Arizona

Canyonlands River Guide (Belknap): Westwater Books, Box 365, Boulder City, NV 89005. $4.95. Includes Green River through Utah and northern Arizona.

Grand Canyon River Guide (Belknap): Westwater Books, Box 365, Boulder City, NV 89005. $4.95. Colorado River from Lees Ferry to Lake Head.

Arkansas

Little published information is available. Contact the Arkansas Fish and Game Commission, State Capitol, Little Rock, AR 72201.

California

Canoeing Waters of California (Ann Dwyer, GBH Press): Westwater Books, Box 365, Boulder City, NV 89005. $3.50.

Sierra Whitewater (Charles Martin, Fiddleneck Press): Westwater Books, Box 365, Boulder City, NV 89005. $5.95.

West Coast River Touring: Touchstone Press, Box 81, Beaverton, OR 97005. $5.95. Includes Northern California waters.

Colorado

Dinosaur River Guide (Evans and Belknap): Westwater Books, Box 365, Boulder City, NV 89005. $4.95. Descriptions of the Green and Yampa Rivers.

Texas Rivers and Rapids (B. Nolen, ed.): Westwater Books, Box 365, Boulder City, NV 89005. $5.95. Includes some waters in Colorado.

Connecticut

Connecticut Canoeing Guide: Department of Environmental Protection, State Office Building, Hartford, CT 06115. Free.

Connecticut River Guide: Connecticut River Watershed Council, 125 Combs Rd., Easthampton, MA 01027. $4.50.

Delaware

A canoeing pamphlet is available from the Bureau of Travel Development, 45 The Green, Dover, DE 19901.

Florida

Canoeing—Your Apachicola, Osceola, and Ocala National Forests: Forest Service, Southern Region, Box 1050, Tallahassee, FL 32302. Free.

Florida Canoe Trail Guide: Florida Department of Natural Resources, Division of Recreation and Parks, Tallahassee, FL 32304. Free.

Guide to the Wilderness Waterway of the Everglades National Park: University of Miami Press, Drawer 9088, Coral Gables, FL 33124. $2.50.

Georgia

Pamphlets are available free from the Costal Plain Area Tourism Council, Box 1223, 327 W.

UNITED STATES CANOEING INFORMATION SOURCES

Savannah Ave., Valdosta, GA 31601, and the Slash Pine Area Planning and Development Council, Box 1276, Waycross, GA 31501.

A Guide to Georgia Flatwater, Sierra Club, in preparation.

Idaho

Lower Salmon River Guide: Department of the Interior, Bureau of Land Management, Area Headquarters, Route 3, Cottonwood, ID 83522.   Free.

Salmon River: U.S. Department of Agriculture, Forest Service, Wild River Ranger, Salmon, ID 83467.   Free.

Illinois

Chicagoland Canoe Trails, Historic Fox Valley Canoe Trails, and *Middle Fork Rendezvous*:   Chicagoland Canoe Base, Inc., 4019 N. Narragansett Ave., Chicago, IL 60634.

Illinois Canoe Trails: Illinois Country Outdoor Guides, 4400 N. Merrimac Ave., Chicago, IL 60630. $1.25 each.

Two volumes. Vol. I: Fox, Mazon, Vermilion, and Little Vermilion Rivers. Vol. II: Dupage, Kankakec, Des Plaines, and Au Sable Rivers.

Illinois Canoeing Guide: Department of Conservation, State Office Building, Springfield, IL 62706.   Free.

Indiana

Indiana Canoe Guide: Department of Natural Resources, 612 State Office Building, Indianapolis, IN 46204. $2.00.

Indiana Canoe Trails: Bureau of Natural Resources, Division of Water Resources, 609 State Office Building, Indianapolis, IN 46204.   30¢.

Includes individual guides for specific rivers.

Iowa

Iowa Canoe Trips: Iowa Conservation Commission, 300 4th Street, Des Moines, IA 50319.   Free.

The Upper Iowa River (Knudson):   Luther College Press, Decorah, IA 52101. $1.25.

Kansas

Kansas Canoe Trail Guide: Don Charvat, Box 798, Belle Plaine, KS 67013. $3.50 plus 50¢ postage.

Kentucky

Kentucky Canoe Trips: Kentucky Department of Public Information, Capitol Annex, Frankfort, KY 40601.   Free.

Sixty-eight canoe trips.

Louisiana

Canoeing in Louisiana: Lafayette Natural History Museum, 639 Girard Park Drive, Lafayette, LA 70501. $3.50.

Maine

Allagash Wilderness Waterway: Department of Parks and Recreation, State House, Augusta, ME 04330.   Free.

AMC New England Canoeing Guide: Appalachian Mountain Club, 5 Joy St., Boston, MA 02108. $6.00.

Canoeing in Maine: Maine Department of Economic Development, State House, Augusta, ME 04330.   Free.

Escape to Maine: Department of Commerce and Industry, State House, Augusta, ME 04330.   Free.

No Horns Blowing (Eben):   Hallowell Printing Co., 145 Water St., Hallowell, ME 04347. $3.95.
Ten major canoe routes.

North Maine Woods: North Maine Woods, Box 1113, Bangor, ME 04401.   Free.

Vacation Planners, Nos. 3 and 4:   Maine Department of Commerce and Industry, State House, Augusta, ME 04330.

Maryland
Blue Ridge Voyages (Corbett and Matacia): Blue Ridge Voyagers, 1515 N. Adams St., Arlington, VA 22201. See also Virginia listing.

Massachusetts
New England Canoeing Guide: Appalachian Mountain Club, 5 Joy St., Boston, MA 02108. $6.00.

Michigan
Guide to Easy Canoeing: State Tourist Council, Commerce Center Building, 300 S. Capitol Ave., Lansing, MI 48926.

Huron River Canoe Map and *Clinton River Canoe Map*: Huron-Clinton Metropolitan Authority, 600 Woodward, Detroit, MI 48226.

Michigan Canoe Trails: Michigan Department of Conservation, Lansing, MI 48926.

Whitewater; Quietwater: Evergreen Paddleways, 1416 21st St., Two Rivers, WI 54241. $7.95.
Guide to streams and rivers in Wisconsin, upper Michigan, and northeastern Minnesota.

Minnesota
Kettle River Canoe Route: U.S. Soil Conservation Service, Box 276, Hinckley, MN 55037.

Whitewater; Quietwater: Evergreen Paddleways, 1416 21st St., Two Rivers, WI 54241. $7.95.
Guide to streams and rivers in Wisconsin, upper Michigan, and northeastern Minnesota.

Wilderness Crow Wing Canoe Trail: Vacation Information Center, Department of Business Development, State Capitol, St. Paul, MN 55101.

Mississippi
No dependable canoe guides. Contact State Fish and Game Commission, Box 451, Jackson, MS 39205.

Missouri
Missouri Ozark Waterways: Department of Conservation, Box 180, Jefferson City, MO 65101. $1.05.

Riverway Map Book of Current River and Jacks Fork: Adams Map Division, Att: L. Mayer, 920 Olive St., St. Louis, MO 63101. $3.12.

Montana
Historic Upper Missouri River: Missouri River Cruises, Box 1212, Fort Benton, MT 59442. $5.00.

Montana's Popular Float Streams: Fish and Game Bulletin 1970, U.S. Forest Service, Missoula, MT 59801. Free.

Nevada
For information write to the Nevada Department of Economic Development, Carson City, NV 89701.

Nebraska
Canoeing in Nebraska: Game and Parks Commission, 2200 N. 33rd St., Lincoln, NB 68503.

New Hampshire
About Stream Canoeing: Department of Resources and Development, State of New Hampshire, Box 856, Concord, NH 03301.

AMC New England Canoeing Guide: Appalachian Mountain Club, 5 Joy St., Boston, MA 02108. $6.00.

Canoeing Fact Sheets: Department of Resources and Economic Development, Box 856, Concord, NH 03301.
Rivers covered include the Magalloway, Androscoggin, Connecticut, Upper Ammonoosuc, Saco, and Contoocook. Specify river.

Canoeing on the Connecticut River: Department of Resources and Economic Development, State of New Hampshire, Box 856, Concord, NH 03301.

Summer Canoeing and Kayaking in the White Mountains of New Hampshire: White Mountains Region Association, Box K, Lancaster, NH 03584.

UNITED STATES CANOEING INFORMATION SOURCES

New Jersey

Canoe Runs in New Jersey: Department of Conservation and Economic Development, State House, Trenton, NJ 08625.   Free.

Delaware River Recreation Maps: Delaware River Commission, 25 Scotch Rd., Trenton, NJ 08628. $1.00.

Exploring the Little Rivers of New Jersey (Cawley):   Rutgers University Press, New Brunswick, NJ. $2.75.

Pine Barrens Canoeing: Eastwood Press, 421 Hudson St., New York, NY 10014.

New Mexico

Rio Grande Gurgle: Route 1, Box 177, Santa Fe, NM 87501. $2.00
A monthly magazine which contains excellent tips on canoeing in New Mexico.

New York

Adirondack Canoe Routes: Conservation Department, Division of Conservation Education, Albany, NY 12226.   Free.

Appalachian Waters, Vol. I: The Delaware and Its Tributaries (Burmeister):   Appalachian Books, Box 249, Oakton, VA 22124. $5.00.

Appalachian Waters, Vol. II: The Hudson River and Its Tributaries (Burmeister):   Appalachian Books, Box 249, Oakton, VA 22124. $6.95.

Barge Canal System and Connecting Waterways: Department of Transportation, Albany, NY 12233.   Free.

Canoe Trips: Department of Environmental Conservation, Albany, NY 12233.   Free.

Delaware River Recreation Maps: Delaware River Commission, 25 Scotch Rd., Trenton, NJ. $1.00.

North Carolina

Carolina Whitewater: A Canoeist's Guide to Western North Carolina (Benner):   Pisgah Providers, Box 101, Morganton, NC 28655. $4.00.

Little Tennessee Valley Canoe Trails: Tennessee Valley Authority, 301 Westcumberland Ave., Knoxville, TN 37902.   Free.

Trails and Streams of North Carolina: Department of Natural and Economic Resources, Travel Development Section, Raleigh, NC 27611.   Free.

North Dakota

Little Missouri Float Trips: U.S. Forest Service, Custer National Forest, Box 2556, Billings, MT 59103.   Free.

Ohio

Boating in Ohio: Publications Center, Ohio Department of Natural Resources, Division of Watercraft, 1350 Holly Ave., Columbus, OH 43212.   Free.

Ohio Canoe Adventures: Publications Center, Ohio Department of Natural Resources, Division of Watercraft, 1350 Holly Ave., Columbus, OH 43212.   Free.

1,000,000 Miles of Canoe and Hiking Routes: Ohio Canoe Adventures, Inc., 5128 Colorado Ave., Box 2092, Sheffield Lake, OH 44054. $1.00.
A catalog of dozens of canoe routes in Ohio and other states.

Oklahoma

Floating the Illinois River: Department of Tourism and Recreation, 504 Will Rogers Building, Oklahoma City, OK 73501.   Free.

Oklahoma Lakes: Department of Tourism and Recreation, 504 Will Rogers Building, Oklahoma City, OK 73501.

Oregon

Oregon River Tours: Binford and Mort, 2536 S.E. 11th, Portland, OR 97202. $5.00.

APPENDIX II

Pennsylvania

Appalachian Waters, Vol. I: The Delaware and Its Tributaries (Burmeister):   Appalachian Books, Box 249, Oakton, VA 22124. $6.95.

Appalachian Waters, Vol. II: The Susquehanna and Its Tributaries (Burmeister):   Appalachian Books, Box 249, Oakton, VA 22124. $6.95.

Canoe Country, Pennsylvania Style: Bureau of State Parks, Room 601, Feller Building, 301 Market St., Harrisburg, PA 17101.   Free.

Canoeing Guide to Western Pennsylvania and Northern West Virginia: Pittsburgh Council, American Youth Hostels, Inc., 6300 Fifth Ave., Pittsburgh, PA 15232. $2.50.

Canoeing in Kinzua (Allegheny National Forest Region) Country (Rusin):   Kinzua Dam Vacation Bureau, 305 Market St., Warren, PA. $1.00.

Pennsylvania Canoe Trails: Commonwealth of Pennsylvania, Department of Commerce, Harrisburg, PA 17120.

Select Rivers of Central Pennsylvania: Penn State Outing Club, Canoe Division, 60 Recreation Building, University Park, PA 16802.   75¢.

See also Delaware, New Jersey, and New York listings for Delaware River sources.

Rhode Island

AMC New England Canoeing Guide: Appalachian Mountain Club, 5 Joy St., Boston, MA 02108. $6.00.

Pawtucket River and Wood River: Department of Natural Resources, Veterans Memorial Building, Providence, RI 02903.   Free.

South Carolina

Canoeing on the Chatooga: P.R.T. Box 1358, Columbia, SC 29202.

The river made famous in the movie *Deliverance*.

South Dakota

For information write to South Dakota Game, Fish, and Parks Department, State Office Building, Pierre, SD 57501.

Tennessee

Mid-South River Guide: Bluff City Canoe Club, Box 5423, Memphis, TN 38104. $1.00.

Principal Floatable Streams in Tennessee: Division of Planning and Development, Department of Conservation, 26111 West End Ave., Nashville, TN 37203.   Free.

Tennessee Buffalo River: Tennessee Fish and Game Commission, 706 Charles St., Nashville, TN 37203.   Free.

Texas

An Analysis of Texas Waterways (Belisle and Josselet):   Parks and Wildlife Department, Reagan Building, Austin, TX 78701.   Free.

Texas Rivers and Rapids: Nolen, Box 673, Humble, TX 77338. $6.55.

Utah

Canyonlands River Guide (Belknap):   Westwater Books, Box 365, Boulder City, NV 89005. $4.95.

Guidebooks to the Colorado River, Part 3 (Ribgy, Hamblin, Matheny, and Welsh; Brigham Young University Press):   Westwater Books, Box 365, Boulder City, NV 89005. $2.00.

Vermont

AMC New England Canoeing Guide: Appalachian Mountain Club, 5 Joy St., Boston, MA 02108. $6.00.

Canoeing the Connecticut River: Department of Forests and Parks, Montpelier, VT 05602.

Canoeing on the Connecticut River: Vermont Board of Recreation and Water Resources Department, Montpelier, VT 05602.   Free.

UNITED STATES CANOEING INFORMATION SOURCES

Virginia

Blue Ridge Voyages—Vol. 1: One and Two Day Cruises in Maryland, Virginia, and West Virginia; Vol. 2: Additional Trips in the Same Area; Vol. 3: One Day Cruises in Virginia and West Virginia: Blue Ridge Voyageurs, Box 32, Oakton, VA 22124. $3.50 each.

Canoeing Whitewater: A Guidebook to the Rivers of Virginia, Eastern West Virginia, and the Great Smoky Mountain Area (Carter): R. Carter, 158 Winchester St., Warrenton, VA 22186. $4.75.

Washington

Water Trails of Washington: Signpost, 16812 36th St. W., Lynnwood, WA 98036. $2.50.

West Virginia

Canoeing Guide to Western Pennsylvania and Northern West Virginia: Pittsburgh Council, American Youth Hostels, Inc., 6300 Fifth Avenue, Pittsburgh, PA 15232. $2.50.

Canoeing Whitewater River Guide (Carter): Appalachian Books, Box 249, Oakton, VA 22124. $5.00.

Whitewater West Virginia (Burrell): Robert Burrell, 1412 Western Ave. Morgantown, WV 26505.

Wisconsin

Canoe Trails of North-Central Wisconsin, Canoe Trails of North-Eastern Wisconsin, and *Canoe Trails of Southern Wisconsin:* Wisconsin Tales and Trails, Inc., Madison, WI 53705. $5.00 each.

Canoeing the Wild Rivers of Northwestern Wisconsin: Wisconsin Indianhead Country, Inc., 1316 Fairfax St., Eau Claire, WI 54701. $3.50.

Whitewater; Quietwater: Evergreen Paddleways, 1416 21st St., Two Rivers, WI 54241. $7.95. Guide to streams and rivers in Wisconsin, upper Michigan, and northeastern Minnesota.

Wisconsin Water Trails: Wisconsin Conservation Department, Box 450, Madison, WI 53701. Free.

Wyoming

Dinosaur River Guide (Evans and Belknap): Westwater Books, Box 365, Boulder City, NV 89005. $4.95. Includes sectional maps for Wyoming.

Family Water Sports in Big Wyoming: Travel Commission, 2320 Capital Ave., Cheyenne, WY 82002. Free.

APPENDIX II

The National Park System

State	Park	Acreage	Mailing Address
Alaska	Mount McKinley	1,939,439	McKinley Park, AK 99755
Arizona	Grand Canyon	673,575	Box 129, Grand Canyon, AZ 86023
	Petrified Forest	94,189	Petrified Forest National Park, AZ 86025
Arkansas	Hot Springs	3,535	Box 1219, Hot Springs, AR 71902
California	Kings Canyon	460,330	Three Rivers, CA 93271
	Lassen Volcanic	106,934	Mineral, CA 96063
	Redwood	57,094	Crescent City, CA 95531
	Sequoia	386,863	Three Rivers, CA 93271
	Yosemite	761,320	Yosemite National Park, CA 95389
Colorado	Mesa Verde	52,074	Mesa Verde National Park, CO 81330
	Rocky Mountain	262,324	Estes Park, CO 80517
Florida	Everglades	1,400,533	Box 279, Homestead, FL 33030
Hawaii	Haleakala	27,283	Box 456, Kahului, Maui, HI 96732
	Hawaii Volcanoes	220,345	Hawaii Volcanoes National Park, HI 96718
Kentucky	Mammoth Cave	15,354	Box 68, Mammoth Cave, KY 42259
Maine	Acadia	41,642	Hulls Cove, ME 04644
Michigan	Isle Royale	539,341	Houghton, MI 49931
Minnesota	Voyageurs	219,000	Regional office: 1709 Jackson St., Omaha, NB 68102
Montana	Glacier	1,013,129	West Glacier, MT 59936
New Mexico	Carlsbad	46,753	Box 1598, Carlsbad, NM 88220
	Guadalupe Mountain	82,279	Box 1598, Carlsbad, NM 88220
Oklahoma	Platt	912	Box 201, Sulphur, OK 73086
Oregon	Crater Lake	160,290	Box 7, Crater Lake, OR 97604
			October-May write to: Box 672, Medford, OR 97501
South Dakota	Wind Cave	28,059	Hot Springs, SD 57747
Tennessee	Great Smoky Mountains	516,626	Gatlinburg, TN 37738
Texas	Big Bend	708,221	Big Bend National Park, TX 79834
Utah	Bryce Canyon	36,010	Bryce Canyon, UT 84717
	Canyonlands	257,640	U.S. Post Office Bldg., Moab, UT 84532
	Zion	147,035	Springdale, UT 84767
Virginia	Shenandoah	193,538	Luray, VA 22835
Washington	Mount Rainier	241,781	Longmire, WA 98397
	North Cascades	505,000	311 State St., Sedro Woolley, WA 98284
	Olympic	896,599	600 E. Park Ave., Port Angeles, WA 98362
Wyoming	Grand Teton	310,350	Moose, WY 83012
	Yellowstone	2,221,773	Yellowstone National Park, WY 83020
Virgin Islands	Virgin Islands	15,150	Box 803, Charlotte Amalie, St. Thomas, VI 00801

UNITED STATES CANOEING INFORMATION SOURCES

National Forest Regional Offices

Eastern Region
633 W. Wisconsin Ave., Milwaukee, WI 53203

Illinois	Shawnee
Indiana	Hoosier
Kentucky	Daniel Boone
Michigan	Hiawatha
	Huron
	Manistee
	Ottawa
Minnesota	Chippewa
	Superior
Missouri	Clark
	Mark Twain
New Hampshire	White Mountain
Ohio	Wayne
Pennsylvania	Allegheny
Vemont	Green Mountain
Virginia	George Washington
	Jefferson
West Virginia	Monongahela
Wisconsin	Chequamegon
	Nicolet

Southern Region
50 Seventh St., N.E., Atlanta, GA 30323

Alabama	William B. Bankhead
	Conecuh
	Talladega
	Tuskegee
Arkansas	Ouachita
	Ozark
	St. Francis
Florida	Apalachicola
	Ocala
	Osceola
Georgia	Chattahoochee
	Oconee
Louisiana	Kisatchie
Mississippi	Bienville
	Delta
	De Sota
	Holly Springs
	Homochitto

	Tombigbee
North Carolina	Croatan
	Nantahala
	Pisgah
	Uwharrie
South Carolina	Francis Marion
	Sumter
Tennessee	Cherokee
Texas	Angelina
	Davy Crockett
	Sabine
	Sam Houston

Northern Region
Federal Building, Missoula, MT 59801

Idaho	Clearwater
	Coeur d'Alene
	Kaniksu
	Nez Perce
	St. Joe
Montana	Beaverhead
	Bitterroot
	Custer
	Deerlodge
	Flathead
	Gallatin
	Helena
	Kottenai
	Lewis and Clark
	Lolo
Washington	Colville
(See also Pacific Northwest Region.)	

Rocky Mountain Region
Denver Federal Building 85, Denver, CO 80225

Colorado	Arapahoe
	Grand Mesa-Uncompahgre
	Gunnison
	Pike
	Rio Grande
	Roosevelt

APPENDIX II

Routt
San Isabel
San Juan
White River

Lincoln
Santa Fe

Nebraska	Nebraska
South Dakota	Black Hills
Wyoming	Bighorn
(See also Intermountain Region.)	Medicine Bow
	Shoshone

California Region
630 Sansome St., San Francisco, CA 94111

California	Angeles
	Cleveland
	Eldorado
	Inyo
	Klamath
	Lassen
	Los Padres
	Mendocino
	Modoc
	Plumas
	San Bernardino
	Sequoia
	Shasta-Trinity
	Sierra
	Six Rivers
	Stanislaus
	Tahoe

Intermountain Region
Federal Office Building, Ogden UT 84401

Idaho	Boise
	Caribou
	Challis
	Payette
	Salmon
	Sawtooth
	Targhee
Nevada	Humboldt
	Toiyabe
Utah	Ashley
	Cache
	Dixie
	Fishlake
	Manti-La Sal
	Uinta
	Wasatch
Wyoming	Bridger
	Teton

Pacific Northwest Region
P.O. Box 3623, Portland, OR 97212

Oregon	Deschutes
	Fremont
	Malheur
	Mount Hood
	Ochoco
	Rogue River
	Siskiyou
	Siuslaw
	Umatilla
	Umpqua
	Wallowa-Whitman
	Willamette
	Winema
Washington	Gifford Pinchot
	Mount Baker
	Okanogan
	Olympic
	Snoqualmie
	Wenatchee

Southwestern Region
Federal Building, Albuquerque, NM 87101

Arizona	Apache
	Coconino
	Coronado
	Kaibab
	Prescott
	Sitgreaves
	Tonto
New Mexico	Carson
	Cibola
	Gila

UNITED STATES CANOEING INFORMATION SOURCES

Alaska Region
Federal Office Building, Juneau, AK 99801

Alaska   Chugach
                 North Tongass
                 South Tongass

Puerto Rico
Box AQ, University Agricultural Experimentation Station, Rio Piedras, PR 00928

Puerto Rico Caribbean

Appendix III

Canadian Guidebooks

Canoeing in Canada can be a very special experience. Great sections of northern Canada are close to the wilderness which existed before Europeans came to the shores of America. Southern Canadian waterways and lakes, though isolated, are much less remote and resemble the backwoods country of the United States.

An indication of how wild the northern bush country can be may be seen in regulations imposed by the provincial government for canoeing in the wilderness regions of Labrador. Nonresidents not only must obtain a forest travel permit but, by law, must be accompanied by a licensed guide during the fire season.

It takes time to plan a wilderness trip where, in the event of an emergency, you may find it impossible to obtain help until those you have notified of your route, travel plans, and arrival date realize that you are not at your destination on the predetermined day and time. As Nick Nickels warns in his excellent book, *Canada Canoe Routes*, "Canoeing and canoe-camping entail long and serious planning months in advance of take-off. Those who disregard the seriousness of the sport by being unprepared invariably end up in making of their dream canoeing vacation a complete shambles. Plan now, paddle later."

Much canoeing in Canada involves only a reasonable amount of skill and sensible wilderness caution. However, there are numerous rivers which are for the expert, experienced wilderness canoeist only. Don't challenge them without as much advance knowledge as you can obtain. When possible, talk to others who have canoed the route before.

CANADIAN GUIDEBOOKS

The following is a list of some guidebooks and information sources in Canada:

Alberta

Canoeing in Alberta: Alberta Outdoor Education Center, Department of Culture, Youth, and Recreation, Box 3018, Hinton, Alta.

Canoeing reference map: Alberta Department of Recreation, Parks, and Wildlife, Edmonton, Alta T5G 0X5.   Free.

Five trip guide pamphlets showing details of routes indicated on the canoeing reference map: Queen's Printer, 11510 Kingsway Ave., Edmonton, Alta T5G 0X5. $1 each.

British Columbia

British Columbia Canoe Routes: Western Heritage Supply Ltd., Box 399, 27247 Fraser Highway, Aldergrove, B. C. V0X 1H0.

Canoe British Columbia: 1606 West Broadway, Vancouver, B. C.

Canoe routes in provincial parks: Parks Branch, Department of Recreation and Conservation, Parliament Building, Victoria, B. C.

Manitoba

Canoe maps of various rivers: Parks Branch, 200 Vaughan St., Winnipeg, Man. R3C 0P8.   Free.

New Brunswick

Guide to Canoe Tripping and *New Brunswick Canoeing*:   Parks Branch, Department of Natural Resources, 575 Centennial Building, Fredericton, N. B.   (Note: While these are free, the New Brunswick Provincial Government frankly discourages nonresidents from canoeing New Brunswick's excellent rivers and lakes. Booklets and river maps are obtainable if the canoeist goes in person to the Parks Branch.)

Newfoundland/Labrador

For information about specific rivers, some of which are exceedingly wild and remote, inquire: Parks Service, Department of Economic Development, 9340, Postal Station B, St. John's, Newfoundland; or Wild Rivers Surveys, National and Historic Parks Branch, Department of Indian and Northern Affairs, Ottawa, Ont. K1A 0H4.

Northwest Territories

This area encompasses about one-third of Canada and ranges from heavily timbered forest to the treeless tundra. It is a combination of polar islands, arctic, and subarctic regions.

Major canoe route guides: Division of Tourism, Government of the Northwest Territories, Yellowknife, N.W.T.   Free. (Note: Specify the river you are interested in.)

Explorer's Guide: Travel Arctic, Yellowknife, N.W.T.   Free. (Note: This is "must" reading for anyone planning a canoe trip in the rugged, remote wilderness regions.)

For further information, inquire: Canadian Government Travel Bureau, Ottawa, Ont.

Nova Scotia

Nova Scotia is an area for short wilderness and nonwilderness canoe trips.

Canoe Routes: Nova Scota (Sport Nova Scotia):   The Trail Shop, 6260 Quinpool Rd., Halifax, N.S.

Ontario

Algonquin Park canoe map: Algonquin Park, Box 219, Whitney, Ont. K0J 2M0.

Canoeing in Ontario (Scott and Kerr):   dePencier Publications, Toronto, Ont.

Northern Ontario Canoe Routes: Ministry of Natural Resources, Queen's Park, Toronto, Ont. M7A 1W3.   50¢.

Ontario Voyageurs River Guide: Ontario Voyageurs Kayak Club, 166 St. Germain Ave., Toronto, Ont. $5. (Note: Generally whitewater routes.)

Quebec

Guides des Rivières du Québec (in French):   Canoe Canada, Lakefield, Ont. K0L 2H0. $4.50 (Note: Even for those who do not read French this can be a helpful guide to the rivers of Quebec.)

APPENDIX III

Saskatchewan
Canoe route maps: Lands and Surveys Branch, Department of Natural Resources, Administration Building, 2340 Albert St., Regina, Sask. S4P 3N2.
Canoeing in Saskatchewan: Department of Tourism and Renewable Resources, Box 7105, Regina, Sask. S4P 3N2.
Yukon Territory
Several guide pamphlets are available through Government of the Yukon Territory, Department of Tourism and Information, Whitehorse, Yukon Territory. Other Yukon rivers are listed in the Wild Rivers *Guide to the Yukon* available from Wild Rivers Surveys, National and Historic Parks branch, Department of Indian and Northern Affairs, Ottawa, Ontario K1A 0H4. $1.50.

ADDITIONAL CANADIAN GUIDEBOOKS
Sixty-five rivers throughout Canada were surveyed by crews from the Department of Indian and Northern Affairs for their potential as canoe routes. The results have been published in a series of booklets on Wild Rivers. Included are routes in Alberta, central British Columbia, Labrador/Newfoundland, southwestern Quebec and eastern Ontario, the James Bay/Hudson Bay region, the Barrenlands, the Yukon Territory, the Northwest Mountains, and Saskatchewan. Booklets are available in either English or French. Order by mail from Wild Rivers Surveys, National and Historic Parks Branch, Department of Indian and Northern Affairs, Ottawa, Ontario K1A 0H4. $1.50 each.
The following is a list of other general Canadian canoe route sources:

Canada Canoe Routes (by Nick Nickels):   Canoe Canada, Lakefield, Ontario K0L 2H0.
Canoe Trips in Canada: Canadian Government Travel Bureau, Ottawa, Ontario K1A 0H4.
Fur Trade Canoe Routes of Canada, Then and Now (by Eric Morse):   Queen's Printer, 11510 Kingsway Ave., Edmonton, Alberta T5G 0X5.
Nick Nickels' Canoe Canada (by Nick Nickels; published by Van Nostrand Reinhold, Toronto):   Canoe Canada, Lakefield, Ontario K04 2H0.   (Note: Covers waterways in every province.)

Appendix IV

Map Sources

The U.S. Geological Survey is the outstanding source in the United States for topographical maps. There is an index for each state which lists the complete series of maps available for that state. The index also contains a list of state libraries which carry USGS maps. Before ordering maps, check the state index for the exact name of the map or maps you need.

Maps for areas west of the Mississippi should be ordered from

Branch Distribution
U.S. Geological Survey
Federal Center
Denver, CO 80225

Maps for areas east of the Mississippi should be ordered from

Branch Distribution
U.S. Geological Survey
1200 S. Eads St.
Arlington, VA 22202

APPENDIX IV

STATE TOPOGRAPHICAL MAP SOURCES

Every state except Rhode Island has an office through which topographical maps may be ordered. Occasionally these may cost more than the same map ordered directly from the USGS, but service by mail generally is quicker from state offices. For information, contact the following agencies:

Geological Survey of Alabama
P.O. Box Drawer O
University of Alabama
University, AL 35486

Department of Natural Resources
3001 Porcupine Drive
Anchorage, AK 99504

Arizona Bureau of Mines
University of Arizona
Tucson, AZ 85721

Arkansas Geological Commission
State Capitol Building
Little Rock, AR 72201

Division of Mines and Geology
Department of Conservation
P.O. Box 2980
Sacramento, CA 95814

Colorado Geological Survey
254 Columbine Building
1845 Sherman St.
Denver, CO 80203

Connecticut Geological and
    Natural History Survey
Box 128, Wesleyan Station
Middletown, CT 06457

Delaware Geological Survey
University of Delaware
16 Robinson Hall
Newark, NJ 19711

Bureau of Geology
Department of Natural Resources
P.O. Box 631
Tallahassee, FL 32302

Department of Mines, Mining,
    and Geology
19 Hunter St. S.W.
Atlanta, GA 30334

Division of Water and Land
    Development
Department of Land and
    Natural Resources
P.O. Box 373
Honolulu, HI 96809

Idaho Bureau of Mines and Geology
Moscow, ID 83843

Illinois Geological Survey
121 Natural Resources Building
Urbana, IL 61801

Department of Natural Resources
Geological Survey
611 North Walnut Grove
Bloomington, IN 47401

Iowa Geological Survey
16 W. Jefferson St.
Iowa City, IA 52240

State Geological Survey of Kansas
University of Kansas
Lawrence, KS 66044

Kentucky Geological Survey
University of Kentucky
307 Mineral Industries Building
120 Graham Ave.
Lexington, KY 40506

Louisiana Geological Survey
Box G, University Station
Baton Rouge, LA 70803

Maine Geological Survey
State Office Building
Room 211
Augusta, ME 04330

Maryland Geological Survey
214 Latrobe Hall
Johns Hopkins University
Baltimore, MD 21218

Massachusetts Department of
    Public Works
Research and Material Division
99 Worcester St.
Wellesley, MA 02181

Michigan Department of Natural
    Resources
Geological Survey Division
Stevens T. Mason Building
Lansing, MI 48926

Minnesota Geological Survey
University of Minnesota
1633 Eustis St.
Saint Paul, MN 55108

Mississippi Geological Survey
Drawer 4915
Jackson, MS 39216

Division of Geological Survey and
    Water Resources
P.O. Box 250
Rolla, MO 65401

Montana Bureau of Mines and
    Geology
Montana College of Mineral Science
    and Technology
Butte, MT 59701

Nebraska Conservation and
    Survey Division
University of Nebraska
113 Nebraska Hall
Lincoln, NB 68508

Nevada Bureau of Mines
University of Nevada
Reno, NV 89507

Geologic Branch, Department of
    Geology
James Hall, University of
    New Hampshire
Durham, NH 03824

New Jersey Bureau of Geology
    and Topography
John Fitch Plaza
P.O. Box 1889
Trenton, NJ 08625

New Mexico State Bureau of Mines
    and Mineral Resources
Campus Station
Socorro, NM 87801

New York Geological Survey
New York State Education
    Building
Room 973
Albany, NY 12224

North Carolina Division of
    Mineral Resources
P.O. Box 27687
Raleigh, NC 27611

North Dakota Geological Survey
University Station
Grand Forks, ND 58202

Ohio Division of Geological
    Survey
1207 Grandview Avenue
Columbus, OH 43212

MAP SOURCES

Oklahoma Geological Survey
University of Oklahoma
Norman, OK 73069

Oregon State Department of
  Geology and Mineral Industries
1069 State Office Building
1400 S.W. Fifth Ave.
Portland, OR 97201

Pennsylvania Bureau of
  Topographic and Geological
  Survey
Harrisburg, PA 17120

South Carolina Division of Geology
P.O. Box 927
Columbia, SC 29202

South Dakota State Geological
  Survey
Science Center
University of South Dakota
Vermillion, SD 57059

Tennessee Department of Conservation
Division of Geology
G-5 State Office Building
Nashville, TN 37219

Texas Bureau of Economic Geology
University of Texas at Austin
Austin, TX 78712

Utah Geological and
  Mineralogical Survey
103 Utah Geology Survey Building
University of Utah
Salt Lake City, UT 84112

Vermont Geological Survey
University of Vermont
Burlington, VT 05401

Virginia Division of Mineral
  Resources
P.O. Box 3667
Charlottesville, VA 22903

Washington Division of Mines
  and Geology
P.O. Box 168
Olympia, WA 98501

West Virginia Geological and
  Economic Survey
P.O. Box 879
Morgantown, WV 26505

Wisconsin Geological and Natural
  History Survey
University of Wisconsin
1815 University Ave.
Madison, WI 53706

Geological Survey of Wyoming
P.O. Box 3008
University Station
University of Wyoming
Laramie, WY 82070

APPENDIX IV

USCGS Topographical Maps

The U.S. Coast and Geodetic Survey also has topographical maps, as well as the aerial photographs from which maps are made. You may order either the maps or the aerial photographs by mail. A state index is free.

Topographical maps may be obtained from

U.S. Coast and Geodetic Survey
Att: Map Information Service, C-513
Rockville, MD 20852

Aerial photographs may be obtained from

U.S. Coast and Geodetic Survey
Att: Photogrammetry Division, C-141
Rockville, MD 20852

Army Corps of Engineers Waterway Maps

Maps of waterways can be purchased from the U.S. Army Corps of Engineers through their field offices. The locations of several of the offices are as follows

U.S. Army Corps of Engineers
P.O. Box 17277
Foy Station
Los Angeles, CA 90017

U.S. Army Corps of Engineers
219 Dearborn St.
Chicago, IL 60604

U.S. Army Corps of Engineers
1217 Post Office and Custom House
180 E. Kellog Blvd.
Saint Paul, MN 55101

U.S. Army Corps of Engineers
111 E. 16th St.
New York, NY 10003

Canadian Topographical Maps

Canadian topographical maps may be ordered from

Map Distribution Office
Department of Energy, Mines, and Resources
615 Booth St.
Ottawa, Ontario
Canada K1A 0E9

MAP SOURCES

Provincial and Local Maps

Provincial and local maps and surveys also may be ordered from the provincial capitals. Some canoe route information can be obtained from the map offices. The offices usually are quite cooperative if you make telephone inquiries. However, be prepared for language difficulties if you contact provincial offices in Quebec, where government employees will often speak only French. Specific inquiries should be sent to the following addresses:

Director, Technical Division
Department of Lands and Forests
Natural Resources Building
Edmonton, Alberta

Director of Surveys and Mappings
Department of Lands, Forests, and
 Water Resources
Parliament Building
Victoria, British Columbia

Director of Surveys
Department of Mines and
 Natural Resources
Winnipeg, Manitoba

Department of Lands and Mines
Fredericton, New Brunswick

Director of Crown Lands
 and Administration
Department of Mines, Agriculture,
 and Resources
Confederation Building
St. John's, Newfoundland

Department of Mines
Halifax, Nova Scotia

Surveys and Engineering Division
Department of Lands and Forests
Toronto, Ontario

Department of the Environment
 and Tourism
Map Library
P.O. Box 2000
Charlottetown, Prince Edward Island

Surveys Branch
Department of Lands and Forests
Quebec City, Quebec

Controller of Surveys
Lands and Surveys Branch
Department of Natural Resources
1739 Cornwall Building
Regina, Saskatchewan

Appendix V

Equipment Sources

Despite the tremendous national interest in self-propelled outdoor activities, there are a limited number of good retail stores throughout the country which carry sophisticated camping, hiking, and canoeing equipment. If you do not have complete faith in a store, you probably will be better off buying merchandise from firms which handle catalog sales.

Start your catalog shopping with the most informative catalog, which is published by Eastern Mountain Supply, Inc., and can be ordered from EMS, 1041 Commonwealth Ave., Boston, Massachusetts 02215. It costs $1. This catalog has lengthy comparative charts and superb information about all types of outdoor gear. It handles some kayaks, but no canoes.

Following is a list of other catalogs, with comments regarding the type and quality of equipment offered by each.

REI
Recreational Co-op Equipment, Inc.
Box 22090
Seattle, WA 98122

This co-op was established in 1938. For $2 you get the catalog and become a member. Equipment is excellent.

Phoenix Products
Tyner, KY 40486

Kayaks, paddles, life vests, and other equipment for the canoeist and kayaker.

Rocky Mountain Kayak Supply
Box 8150
Aspen, CO 81611

All types of whitewater equipment, from river shoes to splash covers for your canoe.

EQUIPMENT SOURCES

Marmot Mountain Works
Box 2433
Grand Junction, CO 81501

Fine equipment. Specializes in Gore-Tex fabrics. Catalog price is $1.

Holubar (Manufacturer)
Box 7
Boulder, CO 80302

Illustrates Holubar products, but also includes specialized camping gear and shoes. Information on down and methods of making equipment.

Sierra Designs (Manufacturer)
4th and Addison Streets
Berkeley, CA 94710

Includes all sleeping bags, tents, and packs made by Sierra, along with limited climbing gear. Deserves a special commendation for beauty of design and photographs.

North Face (Manufacturer)
Box 2399
Berkeley, CA 94702

Primarily devoted to its own down products, but also offers specialized mountaineering and camping supplies, sleeping bags and clothing, very fine tents, and several packs of its own design.

Kelty (Manufacturer)
1801 Victory Blvd.
Box 3645
Glendale, CA 91201

The grandfather of great packs and frames; also includes outstanding lines of tents, down bags and garments, and some camp gear.

Gerry (Manufacturer)
Outdoor Sports Industries, Inc.
5450 North Ave. Valley Hwy.
Denver, CO 80216

Gerry describes its own excellent line of mountaineer tents, clothing, and a compartmented pack with frame; could give more technical information.

The Smilie Company
575 Howard St.
San Francisco, CA 94105

Tends to lack specifics even about its own line of excellent sleeping bags; generally fine outdoor merchandise.

Ski Hut
1615 University Ave.
Berkeley, CA 94703

Similar to EMS; variety not as great; catalog lacks comparative performance charts.

Moor & Mountain
Main Street
Concord, MA 01742

Limited but good selection of sleeping bags and tents; better on camping gear. Their specialty is canoes and kayaks.

Great World
250 Farms Village Rd.
Box 250
West Simsbury, CT 06092

Similar to Moor & Mountain; lots of friendly advice. Conservation-oriented. Excellent camping items, canoes, and kayaks. No comparative or performance data.

Eddie Bauer (Manufacturer)
Expedition Outfitter
1737 Airport Way S.
Box 3700
Seattle, WA 98124

Lots of clothing. Very stylish. Many down items, limited outdoor gear. Excellent guarantee. Copy promises more than it reveals about Bauer products.

Alaska Sleeping Bag Co.
(Manufacturer)
701 N.W. Dawson Way
Beaverton, OR 97005

Like Eddie Bauer, Alaska hits hard at its own line of clothing and down products; light on basic facts. Organization of catalog is haphazard.

The Camp & Hike Shop
4674 Knight Arnold
Memphis, TN 38118

A potpourri of outdoor equipment. Ranges from stock picnic items to a limited number of better mountaineering supplies. Virtually no usable statistics.

Stow-a-Way Sports Industries
166 Cushing Hwy.
Cohasset, MA 02025

Outstanding variety of freeze-dried and lightweight foods. Provides no nutritional information except caloric content of dishes. Some clothing, gear, and tents, but not enough information here, either.

Gokey
21 W. Fifth St.
Saint Paul, MN 55102

Intermixes gifts and novelties with fishing and hunting gear. Carries some quality down items.

P & S Sales
P.O. Box 45095
Tulsa, OK 74145

Scattering of second-level, inexpensive clothing, camp items, and outdoor gear.

Kreeger & Son, Ltd.
30 W. 46th St.
New York, NY 10036

Manufactures some down items. Catalog lists a few items and an invitation to visit an excellent retail store.

The Pinnacle (Manufacturer)
Box 4214
Mountain View, CA 94040

First-rate down sleeping bags.

Camp 7 (Manufacturer)
3235 Prarie Ave.
Boulder, CO 80301

Another manufacturer of superior down bags.

Bugaboo Mountaineering
(Manufacturer)
689 Lighthouse Ave.
Monterey, CA 93940

Again, a maker of top-quality down bags. Also carries down jackets.

Bishop's Ultimate
(Manufacturer)
6804 Millwood Rd.
Bethesda, MD 20034

A few superior tent models for the serious mountaineer or for expeditions.

Forest Mountaineering
(Manufacturer)
Box 7083
Denver, CO 80207

Highly specialized line of excellent technical climbing accessories and packs.

EQUIPMENT SOURCES

Adventure 16 (Manufacturer)
656 Front St.
El Cajon, CA 92020

Catalog features the A16 "hip hugger" adjustable pack, half/dome tent with fly, down sleeping bags.

Chuck Wagon Foods (Manufacturer)
Micro Drive
Woburn, MA 01801

A well-known processor of lightweight freeze-dried, dehydrated, and concentrated foods and complete meals packaged for campers. No nutritional data of any kind is included, not even calories per package.

Canoe Imports
74 S. Willard St.
Burlington, VT 05401

Complete line of Grumman, Old Town, Cadorette, and Langford (canvas) canoes, including covered whitewater canoes, some accessories, and a superb stock of paddles.

Walter Dyer (Manufacturer)
244 Broad St.
Lynn, MA 01901

Quite a selection of leather goods, from moccasins to fringe jackets. *The Whole Earth Catalog*'s description: "Walter Dyer is a human rooster who makes tough moccasins."

L.L. Bean, Inc.
Freeport, ME 04032

Unique among equipment catalogs, this one has a solid, Down East, no-nonsense format; no inflated sales talk here. Bean's has a reputation for Yankee honesty that goes back generations. Emphasizes clothing and its own unique boot, along with some hunting and fishing items; carries several fine lightweight items. Little technical data.

Seda Products
916½ Industrial Blvd.
Chula Vista, CA 92011

In addition to its own canoes, Seda Products produces an outstanding line of stylish and serviceable canoe bags and accessories.

Northwest River Supplies
Box 9243
Moscow, ID 83843

Sells an outstanding selection of canoes, kayaks, and accessories for canoeists.

The Coleman Co., Inc.
250 N. St. Francis
Wichita, KS 67201

Although not especially noted in the past for quality in outdoor gear, Coleman is now handling much more sophisticated equipment, some marketed under the "Peak 1" label.

Wildwater Design Kits, Ltd.
230 Penllyn Pike
Penllyn, PA 19422

Make-it-yourselfers will appreciate a catalog which offers a good variety of accessories, from wet suits to spray skirts.

This list includes by no means all of the manufacturers and retail stores which sell by mail order. There is, for example, the biggest of them all, Sears Roebuck. The purpose behind this appendix is to give you some insight into the use of catalogs for shopping. If you are an outdoor novice, whether you plan to shop by mail or buy from a sporting goods store, I would recommend that you get hold of two or three of the better catalogs listed and compare what these companies sell with the information (or misinformation) you're apt to get when shopping at most commercial stores.

Appendix VI

Canoe Liveries

Most of the following list of canoe liveries in the United States and Canada was compiled by Grumman Boats, Marathon, New York 13803. Neither Grumman nor the author makes any claim that the list is complete, or that it constitutes an endorsement or recommendation of the individual liveries. The list does demonstrate how readily available canoe rentals are throughout the nation.

To avoid disappointment, contact the liveries by mail or telephone well in advance of your planned trip.

Liveries range the gamut from small outfitters with a dozen canoes to large, smoothly run corporations providing every possible service to canoeists along a major river. Typical of the latter is Kittatinny Canoe. The headquarters is at Dingman's Ferry, Pennsylvania 18328, on the shores of the Delaware River. The livery maintains bases at Skinner Falls, 75 miles north; Barryville, 60 miles north; and Matamoras, 35 miles north. It provides take-out service at the Delaware Water Gap, 25 miles south. This livery, with more than 600 canoes and a fleet of 25 trucks, services a 125-mile stretch of the Delaware from its four base launch sites. Three of the sites include camping facilities. Shortwave radio, as well as the usual phone service, links the entire complex together.

Some liveries provide transportation for canoes and canoeists. Some provide transportation only for canoes, or rent canoe racks you can install quickly on the roof of a car. Before you plan on using a livery, make certain you know precisely what it provides, as well as both rental and haulage costs, in advance. We once discovered that the Adirondack livery we had chosen provided the canoes, but not the return transportation from a 90-mile trip. We were lucky: We found a young farmer with a truck.

Fortunately, canoe liveries as a group probably are more interested in the health and welfare of

CANOE LIVERIES

their clients than most commercial services. They usually want to help, and will go out of their way to offer assistance with your planning. Unfortunately, few liveries provide training for either flatwater or whitewater paddling. Some of the larger liveries are so busy running canoes and canoe parties up and down rivers that the employees, though skilled at tossing canoes onto six-tier canoe trailers, don't know a cross draw from a high brace.

When you rent, be careful to select a canoe that can accommodate you and your gear. Make sure that it is equipped with first-quality life jackets and paddles. Do not accept torn or water-logged life jackets. Your life may depend upon the PFD you pick up with your canoe.

Liveries fall into two general classifications: those which provide wilderness service and those chiefly concerned with short-trip paddlers. The former rent a wide variety of outdoor equipment in addition to canoes and can outfit you completely, from maps to menus, for a major wilderness voyage. Should you use these ancillary services, you ought to know well in advance if the equipment meets your needs. As a rule, wilderness liveries charge separately for each item you rent.

Many liveries in remote areas will provide guides, though if you are competent in the use of a map and compass you will not need a guide.

Canoe rental rates in any given region are roughly competitive. However, they vary greatly from region to region. Unless the livery people are personally acquainted with you, they usually ask for payment in advance, in cash, along with a reasonable damage deposit—also in cash—for each canoe. Avoid the embarrassment of showing up with a checkbook or credit card unless you have made advance arrangements. A growing practice among liveries is to offer damage insurance for each canoe, usually at a cost of $1 per day. The insurance may be unnecessary for lake travel, but you may consider it if there is going to be any whitewater that could damage the canoe.

Do not hesitate to ask for special rates if you are organizing a large party, especially early or late in the canoe season. You may not get them, but it is worth the asking.

On the popular canoe rivers of the nation, the liveries set safety precautions for canoe rentals. On the Delaware River, for example, the various liveries do not rent when the water temperature falls below 50 degrees, or when the river is running Heavy after storms.

Alabama

F. D. Sandlin and Associates
4711 Whitehall Drive N. W.
Huntsville, AL 35806

Canoe Trails
5204 S. Maudelayne Drive
Mobile, AL 36609

Piddle Paddle Canoe Rental
801 Deerfield Drive
Mobile, AL 36608

Alaska

Sourdough Outfitters
Bettles, AK 99726

Wilderness Canoe Trails
6-9/10 Mile Chena Hot Springs Rd.
Fairbanks, AK 99701

Arizona

Colorado River Canoe Trips
W. C. "Bob" Trowbridge
Box 1882
Lake Havasu City, AZ 86403

Lynx Lake Store & Marina
Walker Road
Prescott, AZ 86301

Arkansas

Big Ben's Canoe Rental
Hwy. 93 North
(Located at Dalton on Eleven
    Point River)
Dalton, AR 72423

Caddo River Sporting Goods
Hwy. 708 East
Glenwood, AR 71943

Rolling S Ranch
Wilburn Route
Heber Springs, AR 72543

Lake Lene Resort
(Rev. Odell Lene)
Jasper, AR 72641

M & M Canoe Rentals
(Mike Jenks)
Jasper, AR 72641

Many Islands Camp on Spring River
Route 2
Mammoth Spring, AR 72554

Morning Star Canoe Rental
Morning Star, AR 72639

Hedges Canoes on the Buffalo River
Ponca, AR 72670

Lost Valley Lodge
Ponca, AR 72670

APPENDIX VI

Tom Harding
Pruitt, AR 72671

Bill Houston Float Service
Pruitt, AR 72671

Coursey's Float Service
St. Joe, AR 72675

Glen Henderson
c/o Maplewood Motel
St. Joe, AR 72675

Buffalo River Fishing Resort
(Joe Barnes)
Route A
Yellville, AR 72687

Buffalo River Canoe Livery
(Louis Pedersen)
Route A
Yellville, AR 72687

Dodd's Float Service
Route A
Yellville, AR 72687

Robinson's Canoe Rental
(Buffalo River Drive-In)
Route A
Yellville, AR 72687

U. D. Lynch Canoe Rental
(Buffalo River Drive-In)
Route A
Yellville, AR 72687

California

California Canoe Co.
960 E. Gaillard
Azusa, CA 91702

Pack-n-Paddle
476 S. Citrus
Azusa, CA 91702

Canoe Trips West
2170 Redwood Hwy.
Greenbrae, CA 94904

Russian River Canoe Trips
W. C. "Bob" Trowbridge
Box 942
Healdsburg, CA 95448

Sacramento River Canoe Trips
W. C. "Bob" Trowbridge
Box 942
Healdsburg, CA 95448

Gerald F. Smith
Route 1, Box 4
Jamul, CA 92035

Lake Tahoe Canoes
W. C. "Bob" Trowbridge
Box 1226
Kings Beach, CA 95719

A-Rental World
7180 University Ave.
La Mesa, CA 92041

Harold E. Henry
7718 Marie Ave.
La Mesa, CA 92041

Dana's Sporting Goods
547 N. 99-E
Los Molinos, CA 96055

Lane's Marine Sales, Inc.
11120 Atlantic Ave.
Lynwood, CA 90262

American River and Feather River
    Canoe Trips
W. C. "Bob" Trowbridge and
    Al Riolo
P. O. Box 5488
Sacramento, CA 95814

Gray's Rent-A-Canoe
437 E. Fremont St., #3
514 E. Fremont St.
Stockton, CA 95202

Colorado

Colorado Whitewater Specialists
P. O. Box 1416
112 W. Laurel
Fort Collins, CO 80521

Recreation Rentals
Box 414 (west side of Route 34, 4 miles
    south of Grand Lake)
Grand Lake, CO 80447

Connecticut

Mead Rent-A-Canoe
George Bragdon
10 Hiram Lane
Bloomfield, CT 06002

Needle Loft
180 W. Main St. (U.S. Route 2 on
    Hammonhassett River)
Clinton, CT 06417

River Run Canoe Rental
Main Street (Route 126)
Falls Village, CT 06031

Mead Rent-A-Canoe
Dave Meikle
35 Brookside Lane
Mansfield, CT 06250

Boyce Town & Country Marine
126 Main St. Route 25
Monroe, CT 06468

Taylor Rental Center
111 Pane Rd.
Newington, CT 06111

The Inn on Lake Waramaug
Lake Shore Road
New Preston, CT 06777

Gessay's Sport Center
Corner E. Main & Prospect St.
Rockville, CT 06066

Olsen Marine Co., Inc.
76 Ferry Blvd.
Stratford, CT 06497

Mainstream Canoes
Att: John Casey
R.F.D. 2
Winsted, CT 06098

Delaware

Trap Pond State Park
Route 2, Box 331
Laurel, DE 19956

The Suzuki Place
Route 273
New Castle, DE 19720

Wick's Ski Shops, Inc.
1201 Philadelphia Pike
Wilmington, DE 19809

Wilderness Canoe Trips, Inc.
1002 Parkside Drive, Oak Lane
    Manor
Wilmington, DE 19803

Washington, D. C.

Fletcher's Boat House
Reservoir & Canal Rds., N. W.
Washington, DC 20007

CANOE LIVERIES

Florida

Canoe Outpost
Tex Stout, Outfitter
Route 2, Box 301
Arcadia, FL 33821

Alexander Springs
Astor, FL 32002

Vacation Boat Rentals, Inc.
5131 14th St. West
Bradenton, FL 33507

Canoe Outpost
Tex Stout, Outfitter
Box 473
Branford, FL 32008

Manatee Springs State Park
Chiefland, FL 32626

Hopkins-Carter Hardware Co.
3701 N. W. 21st St.
Miami, FL 33142

Tropical Wilderness Outfitters
10635 S. W. 185th Terrace
Miami, FL 33157

Bob's Canoe Rental & Sales, Inc.
Route 8, Box 34
Milton, FL 32570

John's Canoe Rentals
John Peileke
829 N. E. 12th Terrace
Ocala, FL 32789

Circle Canoe Trail
Blue Springs State Park
(On U.S. 17-92, 30 miles north of
    Orlando)
Orange City, FL 32763

Barrett's Marine
4503 N. Orange Blossom Trail
Orlando, FL 32804

Fisheating Creek Campground and
    Wilderness Area
P. O. Box 100
Palmdale, FL 33944

Col. Jack & Betty Carpenter's
    Campers' World
Hwy. 44 Withlacoochee River
(Rutland), Panasoffkee, FL 33538

Bill Jackson, Inc.
1100 Fourth St. South
St. Petersburg, FL 33701

Juniper Springs Recreational
    Services
Route 1, Box 650
Silver Spring, FL 32688

Otter Springs Campground
Trenton, FL 32693

Georgia

Ponderosa Parks—Atlanta North
U.S. Hwy. 41, W. Kemp Road
Acworth, GA 30101

Suwannee Canal Recreation Area,
    Inc.
Route 2, H. Johnson, Concessionaire
Okefenokee National Wildlife Refuge
Folkston, GA 31537

Riverboat—Stone Mountain Park
P. O. Box 778
Stone Mountain, GA 30083

Idaho

Macks Inn Resort
Island Park, ID 83429

Ponds Lodge
Island Park, ID 83429

Illinois

T & V Marine
9436 W. 47th St.
Brookfield, IL 60513

Chockstone Mountaineering Ltd.
216 S. University Ave.
Carbondale, IL 62901

Pirate's Cove Marina
Hwy. 13 East
Carbondale, IL 62901

Robert L. Hardin
1804 Bellamy Drive
Champaign, IL 61820

The Chicagoland Canoe Base, Inc.
4019 N. Narragansett Ave.
Chicago, IL 60634

H₂O Sports, Inc.
716 W. Lincoln
DeKalb, IL 60115

Janet's Sea Gull Outfitters, Inc.
5121 Lee Ave.
Downers Grove, IL 60515

Campertown, Inc.
1337 Dundee Ave.
Elgin, IL 60120

Rent-Rite Equipment Co.
1820 Ridge Ave.
Evanston, IL 60201

Shoppers Center
301 E. Harris Ave.
Greenville, IL 62246

Wooster Lake Park
999 E. Route 134
Ingleside, IL 60041

Seyl Outboard Motors & Boats, Inc.
Routes 59 & 132
Ingleside, IL 60041

A-1 Rental
1010 Kennedy Drive
Kankakee, IL 60901

Reed's Rent All
907 N. Indiana Ave.
Kankakee, IL 60901

Congdon Canoe Co.
828 N. Western Ave.
Lake Forest, IL 60045

Pack & Paddle, Inc.
701 E. Park Ave. (Route 176)
Libertyville, IL 60048

Argyle Lake Concessions
Att: Bronald L. Mead
908 Jamie Lane
Macomb, IL 61455

Two Rivers Sports Center
U.S. Routes 36 & 54
Pittsfield, IL 62363

Zimmerman Canoes
503 Lockport
Plainfield, IL 60544

Merkel's Marine
1720 Broadway
Quincy, IL 62301

H₂O Sports, Inc.
2521 S. Alpine
Rockford, IL 61108

West Side Marine
2936 S. MacArthur
Springfield, IL 62704

188

APPENDIX VI

The Coho Shop
622 Grand Ave.
Waukegan, IL 60085

Wheaton Rental Center
908 E. Roosevelt Rd.
Wheaton, IL 60187

Indiana

Elmer's Marine Sales
Route 5, Crooked Lake
Angola, IN 46703

Lantz's Canoe Rental
c/o Brookville Marine
10 W. 4th St.
Brookville, IN 47012

Morgan's Brookville Canoe Center
Box 118, Route 2 (Blue Creek Road)
Brookville, IN 47012

Whitewater Valley Canoe Rentals,
Inc.
Route 52, P. O. Box 2
Brookville, IN 47012

Clements Canoes Rental & Sales
Robert J. Clements
911 Wayne Ave.
Crawfordsville, IN 47933

U-Rent-It-Center, Inc.
1317 Darlington Ave.
Crawfordsville, IN 47933

Canoes from Kendall's Inc.
1919 N. "B" St.
Elwood, IN 46036

Root's Camp'n Ski Haus
6844 N. Clinton St.
Fort Wayne, IN 46805

Oldfather Canoe Center
State Hwy. 15 North
Goshen, IN 46526

Marsh Rents
Div. of U-Rent-It-Center, Inc.
2370 Lafayette Rd.
Indianapolis, IN 46222

Whitewater Valley Canoe Rentals,
Inc.
Route 1
Metamora, IN 47030

The Outpost Trading Company
100 Center St.
Mishawaka, IN 46544

Myers Bait & Tackle
Don J. Myers
Mongo, IN 46771

The Outdoor Store
1612 W. Jackson
Muncie, IN 47303

J & J Marine & Sales
1728 S. 9th St.
Richmond, IN 47374

Burnham's
1060 W. By-Pass 52
West Lafayette, IN 47906

Iowa

Reynoldson's Service
3rd & Division
Boone, IA 50036

Olsen Boat House, Inc.
120 Center St.
Cedar Falls, IA 50613

Oneota Canoe
(Karl Knudson)
616 Center St.
Decorah, IA 52101

Ahrens & Johnson, Inc.
621–25 Des Moines St.
Des Moines, IA 50316

The Boat Barn, Inc.
Box 185
McGregor, IA 52157

Marina 218 Inc.
U.S. Hwy. 218 North
North Liberty, IA 52317

Adventure Outfitters, Ltd.
314 E. Main St.
West Branch, IA 52358

Kansas

Jim's Champlin Service
700 N. Summit St.
Arkansas City, KS 67005

Lake View Service
U. S. Hwy. 54 & Sante Fe Lake Road
Augusta, KS 67010

Don's Custom Shop
618 Summer St.
Belle Plaine, KS 67013

K-15 Bait Shop
227 S. Baltimore St.
Derby, KS 67037

Herrin's Canoe Rental
221 E. 9th St.
Horton, KS 66439

Webber Rental
15 N. State St.
Iola, KS 66749

Rowley's Canoe Rental
219 S. W. 7th St.
Newton, KS 67114

Tri-C-Canoes
6624 Marty St.
Overland Park, KS 66204

Canoe Float Service
Box 343
Parsons, KS 67357

Canoeing Outfitters Rental
6209 W. 76 Terrace
Prairie Village, KS 66208

Bo's Canoe Rental
Box 33
Raymond, KS 67573

Fairfax Boats
148 S. 7th
Salina, KS 67401

Fairfax Boats
926 S. Santa Fe
Salina, KS 67401

Two Rivers Canoe Rental
R. R. 1, St. George
Wamego, KS 66547

Winfield Bait & Tackle
2013 S. Main St.
Winfield, KS 67156

Kansas Sailing Center
3216 Turnpike Drive
Wichita, KS 67210

West Street Bait & Tackle
232 S. West St.
Wichita, KS 67213

Kentucky

Sage, School of the Outdoors
209 E. High St.
Lexington, KY 40507

CANOE LIVERIES

Rockcastle Adventures
Box 662, Jct. I-75 & Ky. 80
London, KY 40741

Viking Canoe Center
3304 Preston Highway
Louisville, KY 40213

OAK (Outdoor Adventures of
Kentucky)
Box 206A, Route 1
Stanton, KY 40380

Red River Rental
Stanton, KY 40380

All-Sport Canoe Rental
Williams, KY 41300

Louisiana

The Sports Shop
8055 Airline Hyway
Baton Rouge, LA 70815

Ricky's Guide Service
Route 1, Box 375
Bogalusa, LA 70427

Pack & Paddle Wilderness
Equipment
1539 Pinhook Rd.
Lafayette, LA 70501

Canoe and Trail Shop
624 Moss St.
New Orleans, LA 70119

Maine

Cross Rock Canoe Landing
R.F.D. 1, Box 105
Allagash, ME 04774

Wilmer C. Hafford
Box 149
Allagash, ME 04774

McBreairty's Service
Allagash, ME 04774

Clark Marine Co.
426 Western Ave.
Augusta, ME 04330

Twin City Marine
99 S. Main St.
Brewer, ME 04412

Arthur Johnson
Route 160 (located on the Saco River)
Woodland Acres Campground
Brownfield, ME 04010

Maine Wilderness Canoe Basin
Pleasant Lake
Caroll, ME 04420

Maine Waterways
(Deer Isle Sailing Center)
Deer Isle, ME 04627

Pierre Z. Freeman
47 W. Main St.
Fort Kent, ME 04743

Allagash Wilderness Outfitters
Frost Pond, Star Route 76
Greenville, ME 04441

Folsom's Air Service
Greenville, ME 04442

Smith Hardware Inc.
P. O. Box 278
Jackman, ME 04945

Kezar Falls KOA
Route 25
Kezar Falls, ME 04047

Smith Pond Camping
Norman Bud Dionne
Baxter State Park Road
P. O. Box 34
Millinocket, ME 04462

Moose Horn Trading Post
Route 4
North Jay, ME 04262

Davis Marine
Main Street
Rangeley, ME 04970

Hall's Trading Post
Pleasant Avenue
Sangerville, ME 04479

Bronzeback Boat & Canoe Rental
Service
Star Route 1
Skowhegan, ME 04976

Maine Wilderness Canoe Basin
Pleasant Lake
Springfield, ME 04487

Norcross Boat & Motor Service
Norcross Point
Winthrop, ME 04364

York Harbor Marine Service, Inc.
P. O. Box 178
Route 103 "On the Harbor"
York, ME 03909

Maryland

Cycles & Things
165 N. Centre St.
Cumberland, MD 21502

Cycles & Things
Route 4, Box 243
on C & O Canal and Potomac
North Branch
Cumberland, MD 21502

Glen Cove Marina, Inc.
Route 2
Darlington, MD 21034

Pier 7—South River
Route 2
Edgewater (Annapolis), MD 21037

Appalachian Outfitters
8563 Baltimore National Pike
P. O. Box 44
Ellicott City, MD 21043

Springriver Corp.
9235 Baltimore National Pike
Ellicott City, MD 21043

White's Ferry and Landing
White's Ferry Road
Dickenson, MD 20753

Camp Wardeca
4015 Damascus Rd.
Gaithersburg, MD 20760
(By reservation only)

WEF Canoe Sales
1717 Burnside Ave.
Halfway—Greenberry Hills
Hagerstown, MD 21740

River & Trail Outfitters
Box 246, Valley Road
Knoxville, MD 21758

Capital Sailboat Agency, Inc.
Fort Washington Marina
Oxon Hill, MD 20022

Springriver Corp.
5606 Randolph Rd.
Rockville, MD 20852

APPENDIX VI

Massachusetts

Canoe Adventures, Northeast
8 Cherry St.
Belmont, MA 02178

South Bridge Boat House, Inc.
Main Street (Route 62)
Concord, MA 01742

Taylor Rental Center
626 Main St.
Falmouth, MA 02540

Goodhue Enterprises
Route 28 & 39 & 124
Harwichport, MA 02646

Foote Bros.
Top Field Road
Ipswich, MA 01938

Ruby Marine Inc.
Route 122-140
North Grafton, MA 01536

Goose Hummock Shop
Route 6A
Orleans, MA 02653

Frank's Berkshire Marine, Inc.
724 Tyler St.
Pittsfield, MA 01201

Rent-A-Canoe (Hicks)
Apple Hill Rd.
Sturbridge, MA 01566

Paddlers & Packers
1615 Riverdale St.
West Springfield, MA 01089

Michigan

Fox Sporting Goods
624 S. Main St.
Ann Arbor, MI 48104

Skip's Huron River Canoe Livery
3780 W. Delhi Rd.
Ann Arbor, MI 48103

G & L Canoe Livery
Box 92
Atlanta, MI 49709

Rowland Beck
Box 285, Route 3
Atlanta, MI 49709

Baldwin Boat & Canoe Livery
Edward H. Andersen
P. O. Box 265
Baldwin, MI 49304

Ivan's Canoe Livery
R.R. 1, Box 3259
Baldwin, MI 49304

Gardner's Favorite Sports & Marine
741 River View Drive
Benton Harbor, MI 49022

Sport-N-Life Livery
711 Farnsworth St.
Big Rapids, MI 49307

Stubs Bait Shop
Route 1
Branch, MI 49402

Cass River Canoe Livery
4448 Williamson Rd.
Bridgeport, MI 48722

Poser's Park Company
6465 Kensington Rd.
Brighton, MI 48116

Kayak Specialties
Route 1, Box 83
Buchanan, MI 49107

The Sport Corner
320 N. Redbud
Buchanan, MI 49107

Chippewa Landing
111 N. Shelby
Cadillac, MI 49601

Chief Shavehead Recreation Park
Route 3—Union Rd.
Cassopolis, MI 49031

Dick's Canoe Livery
501 W. Ferry St.
Corunna, MI 48817

Nichols Sports & Marine
7048 Greenfield Rd.
Dearborn, MI 48126

Teddy Kotowich Boats & Canoes
Jordan River—109 Main St.
East Jordan, MI 49727

White Birch Canoe Livery
Route 1
Falmouth, MI 49632

Jane's Canoe Rental
4217 S. State Rd.
Glennie, MI 48737

Olson Bros. Sports Center
705 28th St., S. W.
Grand Rapids, MI 49509

Salmon Run Campground
Vic's Canoes
R.R. 2
Grant, MI 49327

Borchers Ausable Canoeing
101 Maple St.
Grayling, MI 49738

Carlisle Canoes
110 State St. P.O. Box 150G
Grayling, MI 49738

Carr's Pioneer Canoe Livery
Grayling, MI 49738

Jim's Canoe Livery
Star Route 1, Box 165
Grayling, MI 49738

Jolly Redskin Canoe Livery
400 Ingham, Ausable Terrace
Box 396
Grayling, MI 49738

Long's Canoe Livery
Manistee River
507 Peninsular St.
Grayling, MI 49738

Manistee River Canoe Livery
R.R. 1
Grayling, MI 49738

Penrod's Ausable Canoe Trips
100 Maple St., P. O. Box 432
Grayling, MI 49738

Ray's Canoe Livery
200 Ingham St.
Grayling, MI 49738

Shel-Haven Canoe Livery
R.R. 1
Grayling, MI 49738

Ray Haywood
Route 1
Hastings, MI 49058

Kellogg's Canoe Livery
White River
Hespera, MI
(Mail: Twin Lake, MI 49457)

Casey's Corner
M-22 at Platte River
Honor, MI 49640

Miller's Marine
M-22 at Platte River
Honor, MI 49640

CANOE LIVERIES

Riverside Canoes
Tom & Kathy Stocklen
M-22 at Platte River
Honor, MI 49640

The Waterwheel
M-22 at Platte River Bridge
Honor, MI 49640

Ashley's Canoe Livery
Howard City, MI 49329

The Sail Shop, Inc.
13589 Cairn Highway
Kewadin, MI 49643

Smithville Landing, Inc.
Box 341
Lake City, MI 49651

Carl's Canoe Livery
State Road
Luther, MI
(Mail: S. 15 Mile Road
    Hoxeyville, MI 49641)

Bear Paw Cabins & Canoe Livery
3670 M-72 West
Luzerne, MI 48636

Manistee Canoe Cruises
354 Third St. or
267 Arthur St.
Manistee, MI 49660

Crystal Harbor, Inc.
  at Glen Lake
Route 2
Maple City, MI 49664

Old Log Resort & Campground
M-115 Route 1
Marion, MI 49665

Happy River Canoe Livery
R.R. 1
Merritt, MI 49667

Johnson's Canoe Livery
Mesick, MI 49668

Eco-Sports Canoe & Kayak Rental
275 W. Liberty
Box 281
Milford, MI 48042

Heavner Canoe Rental
2775 Garden Rd.
Milford, MI 48042

Ausable River Rental
Mio, MI 48647

Hinchman Acres Canoe Rental
702 Morenci
Mio, MI 48647

McKinley Canoe Rental
Route 2, Box 89
Mio, MI 48647

Mio Sport Shop
406 Morenci
Mio, MI 48647

Happy Mohawk Canoe Livery
351 Fruitvale Rd.
Montague, MI 49437

Skippers Landing
4464 Dowling
Montague, MI 49437

Derks Marine Sales
1672 Croton Drive
Newaygo, MI 49337

Dollarville Outdoors
Dollarville Road
Newberry, MI 49868

Dukes Sport Shop
205 Handy
Newberry, MI 49868

Russell's Canoe
Omer, MI 48749

Harbor Boat & Livery
101 Mill St.
Oscoda, MI 48750

Lovell's Canoe Rental & Resort
718 W. River Rd.
Oscoda, MI 48750

Sawyer Canoe Co.
Box 104, 234 State St.
Oscoda, MI 48750

Vagabond Resort & Campground
Route 2, Box 125, County Rd. 513
Rapid River, MI 49878

Campbell's Canoe Livery
1112 Lake St., P. O. Box 327
Roscommon, MI 48653

Hiawatha Canoe Livery
1113 Lake St.
Roscommon, MI 48653

Mead's Canoe Livery
Route 1, Box 936
Roscommon, MI 48653

Chuck & Linda Mires
Paddle Brave Canoe
  Livery–Campground
Route 1, Box 998
Roscommon, MI 48653

Watters Edge Canoe Livery
R.R. 1, Box 990
Roscommon, MI 48653

Beck & Hyde Farmarina
Route 3, 6 miles north of St. John's
  on U. S. 27
St. John's, MI 48879

Wolf's Enterprises
205 Wayne St.
St. Joseph, MI 49085

Gleason's Marina
650 Water St.
Saugatuck, MI 49453

Richard Hoffman
424 Water St.
Saugatuck, MI 49453

D-R-D Canoe Livery
Route 1, 10 miles east of Mt. Pleasant
Shepherd, MI 48883

The Golden Anvil
251 Broadway
South Haven, MI 49090

Cedar Springs Campground &
  Canoe Livery
Box 327 on Rifle River
Sterling, MI 48659

Rifle River Canoe Rental
5825 Townline Rd.
Sterling, MI 48659
(Office: Saginaw Street
    Sterling, MI)

White's "The River"
Old M-70
Sterling, MI 48659

Dudd, Harmon Marina
R.F.D. 2, Klinger Lake
Sturgis, MI 49091

Murray's Boats & Motors, Inc.
507 E. Front St.
Traverse City, MI 49684

Ranch Rudolph
300 State St.
Traverse City, MI 49684

Stark's Cabins & Canoe Rentals
Sylvania Outfitters
Watersmeet, MI 49969

Famous Jarolim Canoes
M-37
Wellston, MI 49689

APPENDIX VI

The Horina Canoe Rental
M-37—Pine River, 20 miles west
  of Cadillac
Wellston, MI 49689

John's Canoe Livery
Wellston, MI 49689

Merrick's Pine River Canoe Service
Route 1
Wellston, MI 49689

Sportsmans Port
Wellston, MI 49689

Jacksonville Canoe Rental
999 E. M-55
West Branch, MI 48661

Minnesota

Rum River Canoe Trails
Anoka County Fairgrounds Park
Route 6, Box 105
Anoka, MN 55303

Duane's Outfitters
Hwy. 21
Babbitt, MN 55706

Big Fork Outfitting Co.
Big Fork, MN 56628

Cliff Wold's Canoe Trip Outfitting
  Co.
1731 E. Sheridan
Bovey, MN 55709

Sports Craft, Inc.
Route 7
Brainerd, MN 56401

Paul's Landing
P. O. Box 355
Cannon Falls, MN 55009

Bob Anderson's Crane Lake Canoe
  Outfitters
Box 66
Crane Lake, MN 55725

Campbell's Trading Post
Crane Lake, MN 55725

Olson's Borderland Lodge &
  Outfitters
Box A-12
Crane Lake, MN 55725

Zup La Croix Outfitters
Lac la Croix, Ontario
Crane Lake, MN 55725

Deerwood Sport Shop
Box 186
Deerwood, MN 56444

Taylor Rental Center
1710 London Rd.
Duluth, MN 55812

B.P.Z. Outfitters
611 E. Harvey St.
Ely, MN 55731

Don Beland's Wilderness Canoe
  Trips
Box 358
Ely, MN 55731

Border Lakes Outfitters
P. O. Box 569
Ely, MN 55731

Boundary Waters Canoe Outfitters
Box 447
Ely, MN 55731

Canadian Waters, Inc.
111 E. Sheridan St.
Ely, MN 55731

Bob Cary's Canadian Border
  Outfitters
Box 117
Ely, MN 55731

Fall Lake Outfitters
State Route 1, Box 3255
Ely, MN 55731

Fishermen's Headquarters & Canoe
  Outfitting
209-223 E. Sheridan St.
Ely, MN 55731

Graystone Canoe Trip Outfitters
1829 E. Sheridan St.
Ely, MN 55731

Kawishiwi Lodge (on Lake One)
Box 480
Ely, MN 55731

Pipestone Outfitting Co.
P. O. Box 780
Ely, MN 55731

Quetico Superior Canoe Outfitters
Box 89
Ely, MN 55731

Bill Rom's Canoe Country
  Outfitters
629 E. Sheridan St.
Ely, MN 55731

Wilderness Outfitters, Inc.
1 E. Camp St.
Ely, MN 55731

Arrowhead Waters Canoe
  Outfitters
Box A
Grand Marais, MN 55604

Bearskin Lodge & Canoe Trail
  Outfitters
East Bearskin Lake
Grand Marais, MN 55604

Beartrack Outfitting Co.
Grand Marais, MN 55604

Blankenburg's Saganaga Outfitters
Grand Marais, MN 55604

Chik-Wauk Lodge & Canoe
  Outfitters
Saganaga Lake
Grand Marais, MN 55604

Grand Marais Northwoods
  Outfitters
Box 110
Grand Marais, MN 55604

Gunflint Northwoods Outfitters
Gunflint Lake
Grand Marais, MN 55604

Janet's Sea Gull Outfitters Inc.
Gunflint Trail, Box 119
Grand Marais, MN 55604

Jocko's Clearwater Canoe
  Outfitters
Gunflint Trail, Box 31
Grand Marais, MN 55604

Northpoint Outfitters
Box 427
Grand Marais, MN 55604

Portage Canoe Outfitters
Grand Marais, MN 55604

Saganaga Outfitters
Grand Marais, MN 55604

Sea Gull Outfitters
Sea Gull Lake
Grand Marais, MN 55604

Tip of the Trail Canoe Outfitters
Grand Marais, MN 55604

Trail Center
Outfitters & Canoe Rental
Gunflint Trail, Box 50
Grand Marais, MN 55604

CANOE LIVERIES

Tuscarora Canoe Outfitters
Gunflint Trail
Grand Marais, MN 55604

Way-of-the-Wilderness Canoe
   Outfitters
Box C-6
Grand Marais, MN 55604

Wilderness Waters
Box 512
Grand Marais, MN 55604

Adventures Unlimited
Hibbing, MN 55746

The Voyageurs Canoe & Bicycle
   Rental
St. Croix State Park
Hinckley, MN
(Mail: 2150 Greenview Drive
      St. Paul, MN 55112)

Point of Pines Marina, Inc.
Island View Route
International Falls, MN 56649

Voyageur Canoe Outfitters
Dan Blais
Box 328
International Falls, MN 56649

Huntersville Outfitters
F. A. Kennelly
Route 4
Menahga, MN 56464

Mr. Outdoors Sporting Goods
8565 Central Ave., N. E.
Minneapolis, MN 55431

Michel's Canoe Landing
North Mankato, MN 56001

Northern Wilderness Outfitters
Box 98 (main base: Ft. Frances,
   Ontario)
Ranier, MN 56668

Earl's Sales & Service, Inc.
Rushford, MN 55971

Bill & Dave's Texaco Service
   Center
I-694 & Lexington Ave. North
St. Paul, MN 55112

Century Camper Center, Inc.
1985 Geneva Ave. N.
St. Paul, MN 55119

Crow Wing Trails Canoe Outfitters
George Gloege
Route 2
Sebeka, MN 56477

Irv Funk Outfitters
R.R. 2, Box 51
Sebeka, MN 56477

Midwest Canoe Rental
3836 Lexington Ave. N.
Shoreview, MN 55112

Hinterland Canoe Outfitters
Spring Lake, MN 56680

Taylors Falls Canoe Co.
Taylors Falls, MN 55084

Sawbill Canoe Outfitters
Sawbill Lake
Tofte, MN 55615

Voyageur Outpost
860 E. Lake St.
Wayzata, MN 55391

Welch Village Canoe Rental
Welch, MN 55089

Marlin Marine, Inc.
1034 S. Robert St.
West St. Paul, MN 55118

Border Lakes Outfitters
(4 miles east of Ely)
P. O. Box 158
Winton, MN 55796

Mississippi

The Wilderness Shop
P.O. Box 6126
Gulfport, MS 39501

Missouri

Harvey's Alley Spring Canoe Rental
Hwy. 106
Alley Spring, MO 65431

Hufstedler's Canoe Rental
Riverton Rural Branch
Alton, MO 65606

Woods Float & Canoe Rental
Don S. Woods, Manager
Jct. Hwy. 19 North & 160
Alton, MO 65606

Midwest Black Rivers Floats
Route 1, Box 138
Annapolis, MO 63620

Sunburst Ranch
Belle & Leroy Webb, Managers
Caufield, MO 65626

Herb & Lea's Resort
Richard Sphar, Manager
Duke, MO 65461

Blue Springs Resort
Eldridge, MO 65463

Bales Canoe Rental
Eminence, MO 65466

Current River Canoe Rental
Located at Pulltite Campground
Eminence, MO 65466

Eminence Canoe Rental
Stanely Smith, Manager
Eminence, MO 65466

Ozark Boating Co.
Two Rivers Canoe Rental
R. R.
Eminence, MO 65466

Windy's Canoe Rental
Box 151
Eminence, MO 65466

Sunburst Ranch
Star Route
Elijah, MO 65642

Bill Rogers Float Fishing Service
   & Canoe Rentals
Tom & June Hammond
Box 185
Galena, MO 65656

Silver Arrow Canoe Rental
George Purcell
Gladden, MO 65478

Wilderness Waters
42 Southridge
Glendale, MO 63122

Everetts Canoe Rental
Bob Price, Manager
Hwy. 63 at 17
Houston, MO 65483

Jadwin Canoe Rental
Jadwin, MO 65501

Ozark Hills Canoe Rental
Hwy. K, Current River
Jadwin, MO 65501

Gunwhale Canoe Rentals
A. Denatale & B. Kallaos,
   Managers
Jennings, MO 63136

APPENDIX VI

Gasconade Valley Canoe Rental
Gene & Gloria Robinson,
   Managers
Jerome, MO 65529

Al Keyes Canoe Rental
Leasburg, MO 65535

Nianqua and Osage Fork River
   Canoe Rentals
Route 3
Lebanon, MO 65536

Sand Spring Resort
Bennett Spring—Brice Route
Lebanon, MO 65536

Vogels' Resort
(Nianqua River Float Service)
Brice Route
Bennett Spring State Park
Lebanon, MO, 65536

Black River Floats & Canoe
   Rental
D. Cook & D. Shaffer, Managers
Lesterville, MO 63654

Big M Resort
Success Route
Licking, MO 65542

Big Piney River Resort
Licking, MO 65542

Midwest Big Piney Floats
Route 7, Box 138
Licking, MO 65542

O. K. Resort
Mrs. Orval Rennick, Manager
Licking, MO 65542

Ray's Riverside Resort
Ray Wallace, Manager
Licking, MO 65542

Roland Meyer
Morrison, MO 65061

Gravens Resort
Hwy. 32 at the Gasconade River
Nebo, MO 65471

Clearwater Stores, Inc.
Jim Wohlschlaeger, Manager
Route 3
Piedmont, MO 63957

Dick's Black River Camp
Dick Goetz, Manager
R.F.D. 3
Piedmont, MO 63957

Pettit's Canoe Rentals
Beryl Pettit, Manager
Pottersville, MO 65790

Eden Resort, John Homan,
   Manager
P. O. Box 775
Richland, MO 65556

Aaron's Boats & Motors
Business Loop 44 W.
Rolla, MO 65401

Dishmann's DX
Current, Big Piney, and Gasconade
   River Floats
1207 Kingshighway
Rolla, MO 65401

Ozark Equipment Co.
Hwy. 63 & Black Street
Rolla, MO 65401

Carr's Grocery and Canoe Rental,
   Inc.
Round Spring, MO 65467

Sullivan Canoe Rental
Round Spring, MO 65467

Fagan's Upper Meramec River Canoe
   Rental
Route 1, Box 160A
Hwy. 8
St. James, MO 65559

Crestwood Boats & Motors, Inc.
9979 Hwy. 66
St. Louis, MO 63126

Eureka Valley Floats
6347 N. Rosebury Ave.
St. Louis, MO 63105

Kemper's Ozark Canoe Rental
12471 Horizon Village
St. Louis, MO 63138

Marlin's Sport Shop
5408 Hampton Ave.
St. Louis, MO 63109

Midwest Floats & Camp Grounds,
   Inc.
4109 Malcolm Drive
St. Louis, MO 63125

Rock Hill Boat & Motor
9225 Manchester
St. Louis, MO 63144

Akers Ferry Resort on Current
   River
Cedar Grove Route
Salem, MO 65560

Current River Canoe Rental
Russell Sandlin, Manager
Gladden Star Route
Salem, MO 65560

Silver Arrow Canoe Rental
Gladden Star Route
Salem, MO 65560

Wild River Canoe Rentals
Arnold Smith & Jack Patton
Cedar Grove Route
Salem, MO 65560

A-B Canoe & Boat Sales & Rental Co.
John Igleheart, Manager
Steelville, MO 65565

B & H Canoe Rental
K. Wood & H. Morgan, Managers
Route 1
Steelville, MO 65565

Bass Canoe & Boat Sales & Rental
Box 61
Steelville, MO 65565

Brown Canoe Rental
Ralph Brown, Manager
Route 1, Box 119
Steelville, MO 65565

Farrar Floats
Carol Farrar, Manager
Steelville, MO 65565

Foggy Valley Floats
Merle Stichnote, Manager
Steelville, MO 65565

Indian Springs Lodge
John Igleheart, Manager
Steelville, MO 65565

Ozark Floats
Bill Hubbard, Manager
Route 1, Box 247
Steelville, MO 65565

Payne's Boat Co.
R. R. 1, Box 10
Steelville, MO 65565

Ray Canoe Rental
Mrs. J. W. Ray, Manager
Box 277, Route 1
Steelville, MO 65565

Thornton Canoe Rental
Box 285, Route 1
Steelville, MO 65565

Stroud & Sons, Inc.
Route 2, Box 107A
Sullivan, MO 63080

CANOE LIVERIES

House's Grocery & Canoe Rental
Tecumseh, MO 65760

Nelson Canoe Rentals
Betty Nelson, Manager
Tecumseh, MO 65760

Ko-Ko Beach Campground
Joe Pautler, Manager
Route 1, Box 267
Union, MO 63087

Garden of Eden Canoe & Jon Boat
  Rental
Ray Randolph, Owner
Box 2
Van Buren, MO 63965

Neil Canoe & Jon Boat Rental
Box 416
Van Buren MO 63965

Roy Reed Guide Service
Van Buren, MO 63965

Willie Parks Guide Service
Van Buren, MO 63965

Indian Ford Resort
Jack Duncan, Manager
Vienna, MO 65582

James Resort
Jim James, Manager
Vienna, MO 65582

Ozark Canoe Rental Service
614 Tuxedo Blvd.
Webster Groves, MO 63119

Twin Bridges Store & Canoe Rental
Twin Bridges Route, Box 230
West Plains, MO 65775

Gipsy Bridge Park
Robert Kerr, Manager
Box 98
Zalma, MO 63787

Montana

Westlake Marina
Box 278, U. S. Hwy. 93
Somers, MT 59932

Nebraska

Archer Arms (canoes only)
3295 "A" St.
Lincoln, NB 68510

Holmes Lake Marina
3150 S. 58th St.
Lincoln, NB 68506

Holmes Lake Marina
70th Normal
Lincoln, NB 68502

Wilderness Expeditions
1820 Brower Rd.
Lincoln, NB 68502

Wilson Outfitters
6211 Sunrise Rd.
Lincoln, NB 68510

New Hampshire

Alexandria Boat Shop
R.D. #1
Bristol, NH 03222

Saco Bound
Route 32
Center Conway, NH
(Mail: Fryeburg, ME 04037)

Derry Marine
Route 28S
Derry, NH 03038

Norman B. Wight
Box 105
Dublin, NH 03444

Harry F. Ashley
c/o Brown Owl Camps
Errol, NH 03579

Northern Waters
Errol, NH
(Mail: Fryeburg, ME 04037)

Sargent's Lakeshore Cottages &
  Boats
P. O. Box 417
George's Mills, NH 03751

Squam Boats, Inc.
Squam Lake
Holderness, NH 03245

Goodhue Enterprises
Route 3, Weirs Blvd.
Laconia, NH 03246

Wilderness Outfitters
121 Nashua St.
Milford, NH 03055

Arey's Marina
Moultonboro, NH 03254

Gralyn Sports Center
North Conway, NH 03860

Village Outfitters
Grove Streeet
Peterborough, NH 03458

Outdoors Unlimited, Inc.
Harriman Hill Road
Raymond, NH 03077

Shir-Roy Camping Area
Route 32
Richmond, NH
(Mail: R.F.D. 3
      Winchester, NH 03470)

White Mountain Canoe Co.
93 Motel, Route 3
West Thornton, NH 03285

Northeast Marina Corp.
36 N. Main St.
Wolfeboro, NH 03894

New Jersey

Sunset Landing
1215 Sunset Ave. (Deal Lake)
Asbury Park, NJ 07712

Morgan's Wharf
589 24th St.
Avalon, NJ 08202

Stanley's Marine & Sport Shop
Route 46
Belvidere, NJ 07823

Walt's Sunoco/Jersey Paddler
900 Route 70
Bricktown, NJ 08723

Walt's Sunoco/Jersey Paddler
1748 Route 88
Bricktown, NJ 08723

Alpine Ski & Sail Center
Route 173 West
Clinton, NJ 08809

Cranford Boat & Canoe Co.
250 Springfield Ave.
Cranford, NJ 07016

Pineland Canoes
Route 70 & 527
Dover, NJ
(Mail: 632 Carroll Fox Rd.
      Bricktown, NJ 08723)

APPENDIX VI

Canal Canoe Rental
Box 21, Amwell Road
East Millstone, NJ 08873

Bel Haven Lake
Green Bank, R.D. 2
Egg Harbor, NJ 08215

Lentine Marine Div.
Route 31
Flemington, NJ 08822

Mercury Outdoor Shop
Route 130 & Klemm Avenue
Gloucester City, NJ 08030

Rutgers Boat Center
127 Raritan Ave.
Highland Park, NJ 08904

Bernard's Boat Rental
Route 27, on the canal
Kingston, NJ 08528

Indian Head Canoes
Box 106, R.D. 1
Lafayette, NJ 07848

Elmer K. Bright
Bright's Boat Basin
Box 305, R.D. 3
Lake Hopatcong, NJ 07849

Lenape Park Recreation Center
Box 57, Park Road
Mays Landing, NJ 08330

Winding River Campground
R.D. 2, Box 246
Mays Landing, NJ 08330

The Outdoor Trader
Stokes Road (Route 541)
Medford, NJ 08055

C. F. Dicks
Dicks Canoes
14 E. Vine St.
Millville, NJ 08332

Hack's Canoe Retreat
100 Mill St.
Mount Holly, NJ 08060

Oscar Jenkins Co.
Route 45 at Jefferson
P.O. Box 98
Mullica Hill, NJ 08062

Indian Head Canoe Rentals
7 Woodside Ave.
Newton, NJ 07860

Cal's Sport Shop
41 River Rd.
Oakland, NJ 07436

Rentals Unlimited
444 Route 23
Pompton Plains, NJ 07444

Recreation Unlimited, Inc.
926 Route 17
Ramsey, NJ 07446

Bowcraft Sport Shop
Route 22
Scotch Plains, NJ 07076

Abbott's Canoe Rental
Route 29, River Road
Titusville, NJ 08560

Pineland Canoes
R. D. 2, Box 4510
Whitesville Road (Route 527)
Toms River, NJ 08753

Adams Canoe Rentals, Inc.
Lake Drive, Atsion Lake
Vincentown, NJ 08088

New York

Larry Piper
179 Colonial Ave.
Albany, NY 12208

Wolf's Boat House
327 S. Ellicott Creek
Amherst, NY 14150

Kittatinny Campgrounds
Kittatinny Canoe Base
Route 97, Box 95
Barryville, NY 12719

Bob Lander's
Minisink Ford Canoe Base
Barryville, NY 12719

Eureka Camping Center
625 Conklin Rd.
Binghamton, NY 13902

Dunn's Boat Service
Big Moose Lake, NY 13307

Blue Mountain Lake Boat Livery, Inc.
Route 28
Blue Mountain Lake, NY 12812

Edw. Griffin Boat Livery
Blue Mountain Lake, NY 12812

Lake George Camping Equipment
  Co.
Ray Smith
Bolton Landing, NY 12814

Lamb Bros., Inc.
Main Street
Bolton Landing, NY 12814

Port Jerry on Lake George
Route 9N
Bolton Landing, NY 12814

R. Bergoffen
Bob's L. I. Canoe Rentals
3 Carol Place
Brookhaven, NY 11719

Bob Lander's
Callicoon Canoe Base
Callicoon, NY 12723

Upper Delaware Campgrounds
Box 188
Callicoon, NY 12745

Loon Lake Marina
Marina Road
Chestertown, NY 12817

Donald P. Kenyon
Pack & Paddles Outfitters
Oneida Lake
Cleveland, NY 13042

Cooperstown Marine & Service
10 Fair St.
Cooperstown, NY 13326

Hulberts Cottages
Cranberry Lake, NY 12927

Maurice Booth
Cranberry Lake, NY 12927

Mountain View Marina
Edgar Beckman
Cranberry Lake, NY 12927

Murray's Copake Lake Marina
Copake Lake Road
Craryville, NY 12521

Pepacton Sport Center
Downsville, NY 13755

Clark's Boat Service
Eagle Bay, NY 13331

Buzz-Arina, Inc.
140 Williamson St.
East Rockaway, NY 11518

A. W. Rollins
Edmeston, NY 13335

Benson, Jessup & Knapp, Inc.
809 Pennsylvania Ave.
Elmira, NY 14904

CANOE LIVERIES

Syracuse Yacht Sales
Lyndon Corners
Fayetteville, NY 13066

H. Chalk & Son, Inc.
Fishers Landing, NY 13646

Roy's Marina, Inc.
R.D. 1
Geneva, NY 14456

Frank & Marge McBride
Hankins House, Route 97
Hankins, NY 12741

Kerst's Boat Livery, Inc.
Indian Lake, NY 12842

Inlet Marine
Inlet, NY 13360

James R. Payne
Payne's Boat Livery
Inlet, NY 13360

Clarence Pierce
Inlet, NY 13360

Inlet Park Marine, Inc.
435 Taughannock Blvd.
Ithaca, NY 14850

Liverpool Sportcenter
125-141 First St.
Liverpool, NY 13088

McDonough Marine
755 Market St.
Lockport, NY 14094

Camp Hillary
Long Lake, NY 12847

Dave Hample's Garage &
Marina
Long Lake, NY 12847

Emerson's Boat Livery
Long Lake, NY 12847

Diane Perkins
Stillwater Reservoir
Star Route
Lowville, NY 13367

The Stillwater Shop
Paul Jacobs
Lowville, NY 13367

Sacandaga Marine, Inc.
Route 30 & School Street
Mayfield, NY 12117

Taconic Sports & Camping
Center
R.D. 2, Rudd Pond Road
Millerton, NY 12546

Mulvey's Marine & Sport Shop
87 Broadway
Monticello, NY 12701

Swinging Bridge Lake Park
Campgrounds
Monticello, NY 12762

West River Marine, Inc.
Route 245, R.D. 1
Naples, NY 14512

Skip Feagles
Box 128, Route 97
Narrowsburg, NY 12764

Hillside Inn
Route 97
Narrowsburg, NY 12764

Bob Lander's
Ten Mile River Enterprises, Inc.
Narrowsburg, NY 12764

Hodges Marine Sales, Inc.
R.D. 3, Route 12
Norwich, NY 13815

McDonough Marine
5852 Main St.
Olcott, NY 14126

Donald Lorez
Old Forge, NY 13420

Old Forge Sports Center, Inc.
Route 28
Old Forge, NY 13420

Rivett's Boat Livery
Lake Trail
Old Forge, NY 13420

Hopkins Marine, Inc.
100 E. Lake Rd.
Penn Yan, NY 14527

Pilot Knob Boat Shop, Inc.
Pilot Knob, NY 12844

Janco's Northern Sports
R.D. 3, Box 90, Lake Shore Rd.
Plattsburgh, NY 12901

Jerry's Canoe Rentals, Inc.
Pond Eddy, NY 12770

Kelly's Canoe Rentals Inc.
Route 97
Pond Eddy, NY 12770

White Water Rentals Inc.
Deerpark Gun Shop
Route 97
Port Jervis, NY 12771

Arlington Sporting Goods, Inc.
794 Main St.
Poughkeepsie, NY 12603

Flushing Meadow Park Boathouse
Flushing Meadow Park
Queens, NY 11380

Bird's Marine, Inc.
Route 28
Raquette Lake, NY 13436

Fred Burke's Boats
Raquette Lake, NY 13436

Raquette Lake Marina, Inc.
Box 37
Raquette Lake, NY 13436

Black Creek Marina
20 Black Creek Rd.
Rochester, NY 14623

Towner Bros. Inc.
710 University Ave.
Rochester, NY 14607

John Monthony
Sabael, NY 12864

Loucks Boat Livery
R.D. 1, Box 200A
Salamanca, NY 14779

Hickok Boat Livery
c/o Stockade Trading Post
Route 30 at Fish Creek Ponds Camp
Site
Saranac Inn, NY 12982

Crescent Bay, Inc.
Boathouse
Saranac Lake, NY 12983

Walter Emmons
Ampersand Bay Boat Club
Saranac Lake, NY 12983

Keough Marine Sales
Saranac Lake, NY 12983

Swiss Marine
Saranac Lake, NY 12983

A & M Canoe Rentals
33 Highview Ave.
Selden, NY 11784

Al's Sport Store
Route 30
Shinhopple, NY 13837

Kittatinny Canoes
Skinners Falls Base

Cycle and Sea, Inc.
Route 25A and Rose Street
Smithtown, NY 11787

Curt's Canoe Livery
Route 97
Sparrow Bush, NY 12780

Clove Lakes Boat House
Clove Lakes Park
Staten Island, NY 10301

Chas. M. Dedrick, Inc.
Next to UCCC
Cottekill Road
Stone Ridge, NY 12484

Edgar Fletcher
Fletcher's Canoes
Moody Road
Tupper Lake, NY 12986

McDonald's Boat Livery
Moody Road
Tupper Lake, NY 12986

Hagner's Marina
Upper Saranac Lake, NY 12983

Taylor Rental Center
150 Orchard St.
Webster, NY 14580

Penningroth Farm Supply, Inc.
Route 11
Whitney Point, NY 13862

North Carolina

Appalachian Outfitters of Carolina
Route 1, Box 88D
Blowing Rock, NC 28605

Appalachian Outfitters
P. O. Box 57, Hwy. 321 South
Boone, NC 28607

Nantahala Outdoor Center
Star Route, Box 68
Bryson City, NC 28713

Trail Shop
405 W. Franklin St.
Chapel Hill, NC 27514

Silver Creek Camping Park & Canoe
  Livery
Silver Creek Rd., Route 2, Box 37
Mill Spring, NC 28756

Tommy McNabb—Rent-A-Canoe
5531 Pinebrook Lane
Winston-Salem, NC 27105

Pack 'n Paddle (Appalachian
  Outfitters)
4240 Kernersville Rd.
Winston-Salem, NC 27107

North Dakota

Larson Marine Inc.
Lake Metigoshe
Bottineau, ND 58318

Dixon Canoe Outfitters
2 miles east of North Unit, Theodore
  Roosevelt National Park
Watford City, ND 58854

Ohio

Molly's Cheese House
Kenneth Hyatt, Route 603
Box 531, R.D. 4
Ashland, OH 44805

Fyffe's Canoe Rental
2750 Washington Mill Rd.
Bellbrook, OH 45305

Richard G. Dailey
Brinkhaven Canoe Livery
Brinkhaven, OH 43006

David Mapes
U. S. Route 62
Brinkhaven, OH 43006

River Bend Canoe Livery
1092 Whetstone River Rd.
Caledonia, OH 43314

Apache Canoe Livery
218 W. Cherry St.
P. O. Box 341
Canal Fulton, OH 44614

Canal Fulton Canoe Rental
Canal Fulton, OH 44614

River Run Canoe Livery
Route 93, 219 Cherry St.
Canal Fulton, OH 44614

Ronald Vaughn
Vaughn's
Hurd Road
Carey, OH 43316

Northmoor Marina
R.R. 4, Box 222D
Celina, OH 45822

Zucker Marine, Inc.
860 E. Washington St.
Chagrin Falls, OH 44022

Flerlage Marine, Inc.
2233 Eastern Ave.
Cincinnati, OH 45211

Western Hills Honda
3110 Harrison Ave.
Cincinnati, OH 45211

Flake's Scenic Route Campgrounds
  & Canoe Livery
9388 State Route 350
Clarksville, OH 45113

All Ohio Canoe
320 S. Ardmore Rd.
Columbus, OH 43209

Alcawi Canoe Base
Route 1
Coshocton, OH 43812

Beaver Creek Canoe Livery
Route 170, Fredericktown Road
East Liverpool, OH 43920

Ehrhart Sport Center, Inc.
308 W. Main St.
Fairborn, OH 45324

Portage Trail Canoe Livery
1773 S. River Rd.
Fremont, OH 43420

Dennis C. Maier
Hinckley Lake Boat House
West Drive, Parkway Route 1
Hinckley, OH 44233

Camp Hi Canoe Livery
Abbott Road
Hiram, OH 44234

Helmick's Haven Marina
Box 89, Route 1
Little Hocking, OH 45742

Camp Oodik
R. D. 2, Box 89
Loudonville, OH 44842

Mohican Canoe Livery
Routes 3 & 97
Loudonville, OH 44842

Mohican Wilderness Canoe Livery
The Wally Road (1 mile south of
  Loudonville, OH)
(Mail: The Walley Road, Route 1
  Glenmont, OH 44628)

CANOE LIVERIES

October Hill
424 W. Main St.
Loudonville, OH 44842

Masek Marine & Woodcraft
131 Union St.
Madison, OH 44057

Miami Canoe Livery
202 Wooster Pike
Milford, OH 45150

Morgan's Canoe Rental
Scenic Route 350
Ft. Ancient
Morrow, OH 45152

Licking Valley Canoe Livery
Route 16, east of Newark
(Mail: Robert Minot
      Route 1
      Newark, OH 43055)

Lake County Canoes
81 Elevator Ave.
Painesville, OH 44077

Pleasant Hill Canoe Livery
P. O. Box 10, R.D. 1
Perrysville, OH 44864

Honda of Piqua
6100 N. County Road 25A
   (S. Main St.)
Piqua, OH 45356

Raccoon Creek Canoe Livery
Route 35 on Bob Evans Farms
Rio Grande, OH 45614

Grand River Recreation
3825 Fobes Rd.
Rock Creek, OH 44084

The Viking Shop
2735 N. Reynolds Rd.
Toledo, OH 43615

East Bay Marina
East of Cedar Point Causeway on
   River Avenue
Sandusky, OH 44870

Ohio Canoe Adventures, Inc.
5128 Colorado Ave.
Sheffield Lake, OH 44054

Barefoot Canoes
3565 W. Frederick-Gingham Rd.
Tipp City, OH 45371

Romp's Water Port, Inc.
5055 Liberty Ave.
Vermilion, OH 44089

Trigg's Marine Supply Co.
4174 Market St.
Youngstown, OH 44512

Oklahoma

Tenkiller Valley Ranch
(3 miles northeast of Gore on Hwy.
   100, or 4 miles southwest of Lake
   Tenkiller Dam on Hwy. 100)
Box 231
Gore, OK 74435

Sparrow Hawk Camp
(5 miles northeast of Tahlequah on
   State Hwy. 10)
Loop Route
Tahlequah, OK 74464

Tahlequah Floats
(2 miles east of Tahlequah on Hwy.
   51)
Tahlequah, OK 74464

Oregon

Riverview Marina
781 N. E. 2nd St.
Corvallis, OR 97330

The Canoe Rack
3003 N. E. Alberta
Portland, OR 97211

Brown's Landing
Route 1, Box 134
Scappoose, OR 97056

Pennsylvania

Yough Lake Marina
Youghiogheny Reservoir
Addison, PA 15411

Wilt P. E.
204 53 St.
Altoona, PA 16602

Towne Marine
614 Catherine St.
Bloomsburg, PA 17815

John Linnot
c/o Ideal Enterprises
Catawissa, PA 17820

Allegheny Outfitters
19 S. Main St.
Clarendon, PA 16313

Jeff's Boats
Black Moshannon State Park
297 W. Market St.
Clearfield, PA 16830

Cook Riverside Cabins, Inc.
Cook Forest State Park
Cooksburg, PA 16217

Kittatinny Canoes
Main Office
Silver Lake Road
Dingmans Ferry, PA 18328

Kittatinny Canoes
Dingmans Bridge Canoe Base
Dingmans Ferry, PA 18328

Forks Valley Sports World, Inc.'s
   "Mountain Shop"
R.D. 2, Route 115
Easton, PA 18042

Pasch Marine Service
North Delaware Drive
Easton, PA 18042

Lagoon Boat Rentals at Presque Isle
   State Park
Erie, PA 16505

Causeway Boat Marina
Pymatuning State Park
Causeway Livery
Espyville, PA

Wick's Ski Shop
403 N. Pottstown Pike
Exton, PA 19341

Baker's Marine Co.
Lake Wallenpaupack
Hawley, PA 18428

Hulmeville Park Association, Inc.
Beaver Street
Hulmeville, PA 19047

Woodrow W. Behney
R.D. 4, Box 320
Hummelstown, PA 17036

Outdoor Specialists
307 S. 13th St.
Indiana, PA 15701

Wilderness Tours
1286 Washington St.
Indiana, PA 15701

Central Service Station
10-12 S. Second St.
Jeannette, PA 15644

APPENDIX VI

Conestoga Marine & Cyclery
1361 Manheim Pike
Lancaster, PA 17601

Louis P. Stefan
Wispering Trails Campgrounds
R.D. 2
Linesville, PA 16424

Hileman's Boat Service on the
   Allegheny
Manorville, PA 16238

James O. Card
Cushetunk Campground
Box 3
Milanville, PA 18443

Milesburg Boat & Trailer Sales
Route 144 & new 220
Milesburg, PA 16853

A House of Canoeing
Laurel Highlands River Tours
Route 381, Box 86
Mill Run, PA 15464

Robbins Marine
2 miles South
Milton, PA 17847

Mountain Streams & Trails
Ralph Wm. McCarty, Rep.
2420 Saunders Station Rd.
Monroeville, PA 15146
(or: Box 106
Ohiopyle, PA 15470)

Whitewater Adventures
Robert Maritta & Wendall Holt,
   Reps.
Box 31
Ohiopyle, PA 15470

Wilderness Voyageurs, Inc.
Box 97
Ohiopyle, PA 15470

Oil City Canoe Sales
Route 62 N., R.D. 2
Oil City, PA 16301

Wilt, P. E.
Prince Gallitzin State Park
   Marina
Patton, PA 16668

The Pocono Boathouse
Route 423
Pocono Pines, PA 18350

Point Pleasant Canoe Rental &
   Sales
Box 6
Point Pleasant, PA 18950

Uniservice, Inc.
Moraine State Park
R.D., Portersville, PA
(Mail: 132 Adele Ave.
          Pittsburgh, PA 15237)

C-B Enterprises, Inc.
835 Hiester's Lane
Reading, PA 19605

Wolfe's Equipment & Rental Co.
208 Revere Blvd.
Reading, PA 19609

Samuel M. Bryan
2032 Second Street Pike
Richboro, PA 18954

Morrows Marina
S. Swarthmore Ave. & Darby
   Creek
Ridley Park, PA 19078

Paul Wick Ski Shops, Inc.
321 W. Woodland Ave.
Springfield, PA 19064

Delaware River Canoe Rental
1527 Spruce St.
Stroudsburg, PA 18360

Tri-Rivers Canoes
Elm Street, Route 62
Tionesta, PA 16353

Valley Buick, Inc. Trailer Center
(1 mile S. Parkway Exit 13)
629 Brown Ave. Ext.
Turtle Creek, PA 15145

Eagle Boat House
Route 100, Box 200
Uwchland, PA 19480

Canyon Cruisers
Edward D. McCarthy, Rep.
% The Antlers Motel
R. D. 4
Wellsboro, PA 16901

John Wright Boats, Inc.
1000 New DeHaven St.
West Conshohocken, PA 19428

Canoe, Kayak & Sailing Craft
701 Wood St.
Wilkinsburg, PA 15221

Harrisburg Seaplane Base, Inc.
333 S. Front St.
Wormleysburg, PA 17043

Sports World
R. D. 11, Hellam Branch
York, PA 17406

Rhode Island

Fin & Feather Lodge, Ltd.
95 Frenchtown Rd.
East Greenwich, RI 02818

Canoes, Inc.
1245 Jefferson Blvd.
Warwick, RI 02886

South Carolina

Fish Creek Landing
Palmetto Dunes Resort
P. O. Box 5354
Hilton Head, SC 29928

South Dakota

Elmen Rental
1701 W. 12th
Sioux Falls, SD 57100

Tennessee

B & B Sports Center
235 Buffalo Valley Rd.
Cookeville, TN 38501

Buffalo Canoe Rental Co.
Flat Woods, TN 38458

Concord Boat Dock
c/o Athletic House
Alcoa Highway
Knoxville, TN 37920

Big Ridge State Park
State Route 61
Maynardville, TN 37807

Buffalo Canoe Rental Co.
2080 Goodhaven Drive
Memphis, TN 38116

Morris Rent-All Center, Inc.
3609 Nolensville Rd.
Nashville, TN 37211

The Crosseyed Cricket
Oak Ridge, TN 37830

Camp'n Aire
State Route 73
Townsend, TN 37882

CANOE LIVERIES

Texas

Spivey Crossing
(Willis Camp)
Route 1, Box 87
Aquilla, TX 76622

Arlington Canoe Rental
2001 W. Pioneer Parkway
Arlington, TX 76015

"Doc" Baker's Canoe Rental
115 E. Woodin Blvd.
Dallas, TX 75216

High Trails Co.
123 E. Woodin Blvd.
Dallas, TX 75216

U. S. Boat Corporation
4230 LBJ Freeway
Dallas, TX 75234

Creek Canoe Co.
605 Pine Drive
Dickinson, TX 77539

Teffy's Hobby House
6179 39th St.
Groves, TX 77619

Houston Canoe Sales & Rentals
3116 Broadway
Houston, TX 77017

Texas Canoe Trails, Inc.
1008 Wirt Rd. #160
Houston, TX 77055

White Oak Service
2520 Houston Ave.
Houston, TX 77009

Wilderness Equipment
638 Westbury Square
Houston, TX 77035

Comanche Outfitters
Horseshoe Bay, P. O. Box Y
Marble Falls, TX 78654

Southwest Canoe 'N Kayak
  Outfitters
200 Broadway Village
Mesquite, TX 75149

Comanche Outfitters
2008 Bedford
Midland, TX 79701

White Water Sports
1311 River Crest
New Braunfels, TX 78130

North Dallas Marine
514 North Central Expressway
Richardson, TX 75080

Stephen Snow
415 Oakleaf
San Antonio, TX 78209

Goynes Canoe Livery
Route 2, Box 43G
San Marcos, TX 78666

Rod Rylander Realty & Boat Sales
2213 Hwy. 75 North
Sherman, TX 75090

Guadalupe Canoe Rental
P. O. Box 8
Spring Branch, TX 78070

Burleson Outfitters
6714 Woodway Drive
Waco, TX 76710

Utah

Tex's Tour Center
Box 67
Moab, UT 84532

Sports Specialties
170 S. State
Orem, UT 84057

Ute Archery & Sporting Goods
3727 S. 900 East
Salt Lake City, UT 84106

Vermont

DeMarco Sporting Goods
200 North Side Drive
Bennington, VT 05201

Eddy's Marine & Sports Center
Route 7 South
Brandon, VT 05733

Canoe Imports, Inc.
74 S. Willard St.
Burlington, VT 05401

West River Canoe
John W. F. Aaron
Route 100 South
East Jamaica, VT 05343

Mead Rent-A-Canoe
Alan R. Mead
River Road
Fairfax, VT 05454

Clearwater Canoe Rental, Inc.
Barry Bender
R.D. 1, Box 24
Moretown, VT 05660

Canoes Unlimited
187 Elm St.
Newport, VT 05855

Tudhope Marine Co., Inc.
U. S. Route 2
North Hero, VT 05474

Chipman Point Marine &
  Campground
Chipman Point
Orwell, VT 05760

Sports Shops, Inc.
139 Lake St.
St. Albans, VT 05478

Waterhouse's
Salisbury, VT 05769

Burlington Rent-All
340 Dorset St.
South Burlington, VT 05401

Stowe Canoe Co.
Route 100
Stowe, VT 05672

Sailing Winds
Box 93
Wells, VT 05774

Woodstock Sports
30 Central St.
Woodstock, VT 05091

Virginia

John E. Shaffer
Route 2, Box 175
Berryville, VA 22611

Blue Ridge Mountain Sports
1417 Emmet St.
Charlottesville, VA 22901

Springriver Corporation
548 S. Main St.
Chincoteague, VA 23336

Rappahannock Canoe, Inc.
1209 Powhatan St.
Fredericksburg, VA 22401

Sport Center Marine
3425 Jefferson Davis Blvd.
Fredericksburg, VA 22401

340 Outfitters
U.S. Route 340 (2 miles south of
   Skyline Drive entrance)
Front Royal, VA 22630

Three Springs KOA Campground
Route 340 South
P. O. Box 274
Front Royal, VA 22630

Downriver Canoe Co.
Route 340
Limeton, VA
(Mail: Route 1, Box 214
       Front Royal, VA 22630)

Shenandoah River Outfitters
Route 3
Luray, VA 22835

Blue Ridge Mountain Sports
1104 W. Little Creek Rd.
Norfolk, VA 23505

Canoe Center
2930 Chain Bridge Rd.
Oakton, VA 22124

Matacia Outfitters
Box 32
Oakton, VA 22124

Lynn's Store, Inc.
313 Mill St.
P. O. Drawer H
Occoquan, VA 22125

Good's Bait & Tackle Shop
Riverton, VA 22651

Louis J. Matacia
2700 Gallows Rd.
Vienna, VA 22180

Camping Servicenter
4975 Holland Rd.
Virginia Beach, VA 23462

Washington

The Lodge, Inc.
P. O. Box 86
Ashford, WA 98304

Cascade Canoe & Kayak
2610 Sunset Drive
Bellingham, WA 98225

Mt. St. Helens Lodge
H. R. Truman
Spirit Lake
P. O. Box 96
Castle Rock, WA 98611

Lake Ozette Lodge
Lake Ozette, WA

Merle's Boat Rentals
Ocean Shores Marina
Ocean Shores, WA 98551

The Boathouse
9808 17th Ave. S.W.
(White Center)
Seattle, WA 98106

Recreational Equipment, Inc.
1525 11th Ave.
Seattle, WA 98122

West Virginia

Don Wolford
Capon Bridge, WV 26711

Appalachian Mountain Sports, Inc.
2120 Pennsylvania Ave.
Charleston, WV 25302

Blue Ridge Outfitters
Route 340
Charles Town, WV 25414

Sunset Beach Marina, Inc.
Box 93A, Route 6, Cheat Lake
Morgantown, WV 26505

Five Rivers Canoe Co., Inc.
231 Virginia St.
Parsons, WV 26287

Canoe & Trail Shop (subsidiary
   of Carpet Services Unlimited)
1 Bridge Street
Reader, WV 26167

The Bike Shop
State Route 2
Wellsburg, WV 26070

West Virginia Canoe & Trail
   Outfitting Company, Inc.
21st & Main Streets & 111-18th
   Street, East
Wheeling, WV 26003

Wisconsin

Cruising Houseboats, Inc.
Alma Marina
125 Hwy. 35N (just off Hwy. 35)
Alma, WI 54610

Rich's Bait & Tackle
Rich Prinsen
Hwy. 35 North
Alma, WI 54610

Wa-Bak-In Sports Equipment
Route 3, Box 85A
Antigo, WI 54409

Rental City
2125 N. Richmond
Appleton, WI 54911

Spangler Sales
134 S. Spring St.
Beaver Dam, WI 53916

Krueger's Cove
Rock River, Hwy. 51
Beloit, WI 53511

Gamble Store
21 S. Second St.
Black River Falls, WI 54615

Steele's Sport Shop
Route 3, Roosevelt Road
Black River Falls, WI 54615

Les Roschi
Little John Lake
Box 62, Hwy. "N"
Boulder Junction, WI 54512

Schauss Woodwork Shop
Box 131
Boulder Junction, WI 54512

Donald McEathron
Route 2 (between Chippewa &
   Flambeau Rivers)
Bruce, WI 54819

Brule River Canoe Rental
Box 150G
Brule, WI 54820

Brule River Tackle Supply, Inc.
P. O. Box 200
Brule, WI 54820

Petrie's Marina
Route 3, Box 98
Burlington, WI 53105

Ed's Service Center, Inc.
Hwys. 63 & "M"
Cable, WI 54821

Mogasheen Resort
Route 2 (north end of Lake
   Namekagon)
Cable, WI 54821

CANOE LIVERIES

Stan's Landing
Mississippi River
Cassville, WI 53806

Jenness Marina
Box 308
Chetek, WI 54728

Wildwood Resort & Trailer Park
Jack Harrison
Route 1
Chetek, WI 54728

C & C Canoe & Bike Rental
220 Main St.
Cornell, WI 54732

McCann's Canoe Sales & Rental
200 Main St.
Cornell, WI 54732

Buoy Marine, Inc.
3115 E. Layton Ave.
Cudahy, WI 53110

Camp One
Route 1, Box 606
Danbury, WI 54830

Rick's Log Cabin, Inc.
Star Route 1, Box 10
Danbury, WI 54830

Sportsmen's Park
Paul & Carole Brahm
P. O. Box 551
Delavan, WI 53115

Norby's Sport Shop
U. S. Hwy. 63
Drummond, WI 54832

Vespies Lodge
Lake Owen
Drummond, WI 54832

Boat-S'-Port
R.R. 3 (3 miles east of Eagle River on
  Hwy. 70)
Eagle River, WI 54521

Deerskin Resort and Campground
R.R. 3 (4 miles north of Eagle River
  on Hwy. 45, east 4 miles to Chain
  Lakes Rd.)
Eagle River, WI 54521

Deywer Boat Works
Eagle River, WI 54521

Holiday Harbor
R.R. 3 (2 miles northeast of Eagle
  River on Chain Lakes Rd.)
Eagle River, WI 54521

Tomlinson Auto & Marine Co.
P. O. Box 579
Eagle River, WI 54521

Half Moon Boat Rental
Lake Drive
Eau Claire, WI 54701

Salter's 66
4317 North Shore Drive
Eau Claire, WI 54701

Wagon Trail Resort
Rowley's Bay
Ellison Bay, WI 54210

Elm Brook Marine Sporting, Inc.
15380 Watertown Plank Rd.
Elm Grove, WI 53122

South Shore Pier
Hwy. 42
Ephriam, WI 54211

Gordy's Ski Boat Rental
147 Lake Ave. (west end of Lake
  Geneva)
Fontana, WI 53125

Lake Shore Marine
Lake Ave.
Fontana, WI 53125

Keith's Campground & Canoe
  Rental
Gordon, WI 54838

Water Trails, Inc.
3½ miles west of Grantsburg on north
  side of Hwy. 70
Grantsburg, WI 54840

Wild River Outfitters
4 miles west of town on Hwy. 70
Grantsburg, WI 54840

Heileman Marine
10549 W. Forest Home Ave.
Hales Corners, WI 53130

Historyland
Hayward, WI 54843

Ross' Teal Lake Lodge
Route 1
Hayward, WI 54843

Voyageur Canoe Outfitters
Hayward, WI 54843

Wild River Inn
Route 6, Namekagon River
Hayward, WI 54843

Flater's Flambeau Point Resort
Route 1
Holcombe, WI 54745

Pine Drive Resort
R.R. 2, Box 191
Holcombe, WI 54745

Horicon Marsh Canoe Outfitters
Hwy. 33 Bridge
Horicon, WI 53032

The Playful Goose
2000 S. Main St. (off Main St. Rd.)
Horicon, WI 53032

Big George's Marina, Inc.
Lake Dr., east shore of Lake
  Sinissippi
Box 386
Hustisford, WI 53034

Bark River Camp Grounds
Route 1, Box 255
Jefferson, WI 53549

Holiday Vacation Cruises, Inc.
1933 Rose St., Hwy. 53
La Crosse, WI 54601

Flambeau Lodge
Route 1
Ladysmith, WI 54848

Beauti-View Resort
Wildcat Mt.
R. 1, Ontario
(Mail: R. 1, Box 197
        La Farge, WI 54639)

Smith's Landing & Canoe Rentals
Route 2 on Kickapoo River
La Farge, WI 54639

Mick's A & W
La Farge, WI 54639

Charles Hysel
La Farge, WI 54639

Farris Boat Rental
Route 1
Lake Delton, WI 53940

Gary's Canoe Rental
Box 3
Lake Nebagamon, WI 54849

Headwaters Marine, Inc.
Box 201
Land O'Lakes, WI 54540

Gannon's Birchwood Resort
R.R. 1, Hwy. 60
Lodi, WI 53555

APPENDIX VI

Brownrigg's Okee Lodge
Route 3
Lodi, WI 53555

A to Z Rent All
2620 E. Washington
Madison, WI 53704

Hanson's Boat Rental
5025 Westport Rd. (Lake Mendota)
Madison, WI 53704

Mazanet Marina
55 Blue Bill Drive
(Lake Mendota, north shore)
Madison, WI 53718

Outdoor Rentals
Wisconsin Union
University of Wisconsin
800 Langdon St.
Madison, WI 53706

Chain O'Lakes Marina, Inc.
Route 51 South
Manitowish Waters, WI 54545

Midway DX Service & Sporting
    Goods, Inc.
1368 Main St.
Marinette, WI 54143

Riverside Rentals
Route 2, Menominee River, Hwy. 180
Marinette, WI 54143

Liske Marine
Hwy. 13
Medford, WI 54451

Waverly Beach Marine
P. O. Box 307
Jct. Rts. 114 & 10 (on the lake)
Menasha, WI 54952

Pine Point Lodge
Route 2
Menomonie, WI 54751

Wolske's Bay
520 E. Locust (Hwy. 194, Lake
    Menomin)
Menomonie, WI 54751

Koss Marine & Sport
Route 3, Hwy. 51 N.
Merrill, WI 54452

M & M True Value Hardware
6305 University Ave.
Middleton, WI 53562

ABC Supply Co.
3203 W. Burnham St.
Milwaukee, WI 53215

Schneider Boat Co.
3133 W. Lisbon Ave.
Milwaukee, WI 53208

Tessners Marine City
3001 W. Lisbon Ave.
Milwaukee, WI 53208

U W M Outing Center
2200 E. Kenwood
Milwaukee, WI 53211

Minocqua Marine Mart
(on Hwy. 51 just north of the town
    of Minocqua)
Minocqua, WI 54548

Jim's Canoe Rental
Box 323
Minong, WI 54859

Zimmerman's Resort
Montello, WI 53949

Riverview Hills
Route 3, Box 67
Hwy. 60, 5 miles west of Gotham
Muscoda, WI 53573

Ken's Marina
R.F.D. 1, Box 777
Necedah, WI 54646

Wa Du Shuda Canoe
115 Welch Prairie Rd.
New Lisbon, WI 53950

Claire Flease (Little Wolf
    River Trips)
Route 3
New London, WI 54961

Kinn Motors Marine
650 E. Wisconsin Ave.
Oconomowoc, WI 53066

Paddle Inn
Ontario, WI 54651

Fox River Marina, Inc.
501 S. Main
Box 2325
Oshkosh, WI 54901

Hideout
2189 Abraham Lane
Oshkosh, WI 54901

Morgan's Sportsland
Hwy. 13 South
Park Falls, WI 54552

Nine Mile Tavern
Route 1, Box 205
(Hwy. 70, 9 miles west of Fifield)
Park Falls, WI 54552

Oxbo Resort
Russell Frey
Route 1, Box 250
Park Falls, WI 54552

Southside Sport & Liquor
Hwy. 13 South
Park Falls, WI 54552

Big Bear Lodge
Phillips, WI 54555

Martwick Bait & Sport Shop
286 N. Lake Ave.
Phillips, WI 54555

Four Seasons Resort
Route 2 (Lake Wisconsin)
Poynette, WI 53955

Helleckson's Resort
Route 2 (Lake Wisconsin)
Poynette, WI 53955

Prairie Du Chien Marina, Inc.
Box 380, Mississippi River
Washington St. off Hwy. 35
Prairie Du Chien, WI 53821

Armour Lake Resort
(1 mile south of CTH "B" on Crab
    Lake Rd.)
Presque Isle, WI 54457

Canoe Trails
Stewart Peterson
Presque Isle, WI 54457

Boom Lake Marine
1520 Eagle St.
Rhinelander, WI 54501

Riverside Marine
Rhinelander, WI 54501

Currier's Lake Aire Motel
Route 4, Box 414
Rice Lake, WI 54868

Ron's Southgate Sport Shop
1822 S. Main
Rice Lake, WI 54868

Richland Canoe Sales & Rentals
Bill's Mobil Service
Hwy. 14
Richland Center, WI 53581

The Voyageurs Canoe Outfitters
Box 582 (Hwy. 87 & U.S. 8)
St. Croix Falls, WI 54024

Clarke's Sport Shop
Hwy. 70
St. Germain, WI 54558

CANOE LIVERIES

Marawaraden Resort
Route 1 (Long Lake)
Sarona, WI 54870

Blackhawk Ridge
Box 92 (Hwy. 78 South)
Sauk City, WI 53583

Sauk Prairie Canoe Rental
106 Polk St.
Sauk City, WI 53583

"W" Sport Shop
2 miles west of Sayner
Sayner, WI 54560

Olson Canoe Rental
c/o Roderick Olson
Kickapoo River
Soldiers Grove, WI 54655

Bob's River Side Camp
R.R. 2 (Wisconsin River)
Spring Green, WI 53588

Otter Lake Resort
Route 2 (south end of Otter Lake)
Stanley, WI 54768

DuBay Marina
R.R. (Hwy. 51 at the point where it
    crosses Lake Dubay on south
    shore)
Stevens Point, WI 54481

Quam's Marine
Hwy. 51
Stoughton, WI 53589

Northwest Outlet, Inc.
1815 Belknap
Superior, WI 54880

Aero Marine
(2½ miles east of Three Lakes on Hwy.
    32)
Three Lakes, WI 54562

Shorewood Marine
(3 miles east of Three Lakes on Hwy.
    32)
Three Lakes, WI 54562

Three Lakes Marina
(1 mile north of Three Lakes on Hwy.
    45)
Three Lakes, WI 54562

Tomahawk Trailer & Boat Sales, Inc.
Hwy. 51 North
Tomahawk, WI 54487

Canfield's Resort & Campgrounds
Namekagon River
Trego, WI 54888

Wild River Canoe Rental & Sales
John Kaas
Route 1
Trego, WI 54888

E. Z. Rental Service
1320 South West Ave.
Waukesha, WI 53186

Ding's Dock, Inc.
Route 1, Hwy. Q
Waupaca, WI 54981

River Boat Rental
Route 3
Waupaca, WI 54981

Edmund's Boat Line
Route 1
Waupaca, WI 54891

Prell's Boat Livery
Route 1
Waupaca, WI 54981

Lake of the Woods Campgrounds
Route 1, Box 207
Wautoma, WI 54982

Marineland, Inc.
7105 W. North Ave.
Wauwatosa, WI 53213

Kickapoo Canoe Rental
c/o Paul Morel
Box 238 (Wis. & Kickapoo & Miss.
    Rivers)
Wauzeka, WI 53826

Crummy's Park Marina
Route 3, Kettle Moraine Drive
Whitewater Lake
Whitewater, WI 53190

Crummy's Sport & Marine
207 Elkhorn Rd.
Whitewater, WI 53190

Rivers Edge
Route 1, Box 89Z
Wisconsin Dells, WI 53965

Beach View Resort
5630 N. Park Rd.
(Lake Wazeecha)
Wisconsin Rapids, WI 54494

Ballagh's & Biermann's
    Big Bear Lodge, Inc.
Star Route
Winter, WI 54896

Wanigan Resort
Route 2 (Chippewa River)
Winter, WI 54896

Indian Shores Campground
Box 12 (Hwy. 47 S.E.)
Woodruff, WI 54568

Thrall's Boat & Canoe Shop
Route 2, Box 4 (2 miles north
    of Woodruff on Hwy. 70 East)
Woodruff, WI 54568

Wyoming

Jackson Hole Ski & Sports
P. O. Box CC
Wapiti Canoe Rentals
Jackson, WY 83001

Canada

The Mountain Shop
10918 88th Ave.
Edmonton, Alberta

Interior Canoe Outfitters
751 Athabaska East
Kamloops, British Columbia
V2H 1C7

Rainbow Canoe Rentals
18601 Lougheed Highway
Pitt Meadows, British Columbia
V0M 1P0

The Happy Outdoorsman, Ltd.
433 St. Mary's Rd.
Winnipeg, Manitoba
R2M 3K7

Stream N'Wood
22 8th St.
Brandon, Manitoba

Vann's Marina
Box 249
Leaf Rapids, Manitoba

Peel Cycle Center (# 1)
1398 Sherbrooke St. West
Montreal, Quebec

Peel Cycle Center (# 2)
4854 Sources Rd.
Dollard des Ormeaux, Quebec

Les Canots Voyageurs
Box 91
Grand Remous, Quebec

The Sportsman Ltd.
Box 162
Yellowknife, Northwest Territories

APPENDIX VI

Back of Beyond Canoe Outfitters
  & Beachside Park Campground
South Milford, Annapolis Co.
R. R. 4
Annapolis Royal, Nova Scotia
B0S 1A0

Box Ahlin's Canoes North
Ogoki Outfitters
Armstrong, Ontario

Mr. D's Camping Park
Thunder Lake
Dryden, Ontario
P8N 2Y4

Algonquin Outfitters
R. R. 1, Box P
(Algonquin Park Area)
Dwight, Ontario

Rent-All Equipment
971 Division St.
Kingston, Ontario

Ranger Lake Holidays Limited
Box 145
Sault Ste. Marie, Ontario

Voyageurs North Canoe Outfitters
Box 507 (Mile 9, Hwy. 72)
Sioux Lookout, Ontario
P0V 2T0
(May 20–Sept. 1)

Leisure Sports
P.O. Box 104, South Hill Shoppers
  Mall
Prince Albert, Saskatchewan

Churchill River Canoe Outfitters
(summer): Box 26
      La Ronge,
      Saskatchewan
(winter): 509 Douglas Park Crescent E.
      Regina, Saskatchewan
      S4N 2R9

The Ski Shop
2146 Albert St.
Regina, Saskatchewan

Olympian Sports
66 33rd St. East
Saskatoon, Saskatchewan

Yukon Canoe Rental
507 Alexander
Whitehorse, Yukon

Appendix VII

Canoe Manufacturers

A. C. MacKenzie River Co.
Box 9301
Richmond Heights, MO 63117
Fiberglass, slalom

Alcan Marine Products
158 Sterling Rd.
Toronto, Ontario M6R 2B8
Canada
Fiberglass, aluminum; general
recreation, whitewater

Alumacraft Boat Co.
315 W. St. Julien St.
St. Peter, MN 56082
Aluminum; cruising, whitewater

American Fiber-Lite
Box 67
Marion, IL 62959
Fiberglass, pressed Fiber-Lite;
cruising, whitewater

Appalachian T & B Plastic Corp.
Isthmus Road
Rumford, ME 04276
Fiberglass; hunting/fishing,
general recreation, whitewater,
cruising

Aqua Sport Canada Ltd.
525 Champlain
Fabreville, Quebec H7P 2N8
Canada
Fiberglass; cruising

Badger Boat Builders
Couderay, WI 54828
Fiberglass; hunting/fishing

Baldwin Boat Co.
Orrington, ME 04474
Fiberglass; whitewater

Bart Hauthaway
640 Boston Post Rd.
Weston, ME 02193
Fiberglass; hunting/fishing

Black River Canoes
South Main Street
Box 527
LaGrange, OH 44050
Fiberglass, Kevlar; general
recreation, racing

Blue Hole Canoe Co.
Sunbright, TN 37872
Royalex (ABS); whitewater,
general recreation

Boat Technology
601 River Rd.
Confluence, PA 15424
Epoxy-glass; whitewater

Canuck Sporting Equipment, Ltd.
30 Bermondsey Rd.
Toronto, Ontario
Canada
Aluminum, fiberglass; cruising

Cedar Creek Canoes
Bog Road
N. Lebanon, ME 04027
Wood; cruising

Chestnut Canoe Co., Ltd.
Box 185
Oromocto, New Brunswick E2V 2G5
Canada
Wood and canvas, fiberglass;
cruising, freighter, general recreation,
hunting/fishing

Chicagoland Canoe Base, Inc.
4019 N. Narragansett Ave.
Chicago, IL 60634
Fiberglass; cruising

Chief Canoes
Chief Manufacturing, Inc.
737 Clearlake Rd.
Cocoa, FL 32922
Fiberglass, Royalex (ABS);
general recreation,
downriver, whitewater

Coldwater Canoe Co.
Box 324
Coldwater, Ontario
Canada
Wood and canvas; general
recreation, whitewater

Core Craft, Inc.
Hwy. 2 W.
Box 249
Bemidji, MN 56601
Fiberglass; cruising,
downriver, whitewater,
hunting/fishing

Dolphin Products
Wabasha, MN 55981
Fiberglass; cruising

Don's Custom Shop
618 Sumner
Belle Plaine, KS 67013
Fiberglass; general recreation

Easy Rider Fiberglass Boat Co.
Box 88108
Tukwila Br.
Seattle, WA 98188
Fiberglass; cruising

Eddyline Northwest Ltd.
8423 Mukilteo Speedway
Everett, WA 98204
Vacuum-bagged vinylester
laminate; cruising

CANOE MANUFACTURERS

Granta Boats Ltd.
West Royalty Industrial Park
Charlottetown,
Prince Edward Island
Canada
Fiberglass, wood and canvas,
Kayel plywood; cruising,
general recreation, camping

Grayling Paddlecraft Ltd.
1271 S. Bannock St.
Denver, CO 80223
Fiberglass; cruising

Great Canadian Canoe
45 Water St.
Worcester, MA 01604
Fiberglass, aluminum,
wood and canvas,
Royalex (ABS), wood;
hunting/fishing,
cruising, whitewater,
downriver.

Green Mountain Outfitters,
Inc.
Cold River Road
North Clarendon, VT 05759
Fiberglass, Royalex (ABS),
polyethylene; general
recreation, cruising,
whitewater

Grumman Boats
Marathon, NY 13803
Aluminum; cruising,
whitewater, lightweight

Hoefgen Canoe
Manufacturing
Menominee, MN 49858
Fiberglass; cruising,
freighter

Hollowform, Inc.
6345 Variel Ave.
Woodland Hills, CA 91364
Zylar; general recreation,
cruising

Indian River Canoe
1525 Kings Court
Titusville, FL 32780
Fiberglass; child's boat,
general recreation, cruising

Langford Canoe Co.
385 The West Mall
Suite 250
Etobicoke, Ontario M9C 1E7
Canada
Wood and canvas, Royalex (ABS),
fiberglass; hunting/fishing,
general recreation,
whitewater

Landau Boat Co.
1015 N. Jefferson
Lebanon, MO 65536
Aluminum; downriver, whitewater

Lincoln Canoes
Route 32
Waldoboro, ME 04572
Fiberglass, Kevlar; general
recreation, cruising,
hunting/fishing

L.L. Bean, Inc.
Freeport, ME 04033
ABS, plastic; cruising

Lowe Industries
Interstate 44
Lebanon, MO 65536
Aluminum; cruising

Lund American Inc.
Box 248
New York Mills, MN 56567
Aluminum; cruising

Mad River Canoe, Inc.
Box 363
No. 1 Spring Hill
Waitsfield, VT 05673
Fiberglass, Kevlar,
Royalex (ABS);
cruising, downriver,
slalom, hunting/fishing

Maxcraft
Box 147
Rapidan, VA 22733
Wood and fiberglass;
racing, cruising,
whitewater

Miami Fiberglass Products
Corp.
Box 420858
Miami, FL 33142
Fiberglass; general
recreation

Michi-Craft Corp.
19 Mile Road at
200th Avenue
Big Rapids, MN 48307
Aluminum; cruising

Mid-Canada Fiberglass
Ltd.
Box 1599
New Liskeard, Ontario
P0J 1P0
Canada
Fiberglass, Kevlar;
cruising, whitewater

Midwestern Fiberglass
Products
Box 247
Winona, MN 55987
Fiberglass, Kevlar;
general recreation,
whitewater, racing

Mohawk Manufacturing Co.
936 N. Hwy. 427
Box 668
Longwood, FL 32750
Fiberglass, Royalex
(ABS); general
recreation, whitewater,
cruising, racing

Monark Boat Co.
Monticello, AR 71655
Aluminum; cruising

Morley Cedar Canoes
Box 147
Swan Lake, MT 59911
Wood; general recreation,
lightweight

Nona Boats
977 W. 19th St.
Costa Mesa, CA 92627
Fiberglass; cruising,
whitewater

Norcal Fabricators, Inc.
Box 250
Callander, Ontario P0R 1H0
Canada
Aluminum; cruising

Northeast Canoe
Manufacturing
284 Indian Point St.
Newport, VT 05855
Fiberglass, light lay-up
fiberglass with
carbon fiber, carbon fiber;
hunting/fishing,
cruising, slalom,
downriver, racing

Northern Fiberglass
Industries, Inc.
747 Payne Ave.
St. Paul, MN 55101
Fiberglass; cruising

Old Town Canoe Co.
Old Town, ME 04468
Fiberglass, Oltonar
(ABS), wood
and canvas; general
recreation, cruising,
racing, sailing

Osagian Boats, Inc.
Hwy. 5N, Route 3
Lebanon, MO 65536
Aluminum; general
recreation, whitewater

CANOE MANUFACTURERS

Pack 'N Paddle, Inc.
Libertyville, IL 60048
Fiberglass, fiberglass
and foam; cruising,
racing

Pat Moore Canoes, Inc.
5256 E. 65th St.
Indianapolis, IN 46220
Fiberglass

Perception, Inc.
Box 64
Liberty, SC 29657
Royalex (ABS) with wooden
rails or aluminum rails;
whitewater, general
recreation, slalom

Pinetree Canoes, Ltd.
Box 824
Orillia, Ontario L3V 6K8
Canada
Epoxy Kevlar; cruising,
downriver, general recreation

Quapaw Canoe
600 Newman Rd.
Miami, OK 74354
Fiberglass, aluminum,
Royalex (ABS);
hunting/fishing, cruising
whitewater, general recreation

Quicksilver Fiberglass
Canoes
Quicksilver Ltd.
Box 104
Strome, Alberta
T0B 4H0
Canada
Fiberglass, Kevlar; general
recreation, downriver

Quintus Enterprises, Inc.
444 Lake Mary Rd.
Flagstaff, AZ 86001
Fiberglass; cruising,
hunting/fishing

Ranger Canoes
Box 426
Route 25
Plymouth, NH 03264
Fiberglass; hunting/fishing,
racing, downriver, freighter

Rich-Land Manufacturing Co.
Box 420
Arkadelphia, AR 71923
Aluminum; cruising,
whitewater

River Marine Corp.
Box 420
Arkadelphia, AR 71923
Aluminum; cruising,
whitewater

Rivers & Gilman Moulded
Products, Inc.
Main Street
Hampden, ME 04444
Fiberglass, Royalex (ABS);
hunting/fishing,
cruising, whitewater

RKL Canoes and Boats
Pretty Marsh
Mt. Desert, ME 04660
Wood sheathed in epoxy
and fiberglass;
general recreation,
cruising

Sawyer Canoe Co.
234 S. State St.
Oscoda, MI 48750
Fiberglass; cruising,
hunting/fishing,
whitewater, racing

Sea Nymph Boats
Box 298
Syracuse, IN 46567
Aluminum; cruising,
whitewater

Sears, Roebuck and Co.
Sears Tower
BSC 37047
Chicago, IL 60684
Aluminum, Fiber-Lite;
cruising,
hunting/fishing,
downriver, child's boat

Seda Products
916½ Industrial Blvd.
Chula Vista, CA 92011
Fiberglass, Kevlar,
Royalex (ABS);
general recreation

Seminole Boat Co.
Box 43
Sanford, FL 32771
Fiberglass; general
recreation,
hunting/fishing,
whitewater

Shenandoah Canoe Co.
Shenandoah River
Outfitters, Inc.
R.F.D. 3
Luray, VA 22835
Royalex (ABS);
whitewater

Sierra Canoes
735 Riverview
Orange, CA 92665
Fiberglass; general
recreation, sailing

6-H Products, Ltd.
80 Hickson Ave.
Kingston, Ontario
Canada
Fiberglass foam sandwich,
Kevlar-Airex foam
sandwich; cruising

Smoker-Craft, Inc.
Box 65
New Paris, IN 46553
Aluminum; cruising

Sportspal, Inc.
Industrial Park Road
Johnstown, PA 15904,
Aluminum; hunting/fishing,
cruising

Starcraft Canoes
2703 College Ave.
Goshen, IN 46526
Aluminum; cruising,
whitewater

Stowe Canoe Co.
Route 100
Stowe, VT 05672
Fiberglass with wood;
hunting/fishing

Sunspot Plastics
734 Kennedy Rd.
Scarborough, Ontario M1K 2C7
Canada
Polyethylene, Marlex;
general recreation,
cruising

Terry-Delhi/Woodstream
Delhi Manufacturing Corp.
Box 7
Delhi, LA 71232
Aluminum; general
recreation

The Coleman Co., Inc.
250 N. Francis
Wichita, KS 67201
Ram-X polyethylene;
general recreation

Thompson Canoe Co.
Box 2
Hairy Hill, Alberta T0B 1S0
Canada
Wood and canvas; cruising

CANOE MANUFACTURERS

Tip-A Canoe Stores, Inc.
Box 87E
Hwy. 70
Kingston Springs, TN 37082
Royalex (ABS); whitewater

Tremblay Canoes Ltd.
Box 97
Station D
Toronto, Ontario M6P 3J5
Canada
Verilite-wood; general
recreation, freighter

Troy Manufacturing
R.R. 3
Athens, Ontario
Canada
Fiberglass, Kevlar;
cruising, whitewater

Voyageur Canoe Co., Ltd.
King Street
Millbrook, Ontario L0A 1G0
Canada
Fiberglass, Kevlar;
cruising,
freighter, lightweight

Wabash Valley Canoes
506 Rd. 225 W.
Crawfordsville, IN 47933
Kevlar, fiberglass;
racing, cruising,
whitewater

Whitewater Boats
Box 843
Cedar City UT 84720
Fiberglass, Kevlar;
cruising, racing

Yukon Boat Works
1500 W. North Ave.
Milwaukee, WI 53205
Fiberglass, aluminum;
general recreation,
whitewater, racing

Appendix VIII

Paddle Manufacturers

Firm	Type of Paddle	Prices start at:
Blue Hole Sunbright, TN 37872	Aluminum shaft, ABS blade	$38
Cardorette, Keter Canoeing 101 79th Ave. N. Minneapolis, MN 55444	Laminated wood	$10
Calpino 433 St. Mary's Rd. Winnipeg, Manitoba R2M 3K7 Canada	Laminated wood	$18
Cannon P.O. Box 835 Faribault, MN 55021	Aluminum shaft, ABS blade	$9
Carlisle Ausable 110 State St. P.O. Box 150 Grayling, MI 49738	Aluminum shaft, ABS blade	$11
Clement 1625 Broadway Nile, MI 49120	Laminated wood	$17
Feather Brand P.O. Box 710 Calhoun City, MS 38916	Laminated wood	not available

APPENDIX VIII

Firm	Type of Paddle	Prices start at:
Foster P.O. Box 1185 Canway, AK	Wood	not available
Great Canadian 45 Water St. Worcester, MA 01604	Laminated wood	$10
Grumman Marathon, NY 13803	White ash	$15
Hauthaway 640 Boston Post Rd. Weston, MA 02193	Fir shaft, fiberglass blades	$28
Iliad 168 Circuit St. Norwell, MA 02061	Aluminum shaft, epoxy-fiberglass blade	$43
Kruger 243 S. Webb Rd. DeWitte, MI 48820	Aluminum shaft, fiberglass blade	$20
Kober, Hyperform 25 Industrial Park Rd. Hingham, MA 02043	Laminated wood	$40
Nona 977 W. 19th St. Costa Mesa, CA 92627	Fiberglass shaft and blade	$30
Norse P.O. Box 77 Pine Grove, Mills, PA 16868	Fiberglass-reinforced aluminum shaft with epoxy-fiberglass blade	$38
Old Town Old Town, ME 04468	Wood	$21
Sawyer 234 South State St. Oscoda, MI 48750	Ponderosa shaft, fiberglass-wood blade	$17
Seda P.O. Box 41B San Ysidro, CA 92073	Vaulting pole shaft, epoxy-fiberglass blade	not available
Smoker Camp New Paris, IN 46553	Ash shaft, hardwood blade	not available
Tuft-Lite P.O. Box 958 West Point, MS 39773	Polyproylene shaft and blade	$5
Wonacott Cherry Paddle P.O. Box 1902 Wenatchee, WA 98801	Laminated, oil-soaked cherry	$40
Wood-Lyte P.O. Box 204 Lemont, PA 16851	Laminated woods	$20

Appendix IX

Additional Reading

A Guide to Paddle Adventure: How to Buy Canoes and Kayaks and Where to Travel, Rick Kemmer, Vanguard Press, Inc., New York 10017, 1975.

Back to Nature in Canoes, A Guide to American Waters, Rainer Esslen, Columbia Publishing Company, Inc., Frenchtown, New Jersey 08825, 1976.
   An outstanding compilation of waterways throughout the United States. It is invaluable to the restless nomad of the canoe forever searching for a new waterway.

Basic Canoeing, The American Red Cross.
   Better suited for youngsters at summer camp than for the serious downriver canoeist. Sound but elementary.

Basic River Canoeing (2d Edition), Robert E. McNair, American Camping Association, Bradford Woods, Martinsville, Indiana 46151, 1968.
   Outstanding booklet for the novice.

Boat Builder's Manual, Charles Walbridge, Wildwater Designs, Inc., Penllyn Pike and Morris Road, Penllyn, Pennsylvania 19422, 1974.
   A "how-to-build" book on whitewater fiberglass canoes and kayaks.

Canoe Poling, Al, Frank, and Syl Beletz, A.C. Mackenzie Press, Box 9301, Richmond Heights Station, St. Louis, Missouri 63117, 1974.
   The authors are poling chairmen, respectively, of the American Canoe Association and the Meramec Canoe Club.

Cooking for Camp and Trail, Hasse Bunnelle and Shirley Sarvis, a Sierra Club Totebook, 1972.
   Recipes and more recipes for base-camp use.

ADDITIONAL READING

Explorers, Ltd. Source Book, Alwyn Perrin, Editor, Harper & Row, New York, 1977.
   A source for source books and catalogs on everything you'll need outdoors under the sun, stars, or rain.

Food for Knapsackers: and Other Trail Travelers, Hasse Bunnelle, a Sierra Club Totebook, 1971.
   Recipes; how to figure quantities. Excellent for wilderness travelers.

Kayaking, Evans and Anderson, Stephen Greene Press, Brattleboro, Vermont 05301.
   An excellent book on kayaking. As former U.S. Olympic whitewater coach and a National Senior Kayak Champion, Evans knows what it is all about.

North American Canoe Country, Calvin Rutstrum, Macmillan, New York, 1965.
   A general book with some pleasant musings about canoe life.

The Canoe and White Water, C.E. Franks, University of Toronto Press, Toronto, 1977.
   Filled with fascinating information about the history of canoes and canoeing. A compendium of canoeing advice.

The Complete Light-Pack Camping and Trail-Foods Cookbook, Edwin P. Drew, McGraw-Hill Paperbacks, New York, 1977.
   Lots of fine advice about preparing your own lightweight foods; good trail and canoe menus and recipes; information about cooking equipment.

The Complete Wilderness Paddler, Davidson and Rugge, Alfred A. Knopf, New York, 1976.
   Davidson writes history and is a canoeist. Rugge is an M.D. and a canoeist. Their book is as interesting as it is informative.

White Water Handbook for Canoe and Kayak, John T. Urban, Appalachian Mountain Club, 5 Joy St., Boston, Massachusetts 02108, 1972.
   Outstanding booklet for the serious student of whitewater canoeing and kayaking.

Wilderness Canoeing & Camping, Clifford Jacobson, Dutton, New York, 1977.
   Another good general-purpose canoe book.

Appendix X

Outdoor Magazines

Traditionally, hunting and fishing magazines have been the primary source of information about the out-of-doors. In recent years, they have begun to include articles of basic interest to the person who would rather canoe the Big Horn River than blast a bighorn sheep with a high-powered piece of artillery. They still approach anything but shooting and fishing with a sense of diffidence, however.

This trend has led to an increase in the publication of magazines for those who want to know about canoe-camping, rock climbing, backpacking, or conservation. You should find the following publications informative and entertaining:

General Outdoor Magazines

Camping Journal
229 Park Ave. S.
New York, NY 10003

A good general-interest magazine with emphasis on recreational-vehicle camping.

Better Camping
Woodall Publishing Co.
500 Hyacinth Place
Highland Park, IL 60035

Somewhat similar to *Camping Journal* but more emphasis on outdoor activities. On a novice level.

OUTDOOR MAGAZINES

Magazines for the Self-Propelled

Back Packer
28 W. 44th St.
New York, NY 10036

Lots of interesting material for the real hiking enthusiast; beautiful pictures; excellent comparative studies of outdoor gear.

Wilderness Camping
Fitzgerald Communications, Inc.
1654 Central Ave.
Albany, NY 12205

Articles cover backpacking, ski touring, canoeing, bicycle camping; a workmanlike magazine with very positive, and welcome, views on conservation.

Mountain Gazette
Write On Publishing House, Inc.
1801 York St.
Denver, CO 80206

A tabloid magazine whose heart is in the right place.

Mariah
Box 2690
Boulder, CO 80321

Slick quarterly, devoted to wilderness, sports expeditions, and excellent photography.

Conservation Organization Magazines

A number of distinguished national organizations publish superb magazines devoted to conservation in the broadest meaning of the word. No true conservationist can blind himself to the basic truth of technological change, nor should one oppose all change merely for the sake of opposition. Occasionally it *is* necessary to build a new highway, just as there are forest areas which must be closed to timbering and changed back to wilderness.

The following magazines are all involved with the out-of-doors, the wildlife that walks, swims, crawls, and flies therein, and the welfare of man in an atmosphere free from industrial destruction. All of the magazines listed are included with membership in the organizations that publish them. Membership is open to anyone interested. Write to the addresses listed for more information.

The Living Wilderness
The Wilderness Society
1901 Pennsylvania Ave. N.W.
Washington, DC 20006

The Wilderness Society is one of the nation's oldest conservation societies. Articles are especially sensitive to Congressional behavior toward the environment. A quarterly.

Animal Kingdom
New York Zoological Society
The Zoological Park
Bronx, NY 10460

The magazine does contain articles about the Bronx Zoo, but its major emphasis is on wildlife throughout the world. Bimonthly.

Defenders of Wildlife News
Defenders of Wildlife
2000 N St. N.W.
Washington, DC 20036

Similar to but younger than the Wilderness Society, Defenders and their excellent magazine are "dedicated to the preservation of all forms of wildlife." Bimonthly.

National Wildlife
National Wildlife Federation
1412 16th St. N.W.
Washington, DC 20036

Beautifully printed, thought provoking articles

Natural History
The American Museum of Natural History
Central Park West at 79th Street
New York, NY 10024

Its interests are as diverse as the museum's collections, ranging from bird life in the Falklands to the tragic history of P.T. Barnum's greatest attraction, "Jumbo." Ten issues annually.

Smithsonian
Smithsonian Institution
900 Jefferson Drive
Washington, DC 20560

There is a similarity between this and *Natural History*, though the venerable institution's exceedingly well edited magazine is more involved with man and science than with nature. Monthly.

Sierra Club Bulletin
Sierra Club
1050 Mills Tower
San Francisco, CA 94104

The official publication of the famed Sierra Club; filled with compelling articles about the fight to defend our environment. Ten issues annually.

Audubon
National Audubon Society
950 Third Ave.
New York, NY 10022

Audubon may well be the most beautiful regularly published magazine in the world. Its color plates of birds, plants, animals, and scenery are simply magnificent; its articles are excellent. Bimonthly.

Special-Interest Magazines

American Forest
American Forestry Association
919 17th St., N.W.
Washington, DC 20006

Devoted to making the interests of the forest industry palatable to outdoorsmen.

Appalachian Trailway News
Appalachian Trail Conference
1718 N St., N.W.
Washington, DC 20036

This official publication of the ATC is a three-times-a-year report on the magnificent Appalachian Trail.

Directory of Walking, Mountaineering & Nature Clubs of America
Walking News
556 Fairview Ave.
Brooklyn, NY 11237

Published annually—almost; the *Directory* is the best available source on outdoor clubs in the United States.

OUTDOOR MAGAZINES

American Publications

AWA Journal
P.O. Box 321
Concord, NY 03301

The official journal of the American Whitewater Affiliation, whose members chiefly are interested in whitewater paddle sports. Bimonthly. $5 a year

Canoe
1999 Shepard Rd.
St. Paul, MN 55116

The official magazine of the American Canoe Association, and the best canoeing magazine on the market. Bimonthly. $6 for six issues.

Down River
Box 366
Mountain View, CA 94040

This is an outstanding small magazine thoroughly devoted to all phases of canoeing. Monthly. $8 a year.

Canadian Publications

Canadian Alpine Journal
The Alpine Club of Canada
Box 1026
Banff, Alberta
Canada

Climbs and first ascents in Canada; reports on ice and snow research.

Canadian Outdoorsman
PenReid Publications
2347 Yonge St.
Toronto, Ontario
Canada

A general outdoor magazine.

Skyline Trail Hikers of the Canadian Rockies
Box 590, Station A
Calgary, Alberta
Canada

An annual bulletin.

British Publications

Mountain
Mountain Magazines Ltd.
102A Westbourne Grove
London W2
England

Mountain Life
1 Meadow Close
Goring, Reading
Berkshire RC80AP
England

Canoeing Magazine
Canoeing Press
25 Featherbed Lane
Croydon CR09AE
England

Glossary

Canoes are watercraft; they are addressed in the language of the sea. They do not have floors; they have decks, beams, thwarts, keels, and bilges. A glossary of every term related to canoeing would be excessive for general use, but a knowledge of many of the terms is necessary not only to understand canoeing but also to communicate with others about canoeing.

Here is a glossary of some terms which will prove helpful in understanding canoeing, canoes, and canoeists.

ABEAM. To the right, or at right angles to the center of a craft.

ABOARD. On, or in, the canoe.

A.C.A. American Canoe Association.

ACCESS or ACCESS POINT. The place on the shore of a lake or river where you put in or take out.

ACTIVE BLADE. When using a double, or kayak, blade, that blade which is in the water at any given time.

AFLOAT. Floating. Not stuck on a rock or sandbar.

AFT. Toward the rear, or stern, of the canoe.

AGROUND. Stuck—usually on a shoal or rock—when you didn't intend to be.

AHEAD. Forward—as in the nautical phrase "Full speed ahead."

AIR LOCK. The pressure of air which holds water inside an overturned canoe if you attempt to lift it straight up.

ALONGSIDE. "Hey, bring your canoe up *alongside* this rock."

AMIDSHIPS. In the middle of the canoe.

ANCHOR, SEA.   Your largest kettle tied to the end of a 20-foot rope and tossed over the stern when you are being driven by a heavy tail wind in a running sea.

ASTERN.   Toward the rear, behind, or in back of your canoe.

AZIMUTH.   The angle of horizontal deviation from north. When using a compass, the direction in degrees. East, for example, is on an azimuth of 90 degrees.

BACK FERRY.   Paddling the canoe backward at an angle to the current when crossing a stream laterally.

BACKCOUNTRY.   Distant wilderness invaded by those with a sense of adventure.

BACKPADDLE.   Paddling backward to slow or reverse the forward motion of a canoe.

BAIL.   To empty water from a craft by scooping it out with anything from a sponge to a tin can.

BAILER.   Anything used to bail out a canoe. One of the most effective is an old plastic bottle with the bottom cut off.

BANG PLATE.   *See* Stem Band.

BEAM.   Width of a canoe when measured at its widest point.

BEAM ENDS.   A canoe tipped on its side is said to be "on her beam ends."

BEAR OFF.   To push off from an obstruction or an object.

BEARING.   A direction with respect either to a compass point, such as north, or to the craft.

BEFORE.   What lies ahead; in front of.

BELOW.   Downriver.

BILGE.   When a hull is cut in a cross section, the bilge is the point of maximum curvature between the bottom and the side of the canoe below the waterline.

BILGE KEEL.   Two additional keels, one on each side of the keel, which protect canvas-covered canoes.

BLADDER.   An air bag inside a kayak which adds to the buoyancy of the craft in event of a capsize.

BLADE.   The wide, flat end of the paddle.

BOIL.   Where current foams upward when it is deflected by obstructions under the water.

BOTTOM.   The part of the canoe that is under the water.

BOW.   The front or extreme forward end of the canoe.

BOW-IN.   With the bow forward.

BOW PADDLER, BOWMAN, BOW PERSON.   The person who paddles in the bow.

BOW PLATE.   Another term for the stem band.

BOW SEAT.   The seat located at the front end of a canoe.

BRACE.   A stroke used somewhat like an outrigger to stabilize a canoe. The brace may be a high or low brace. The usual reference is to "throw" or "hang" a brace.

BRIDLE.   A line looped around the front end of the canoe to which another line is attached under the canoe and used for towing the craft.

BROACH.   Broadside to any obstacle—wind, waves, current, or rocks; usually the prelude to an upstream capsize. Don't broach!

BULKHEAD.   A partition under the forward and aft decks inside which flotation blocks are attached.

BULL COOK.   An ancient and honorable north woods term for the person whose job is washing pots and pans and cleaning up the kitchen.

BUSH.   In Canada, the deep wilderness.

C-1.   A one-man covered canoe in which the paddler may kneel or sit. At one time C-1's were made with the bow and stern higher than the middle, but this is no longer standard practice. While a C-1 looks much like a kayak, it has a larger volume and rides higher.

GLOSSARY

C-2. A two-man covered canoe.

CANADIAN CANOE. In Europe the open canoe is referred to as a Canadian or North American Indian canoe.

CANOE POLE. *See* Pick Pole.

CAPSIZE. What happens when you are gobbled up in whitewater, or flipped by a combination of wind and waves, or— Well, it shouldn't happen.

CARRY. *See* Portage.

CARVEL-BUILT. A wooden canoe built so the longitudinal sides are laid edge to edge, smoothed, and the gaps sealed with waterproofing material.

CFS. The flow of water measured in cubic feet per second. A cubic foot contains about 8 gallons of water.

CHANNEL. A stretch of passable water through shallows or among obstructions.

CHART. A map especially prepared for navigation.

CHINE. Where the curving sides of the hull gradually merge into the bottom.

CHUTE. A fast current where part of a stream is compressed and flows between two obstructions.

CLOSED BOAT, COVERED CANOE. Any kayak or C-1 or C-2 where the deck is not detachable but built as an integral part of the craft.

COAMING. A rim around a kayak or C-1 or C-2 cockpit to which a spray skirt is attached.

CREST. The summit of a standing wave; the top of a ridge.

CURLER. A steep wave, usually at the base of a drop or chute, that curls back onto its upstream side.

DEAD RECKONING. A way of figuring your position based upon the influence of such things as currents and wind upon your projected course and anticipated speed.

DECK. The triangular piece of material, usually metal or wood, to which the gunwales are attached at the bow and stern. A deck also may be the entire top covering built as an integral part of a kayak, C-1, or C-2.

DEPTH. The depth of a canoe measured from gunwale to bottom amidships.

DOUBLE-BLADE PADDLE. A paddle with a blade at each end, used basically in kayaks but occasionally favored by some canoeists.

DOWNRIVER RACE. A race, usually including whitewater, over a long distance on a river.

DRAFT. The depth of water necessary for a craft to float; the distance between the waterline and the bottom of the keel.

DRAG. The resistance to forward motion. Drag may be decreased by use of special waxes.

DRAW or DRAW STROKE. A stroke in which the blade is placed well out from the canoe and pulled directly toward the side of the canoe; designed to move the craft sideways.

DUFFEK STROKE. *See* High Brace.

DUFFLE. *See* Gear.

EDDY. A current at variance with the main current, and where the main current either stops or reverses its flow upstream; caused by rocks, obstructions, or the bends in a river or stream. Once avoided as dangerous, eddies now are routinely used in maneuvers and for rest stops.

EDDY HOPPING. Using eddies to maneuver upstream or downstream.

EDDY LINE. The boundary between a downstream and an upstream current.

EDDY TURN. A dynamic maneuver used to enter or leave an eddy.

FACE. The flat side of a blade.

FALLS. A sudden drop in which the water falls free for at least part of the way.

GLOSSARY

FATHOM.   A nautical measure of depth: 6 feet.

FEATHER.   To turn the paddle so that the blade is parallel to the current or wind and the resistance is reduced.

FERRY.   To move a canoe laterally across a current.

FIBERGLASS.   Glass threads formed into matting or fabric and used with special resins to form a covering of high strength-to-weight ratio for a canoe or kayak.

FLATWATER.   Calm river water without rapids; lake water.

FLOORBOARDS.   Slats placed in the bilge of a wooden canoe to protect the ribs.

FLOTATION.   Styrofoam or air bags placed in a canoe or kayak to help keep the craft afloat in the event of a capsize.

FOLDBOAT.   Ingeniously designed kayaks or canoes made of a rubberized fabric with a collapsible wooden frame; can be packed into carrying bags for transportation.

FORWARD FERRY.   Paddling with the canoe at a downstream angle to the current in crossing laterally.

FREEBOARD.   The part of the canoe which lies above the waterline.

FREIGHTER.   Canoe with large carrying capacity; often used in wilderness regions as work craft.

GAUGING STATION.   A permanent device measuring the level of water at a given point.

GEAR.   Everything you carry in your canoe, from food to foolish items; something you always wish you had more of in camp and less of on a portage.

GIRTH.   The circumference of the hull at its widest section.

GRAB LOOP.   A loop of rope on the bow or stern of a kayak which is useful for grabbing onto in an upset.

GRADIENT.   The degree of inclination of a riverbed, usually described as the number of feet the river drops per mile.

GRIP.   The top of a paddle. The two most popular shapes are the pear grip and the T grip. The former is used for general canoeing; the latter is favored by whitewater canoeists.

GUNWALE.   The section along the top of the canoe from stern to bow where the sides meet; a strip along the top of the canoe's sides. Pronounced "gunnel."

HEAVY WATER.   A huge flow of water through rapids marked by extreme velocity differences in currents and violent turbulence.

HIGH BRACE.   A powerful, dynamic kayak or canoe stroke for entering or leaving an eddy. Also called the "Dúffek stroke", because it was developed by Milovan Dúffek of Czechoslovakia.

HULL.   The lower half of a kayak or closed canoe, or the main structure of an open canoe.

HUNG UP.   When a craft is caught on a rock.

HYDRAULIC.   An area of major current changes which in turn create problems normally associated with rocks. Also, the formation of a backflow at the base of a ledge where the current reverses itself.

HYPOTHERMIA.   The dangerous lowering of body temperature under wet, cold conditions. Can lead to death due to "exposure."

ICF.   International Canoe Federation.

INWALE.   The inside of the gunwale.

K-1.   A one-man kayak.

K-2.   A two-man kayak.

KAYAK.   A decked craft in which the paddlers sit with legs extended and propel the craft with a double blade paddle.

GLOSSARY

KEEL. A projection below the hull, running from stern to bow, which adds strength to the hull, protects it from damage, and helps the craft maintain straight movement, though the last is a result of the use of a keel, not the reason keels are built into metal and wooden craft. Keels usually are found only on aluminum and wooden canoes.

KNEE BRACE. Supports attached to the canoe into which the canoeist may slide his knees to gain greater control.

LAPSTRAKE. Construction of a wooden canoe so that each longitudinal board overlaps the one below, like a clapboard house; also—clinker built.

LASH. To make gear secure, usually with a rope.

LAUNCH. To slide a craft into the water.

LEAN. A deliberate tipping of the canoe as a maneuver in ferrying or to regain stability.

LEDGE. Rock shelf which extends at right angles to the current and acts as a natural dam over which the water flows.

LEE, LEEWARD. Away from the wind; downwind. Opposite of windward.

LEFT BANK. The left side of the river when facing downstream.

LIFE JACKET, LIFE VEST. A flotation device to provide buoyancy in the water. Wear one when canoeing! *See also* PFD.

LINE. *See* Painter.

LINING. The use of ropes, one fore and one aft, to maneuver an empty canoe downstream. When a canoe is hauled upstream, this is known as "tracking."

LIVERY. Where you rent canoes and equipment.

LOB TREE. A tall tree with some or all of the top branches removed to make it a distinct landmark. Lob trees were once used to mark portages.

LONG-DISTANCE RACING. A term usually used for downriver races of at least 10 miles for senior canoeists and 5 miles for junior canoeists.

MOLD. A form used to make a canoe. A female mold is said to produce a male canoe; a male mold to produce a female structure.

MOUTH. Where a river empties into another body of water.

OFF SIDE. The side opposite to the side where the canoeist is paddling.

OPEN CANOE. The standard North American canoe.

OUTFIT. To equip a canoe for a particular purpose.

OUTFITTER. Commercial companies which supply all necessary equipment for wilderness travel.

OUTSIDE BANK. The outside of a bend.

OUTWALE. The outside gunwale.

OVERBOARD. "Man overboard!"

PADDLE. The instrument used to propel a canoe through the water; it is not an "oar."

PAINTER. A rope attached either to the bow or stern, usually from 15 to 25 feet long.

PFD. Personal Flotation Device. The term now used by the U.S. Coast Guard to designate life jackets. Do not use any PFD that is not approved by the U.S. Coast Guard for a person of your weight.

PICK POLE. A pole used to propel a canoe. Also called a "canoe pole."

PIKE. The iron point on a canoe pole.

PILLOW. A gentle bulge on the surface of the water caused by an underwater obstruction. All such pillows have hard centers.

PITCH. A sudden drop in, or steeper section of, a set of rapids.

GLOSSARY

PIVOT. To turn sharply, or to pivot the craft around a point.

PLAYING. Enjoying running a particular set of rapids several times.

POLE. *See* Pick Pole.

POOL. A stretch of river with little current.

PORT. The left side of the canoe when facing the bow.

PORTAGE. How you get your gear and canoe across a stretch of land between two bodies of water. A solid reason why canoe-campers, like backpackers, attempt to reduce their gear to the lightest load possible.

POWER FACE. The face of the blade which pushes against the water.

PRY STROKE. A paddle stroke used to move the craft sideways, away from the paddle.

PURCHASE. The application of power on a paddle to get leverage.

PUT-IN. Where a canoe is placed in the water; a launching site; the start of a trip.

QUARTERING. Running at an angle to wind or waves; a technique for riding over waves at a slight angle to avoid burying the bow in a standing wave.

RAPIDS. Waves, whitewater, haystacks, and similar contortions of water in a fast and turbulent stretch of river.

READING THE WATER. Determining water conditions by the appearance of water formations; used in determining the appropriate route through rapids.

RECOVERY STROKE. Not really a stroke, but getting ready for the next stroke.

REVERSAL. Where the current curls back on itself; usually treacherous. May be caused by large obstructions, either on the surface or underwater. Reversals also may be known as souse holes, hydraulics, curlers, or back rollers.

RIBS. Curved strips from gunwale to gunwale which form the shape of the hull; may also be used to add strength to the hull.

RIFFLES. Light rapids where water flows across a shallow section of river.

RIGHT BANK. The right side of the river when facing downstream.

ROCK GARDEN. A navigable waterway filled with rocks; requires constant maneuvering by the canoeist.

ROCKAGATOR. A sullen rock hiding in the rapids which the bow paddler failed to detect until after it reached up and smacked the canoe, sometimes hard enough to cause a capsize or hang-up.

ROCKOPOTAMUS. A huge, sleepy rock over which water flows in a gentle pillow so unobtrusively that no one recognizes it until the canoe slides to a stop atop it.

ROCKER. The upward sweep of the keel toward the bow and stern. The more pronounced the rocker, the easier the canoe is to pivot.

RUNNING. To sail with the wind; in canoeing, to hoist a jury sail and let the wind sweep the craft along.

SCOUTING. To check an unknown stretch of water before attempting it.

SCULLING STROKE. A figure-eight stroke with the paddle in the water at all times; used for fine adjustments, or when necessary to keep the paddle in a ready position when running a tricky set of rapids.

SHAFT. The handle of the canoe paddle between the grip and the blade.

SHEER. The fore and aft curving sides of a hull.

SHOAL. Shallows caused by a sand bar or sand bank, especially those which may be exposed at low water. Swift current shoals also are known as riffles.

SHOE KEEL. A wide, flat keel used on river canoes.

GLOSSARY

SHUTTLE. The art of maneuvering cars and canoes from put-in to take-out points.

SKIN. The covering of a craft; may be fiberglass, canvas, or a sheath placed over a fiberglass or wood canoe to protect the craft from chafing.

SLALOM. A race in which craft are maneuvered through a series of gates.

SMOKER. A single violent set of rapids.

SPOON. The curved shape of some types of kayak paddle blades.

SPRAY COVER. A fabric deck used to enclose open canoes when running whitewater. Also called a "spray deck."

SPRAY SKIRT. A garment worn by the canoeist which attaches to the spray cover to keep water out of the craft.

SQUALL. A quick, driving gust of wind or rain.

SQUARE STERN. A canoe with the stern cut off to provide a "transom" for attaching a motor.

STANDING WAVE. Perpetual waves which remain in one place; may be caused by decelerating current when fast water meets slower-moving water, or by obstructions.

STARBOARD. The right side of the canoe when facing the bow.

STEM. The curved outer section of the frame which forms the extreme forward and stern sections of the canoe.

STEM BAND. Also known as a "bang plate." A strip attached to the stem to protect it from damage.

STERN. The rear of the canoe.

STERN PADDLER. The person who paddles from the rear of a two-man canoe or C-2.

STRAINER. Brush or trees which have fallen into a river, usually on the outside of a bend. Current may sweep through, but the obstruction will stop a craft. Can be deadly.

STROKES. The various movements used by the paddler to control the direction and speed of the craft.

SWAMP. When a canoe is accidentally filled with water.

TAKE-OUT. Where you end your trip; the take-out point.

TECHNICAL PASSAGE. A route through a rock garden in which considerable maneuvering is required for safe transit.

THROAT. Where the paddle shaft flares into the blade.

THROWING LINE. An emergency rope used to throw out to a canoe in trouble.

THWART. The cross braces which stretch from gunwale to gunwale to strengthen an open canoe.

TIP. The end of the paddle blade opposite the shaft.

TONGUE. The V of smooth water which indicates a safe passage between two obstructions.

TOP SIDES. The part of the hull above the water.

TRIM. The angle at which a canoe rides in the water. A canoe may be trimmed so it rides even, down at the stern, or down at the bow.

TRIP LEADER. The person in charge.

TROUGH. The bottom between two waves.

TUMBLEHOME. The curving inward of the upper section of a canoe. This produces a canoe narrower at the gunwales than at the bulging sides. An aid in keeping open canoes dry.

TUMPLINE. A strap which slips around either the chest or forehead and is used to help support a heavy pack.

UNDERWAY. Moving, at last.

UPSTREAM, UPSTREAM SIDE. The side of the boat facing the oncoming current.

GLOSSARY

VOYAGEURS. The canoe trappers and traders of another era.

WAKE. The temporary trail in the water behind the canoe; also called the "wash." Beginning canoeists should peek occasionally at their wake to see if it is a straight line, which indicates good directional control.

WATERLINE. The line of the water on the side of the canoe when it is afloat. The waterline will vary with the load.

WATERSHED. The entire region drained by a single river.

WEIR. A low dam used to divert water; frequently built by commercial eel-trap operators to catch eels and confuse canoeists.

WET SUIT. A garment made of neoprene foam which insulates canoeist, kayakers, and scuba divers against the chill of cold water. Essential for cold-water canoeing to avoid hypothermia.

WHITEWATER. A long stretch of foaming waves and rapids. Also called "wild water."

WINDWARD. The direction from which the wind is blowing; into the wind. Opposite of leeward.

WRAPPED UP or WRAPPED AROUND. Said of a canoe or kayak which has slammed sideways into an obstruction with sufficient force to physically bend it in a horseshoe shape around the rock.

YAW. When a canoe swerves from its course.

YOKE. Cushioned shoulder blocks that clamp onto the gunwales or midthwart of a canoe to make portaging by one person easier.

Index

INDEX

Catalog

If you are interested in a list of fine Paperback
books, covering a wide range of subjects
and interests, send your name and address,
requesting your free catalog, to:

McGraw-Hill Paperbacks
1221 Avenue of Americas
New York, N.Y. 10020

8823